Quite A Curiosity
The Sea Letters of Grace Ladd

Copyright © Louise Nichols, 2003

All rights reserved. No part of this book may be reproduced, stored in a retrieval system or transmitted in any form or by any means without the prior written permission from the publisher, or, in the case of photocopying or other reprographic copying, permission from CANCOPY (Canadian Copyright Licensing Agency), 1 Yonge Street, Suite 1900, Toronto, Ontario M5E 1E5.

Nimbus Publishing Limited
PO Box 9166
Halifax, NS   B3K 5M8
(902) 455-4286

Printed and bound in Canada

Design: Denise Williams

Title page: The figurehead of the *Belmont* was a sculpture made in the image of Grace Ladd.

National Library of Canada Cataloguing in Publication

    Ladd, Grace F.
    Quite a curiousity : the sea letters of Grace F. Ladd / [edited by] Louise Nichols.

Includes bibliographical references.
ISBN 1-55109-430-4

1. Ladd, Grace F.—Correspondence. 2. Women merchant mariners—Nova Scotia—Correspondence. 3. Seafaring life—History—19th century—Sources. I. Nichols, Louise, 1959- II. Title.

G540.L29 2003   387.5'092   C2003-900430-9

We acknowledge the financial support of the Government of Canada through the Book Publishing Industry Development Program (BPIDP) and the Canada Council for our publishing activities.

Introduction
1

The Letters of Grace Ladd
21

Ladds at Sea
137

Kathryn Ladd's Travel Journal
149

Retirement Years
155

Kathryn's Recollections
161

Kathryn's Notebook
169

Endnotes
173

Glossary
185

Bibliography
193

Image Sources
196

Acknowledgements

I'd like to express my gratitude to a number of people who have helped along the way. To my colleagues from the English department at l'Université de Moncton for their encouragement and support. To John G. Arrison (Penobscot Marine Museum, Searsport, ME), Richard (Duke) Campbell, Gregg Cina (The Mariner's Museum, Newport News, VA), Esther Dares, Gregg Finley, Lorain Lounsberry (Glenbow Museum, Calgary, Alta), Leslie McGrath (Toronto Public Library), Bent Nielsen, and Rick Wiggins, O.D. (University of Waterloo) for answering my questions at various times. To Mary Clulee, Jim Day, and Cynthia Roberts for generously sharing their stories and memories with me. To the staff and volunteers of the Yarmouth County Museum Archives, especially Janice Stelma and Helen Hall. And finally, a very special thank you to Laura Bradley (former archivist, Yarmouth County Museum Archives) for her expertise and her help in providing me with the materials for this book, and to Eric Ruff (curator, Yarmouth County Museum) for reading through much of the manuscript and generously sharing his knowledge and love of nautical history with me.

This book is dedicated to Grace and Kathryn Ladd.
And to Glen, who was always interested in their story.

Introduction

A film entitled *Empty Harbours, Empty Dreams*, produced by the National Film Board of Canada[1] to document the decline of the Maritime region after Confederation, shows an elderly lady clipping flowers in a beautiful Yarmouth garden while reminiscing about the past. The lady is Kathryn Ladd, 78 years old at the time the film was made, and one of the few remaining witnesses to Nova Scotia's declining days of sail at the beginning of the twentieth century. She is speaking about the vessel her father sailed, a steel barque called *Belmont*, and its encounter one day with a particularly fast ship, also of steel, the *Pass of Balmaha*:

One time when we were sailing...up the north Atlantic, she came along and slowly went by us and as she turned—her sails were just glistening.... She was painted grey with black and white ports and...she went by with a switch like that—[Kathryn swivels her hips]—*the most flirtatious and happy-looking vessel you ever saw. The* Belmont, *of course, was a very prosaic...vessel; and she was very proud of herself, with a beautiful line. She was very matter-of-fact and she'd just go about her business. It nearly broke my heart to see the* Pass of Balmaha *go sailing past. We had the same wind—there was no reason—except she was a faster ship.*

When watching this scene, one is touched by Kathryn's emotional connection with the *Belmont* as well as her description, which gives each vessel a personality—like two women silently competing at a posh social gathering. It wasn't uncommon for a ship to instill feelings of pride in those who sailed her—but perhaps the surprise here is that it is not the captain who is speaking, but the captain's daughter. Kathryn was the one standing on the *Belmont*'s deck watching the other vessel pass and the one who was disheartened when the *Belmont* lost the race. Also aboard the vessel (and perhaps watching the same scene) would have been Kathryn's mother, Grace Forrest Ladd. She too must have been very proud of and attached to the *Belmont*, which was her home for almost 25 years.

This book focuses on Grace Ladd's story as she sailed with her sea captain husband, Frederick Arthur Ladd, in the final fourteen years of the 1800s. The story is told primarily through her own words, as recorded in the letters she wrote. Her daughter Kathryn's voice emerges later, first in a travel diary she kept as a young girl on a trip to England, and finally in the fond recollections of an older woman concerned with preserving a fascinating past. These two women, along with countless others, played their part in the Maritime culture of the sea. They left the security of a home on shore to join their husbands and fathers in a different kind of home, one that was often cold and wet, that presented many risks, and that moved across the globe offering those aboard experiences in travel and culture most of us will never know.

Grace Ladd was born Grace Forrest Brown on December 2, 1864, in Yarmouth, Nova Scotia, the third child of Charles Edward Brown (1830-1900) and Azuba Davis (Rose) Brown (1838-1891). She grew up in a distinguished family. Grace's grandfather, the Honourable Stayley Brown (1801-1877), was a successful merchant and ship owner, in addition to holding a number of prestigious posts. Stayley Brown was a director in the early years of the Bank of Nova Scotia in Yarmouth. Following this, he served as a member of the Nova Scotia legislature's Upper House for 34 years, acting as receiver general from 1857 to 1860. When Grace was just ten years old, her grandfather, who was known to be a strong opponent to Confederation, was appointed president of the Council, and one year later he became provincial treasurer.

Grace's paternal grandfather, the Honourable Stayley Brown, circa 1870

Grace's father, Charles E. Brown, was educated at Harvard, suggesting that Grace grew up in a household that exposed her to books and intelligent discourse. When he returned to Milton (the north side of Yarmouth where the Brown residence was located, and so named because of the mill at the head of the harbour), Charles Brown, like his father before him, became a

Introduction

Grace's father, the "dear Papa" of her sea letters, Charles E. Brown

profitable merchant. He too was receiver general for Nova Scotia for a number of years, and was also an agricultural and horticultural expert (an interest that a number of his children seemed to share) and a founding member of the Yarmouth County Agricultural Society. In fact, his store (located close to the home he inherited from his father) was in part a supplier of agricultural merchandise including English agricultural periodicals and other publications on the subject of farming.

The Brown family was a large one, but Grace's letters suggest that she remained close to her nine brothers and sisters. She mentions them frequently in queries and references to their successes and difficulties. Two of her younger brothers (Stayley and Ron) sailed with Grace and Fred in the 1890s, and her letters reflect her pride in the good work they performed while on board the vessel. Because the names of her siblings are frequently mentioned in Grace's letters, I have listed them, with the years of their births and deaths where known, and indicated the nicknames Grace used when referring to them. I have also given the names of spouses relevant to the period of Grace's letters. Since the birth of the Brown children spanned a period of over twenty years, Grace's youngest brother, Hermann, was only four years old when Grace departed on her first voyage at sea.

Mary Fletcher (Fletch)—b. 1860; d. 1942 did not marry
Charlotte Ethel (Eth)—b. 1862; d. 1929; m. Thomas W. Stoneman in 1884
Arthur White (Arth)—b. 1866; d. 1943
Charles Frederick—b. 1868; d. 1965; m. Maria Tilley in 1896
Florence Isabel (Flo)—b. 1869; d. 1961; m. Hamilton Byers in 1899
Georgina Everett (Georgie)—b. 1872; ? m. John Allen in 1899

Quite A Curiosity

Stayley—b. 1876; d. 1918
Ronald Laurie—b. 1879; ?
Hermann Hoffendahl—b. 1882; d. 1961

Grace also had strong ties to her "Aunt Maggie," (another relation mentioned frequently in her letters), who was Margaret (Rose) Robbins (1850-1926), her mother's sister, and who married a sea captain, Lemuel Robbins. The Robbinses were living in Ainsdale (close to Liverpool), England, at the time Grace wrote her letters. Grace kept in contact with her aunt, visiting her several times whenever circumstances brought her close to the area.

Grace's marriage to Captain Frederick Arthur Ladd (1858-1937) took place on May 20, 1886. They had known each other most of their lives; in fact, Grace and Fred were related (their mothers, Azuba Davis and Mary E. Davis [1830-1926] were first cousins) and their families were well-acquainted. In one of her letters, Grace recollects the last Christmas Fred was able to spend at home in Yarmouth, thirteen years before their marriage when she was only nine years old: "Fred has not spent a Christmas at home since 1873. ...the last Christmas evening in Yarmouth he spent at our house. I can remember we had a fine tree in the back office in the old house. In the evening all the Ladds came up." The Ladds also settled in Milton and, like the Browns, were a prominent family in Yarmouth County. Fred's father, Byron Parker Ladd

The Brown residence on Vancouver Street owned by the Hon. Stayley Brown and passed down to Charles E. Brown. Extensively damaged by fire in 1990, the house was restored and is now a bed and breakfast operated by Gilford and Esther Dares.

Introduction

The five daughters of Charles and Azuba Brown. The original photo was not labelled, but the woman in the upper left corner most resembles Grace.

The five sons of Charles and Azuba Brown. The youngest, Hermann Hoffendahl, sits in the centre.

(1825-1904), was born in Boston, moved to Westport (Nova Scotia) when young, and arrived at Yarmouth in 1870, where he formed a partnership with George H. Porter in the firm, Ladd, Porter & Co. Fred was one of four children—a brother died young and there were two sisters, Frances Susan, or "Fannie" (1855-1906), and Mary Byron, or "Minnie" (1861-?), who married Charles Pratt of Boston in 1888, and later resided in New Jersey. Just after his last Christmas in Yarmouth in 1873, Fred, at sixteen years old, joined the crew of the Nova Scotian ship *Cambridge* (built in Meteghan). Before long, he progressed in rank to become mate of this vessel, and by the end of the decade, he was mate on the barque, *Herbert C. Hall* (also of Meteghan), of which his uncle, Samuel Davis, was captain. In 1880, Fred obtained his master's papers from the marine school in Liverpool, England, and took over command of the *Herbert C. Hall* for several years. In 1883, he became master of yet another Meteghan vessel, *Morning Light*, a command he held until 1890. After a short break from the sea, Fred took charge of his next and final vessel, the barque *Belmont*, built in New Glasgow, Scotland, in 1891. His profitable relationship with the *Belmont* lasted for a remarkable 24 years.

As captain and part owner of the vessels he sailed, Fred had a personal interest in the business he carried out. Each vessel was owned by a number of people who bought one or more of its 64 shares, and it was not unusual for the captain to be one of the

Quite A Curiosity

Mary Elizabeth (Davis) Ladd, circa 1867

Byron P. Ladd, circa 1867

shareholders, a good arrangement in that the person in whose hands the vessel rested had a vested interest in what happened to it. Fred owned four shares of the *Morning Light* at the time he sold it, and he was part of a corporation of predominantly Yarmouth citizens who owned the *Belmont* under the name "The Belmont Shipping Company." Among vessel shareholders was also a managing owner who would take charge of obtaining cargos through agents located at various ports, and who would look after the essential business of the vessel. The Halls of John G. Hall & Co., located in Boston, were the managing owners of the *Belmont*.

By the late nineteenth century, communications between the captain and the managing owner was by letter and telegraph. The captain would telegraph his arrival in port. Normally he would find letters from the managing owner waiting for him, telling him of the details and arrangements for the vessel's next cargo. A document called the "charter party," which constituted the agreement made with a shipper to provide the vessel with a particular cargo, would be drawn and signed. The charter party would specify the amount of cargo, freight rate, date of delivery, loading time, destination port, and discharging time. The time indicated for loading and discharging was termed "lay days," and any extra time a vessel had to wait in port outside of the specified lay days could result in a demurrage fee charged to the shipper. Sometimes upon reaching one port, a captain was given orders to go to an alternate port for a cargo that had been obtained there. If there was no cargo to be obtained, the vessel would sail in ballast.

Introduction

Although subject to the dictates of the managing owner, the captain of a vessel had considerable power himself. Occasionally he would arrange cargos in lieu of the managing owner. Moreover, he was responsible for overseeing the business of the vessel, for obtaining and managing a crew, for supervising the maintenance and any necessary repairs of the vessel, for navigation, and, while at sea, for the health and well-being of the crew, including the provision of medical treatment. If the shareholders decided to sell the vessel, the captain might also oversee the sale. All things considered, seafaring was a stressful life, as Grace points out several times in her letters, and Captain Fred Ladd was about as successful at it as they come.[2]

Grace became Fred's wife while he was captain of the *Morning Light*. This ship was to be Grace's first home at sea, the one she sailed in with Fred from New York, just nine days after their marriage, on a "honeymoon" voyage to Shanghai.

Grace wrote her first letter on this voyage and she continued to keep in touch with those back home by mail for many years. The letters that have survived are the ones she wrote to her father, Charles E. Brown, over a span of time that began in 1886 and ended in 1899, not long before his death. Grace's letters form part of a slowly emerging and much larger collection of documents (letters and journals) written by women who went to sea. Such writings are a valuable contribution to our knowledge of this period in Maritime history, partly because the sheer volume of writing is witness to the regular presence of wives and daughters onboard merchant vessels. Grace, moreover, was not only an occasional traveller, but one who occupied a place in the captain's quarters for many years. Consequently, her letters provide insight into her own role aboard the vessel and her relationship with the captain and crew. They also give us insight into the day-to-day routine of a woman's life at sea—the challenges and difficulties that arose as well as responses to emergencies.

But perhaps most importantly, letters such as those written by Grace Ladd simply reveal just

Captain Frederick Arthur Ladd, circa 1886

how courageous these women were. They call into question our tendency to view Victorian women as fragile or weak, and put us instead face to face with the strength and daring many of them possessed. The stereotypical image of the Victorian woman gives us a false sense of superiority, as though women from Grace's age were less empowered than we are. We mistakenly judge them as a collective, confining them to certain tasks and social positions. But in truth the position of women in society has always been in flux, and during the lengthy Victorian period many changes took place. Letters and journals that Victorian women left behind show that many could and did live unusual and challenging lives, and that in many cases they were mistresses of their own destinies.

It is possible, of course, to view wives at sea as stereotypical of women so devoted to their husbands that they would give up everything for them, even if it meant risking their comfort and safety, to follow them.[3] But documents such as Grace's letters contest such a view. Grace does not discuss her decision to go to sea in her letters to her father, but the letters themselves strongly suggest that Grace wanted to be there, not just to support Fred, but because she herself enjoyed it and possessed an obvious hankering for adventure. Not only do her letters reflect a sense of Grace's independence and self-determination, but they also show a strong bond between her and Fred, a relationship not so different from what we would consider today to be a modern marriage of equality between partners. There is no sense that Fred dominates in the relationship or that Grace has no freedom. Instead, they are mutually supportive, appreciating the company of the other. Neither do the letters to Grace's father imply anything other than a close companionship and mutual respect between father and daughter. Their exchange is light and good natured with no hint that her

The Cambridge *was the first ship Fred Ladd sailed on, initially as a member of the crew and finally as mate. At 1,135 tons, the* Cambridge *was built at Meteghan, Nova Scotia in 1874. The portrait was done by S.F.M. Badger.*

father objects to Grace's nomadic life. He grumbles on one occasion in his journal that Grace had to leave Yarmouth sooner than expected in order to sail across the Atlantic to meet Fred in England so that she could be with him on his next passage to Cape Town. But it is obviously her decision to go when she wishes, and Grace makes the trip accompanied only by Forrest, her two-year-old son.

Grace's letters then are not only important for the information they impart, but also for what they imply about lifestyle, expectations and relationships. Part of their fascination stems from their nature as personal documents, different from the often more public and deliberate writing of men. The same can be said for a diary (which Grace claimed in her early letters to be keeping, but unfortunately has never been found) that may consist of private reflections or merely a summary of daily routine, but in each case quite likely communicates more to a reader of later years than the original writer intended. A diary too may have been written only for the eyes of the writer or, in the case of a travel journal, with the objective of showing it to others back home, intentions which obviously influenced its content. Grace's daughter, Kathryn Ladd, kept a travel diary on her trip to England in 1915, and in a preface to it written much later, the older Kathryn records: "This is a copy of my original diary. It was copied in 1915 when I returned home—as Mother wanted her friends to read it and I had written some rather personal and uncomplimentary remarks about some of her friends, especially poor Miss Kelly who had not passed me any cake." Grace considered her daughter Kathryn's diary as a kind of public record, suitable to be read by others. Kathryn, however, evidently fretted about some of the more private content, and chose to edit her diary before allowing others to see it.

After the Cambridge, *Fred became mate, and later master, of the* Herbert C. Hall, *a 650-ton barque built at Meteghan in 1873. Portrait by John Loos, 1876.*

Quite A Curiosity

When looking at personal documents, it is important to consider the writer's intentions. With letters we know there is at least one other individual who is meant to read them, and the writer's relationship with this reader is bound to influence what the writer decides to write. The content of Grace's letters to her father may well have been different from the content of those she wrote to her siblings or friends—or indeed to her husband, on those rare occasions when she stayed home. Moreover, the experience of reading someone else's letters is something like listening to a one-sided conversation; without the other voice, certain comments, stories and responses remain clouded in mystery. In Grace's letters, we often sense that she is responding to a remark of her father's in a previous letter, or telling him a story that would be of particular interest to him—and we cannot always understand the full impact of such things or the context that surrounds them from the letters alone.

We can, however, get a feel for the personality Grace is writing to. Charles E. Brown was an educated man and his knowledge of the world is hinted at several times in Grace's letters. Early on, when Grace writes to him from Shanghai to describe her experiences there, she suddenly interrupts her own narrative of a wedding she attended with the comment: "I know you have read better descriptions of Chinese weddings than I could give you." Not long after this is her comment in a letter from Cardiff that looks back on their recent visit to Denmark: "I am afraid you were disappointed in the letters I wrote after visiting Copenhagen, but really we saw so much that I could not begin to write about it all." It becomes evident that Grace takes great care in relating her experiences in her letters to her father because they are of great

The Morning Light, *1,327 tons, was built in Meteghan in 1878. Fred became master in 1883. Portrait by W.H. Yorke of Liverpool, 1884.*

Introduction

importance to *him*. Perhaps his greatest demand on her was to get the most out of the opportunities given to her and to absorb as much knowledge as possible about the world she would be seeing. Mr. Brown's close ties with his daughter and his interest in the life she chose to lead were confirmed with the discovery of close to fifty years of journals he kept in which his daily entries were filled with news of Grace and his nine other children. He wrote to Grace often, judging by his and Grace's numerous references to their correspondence. Moreover, he meticulously kept a schedule of the years Grace accompanied Fred at sea, a schedule that included dates of departure and arrival at ports, periods of time Grace spent at home, and various other events that happened in their personal lives (such as the loss of Grace's first child or the birth of Forrest, their son). These schedules, along with Charles E. Brown's journals and two letters he wrote to Grace that are extant, allow us the privilege of hearing the other voice from time to time, and they occasionally provide insights into the content of Grace's letters.

Charles E. Brown's passion for horticulture was also something that Grace shared with him. Mr. Brown was known to be a collector of plants from around the world. Grace frequently detailed her horticultural findings in her letters to her father, sending seeds back to him and collecting seeds from him (or occasionally from her older sister, "Fletch") for exchange. Such seems to be the case when she writes to him from Cardiff (June, 8, 1888): "I received the Sequoia and Parsley seeds alright. I shall be able to exchange the Sequoia seeds in Cape Town. I will plant some too. The little envelopes are just the thing. I shall be very careful of them." Grace happily kept her father up to date on the plants she grew aboard the vessel, taking a great deal of pride in their success. For his

Fred Ladd sailed the Belmont *from 1891 to 1915 with only a small break from late 1899 to September 1901. The* Belmont *was made of steel, 1,415 tons, and built in Port Glasgow, Scotland. Portrait by S.F.M. Badger.*

part, Mr. Brown kept Grace up to date on the people back home, providing her with news of relations, friends and acquaintances, and sending her numerous copies of the latest Yarmouth newspapers.

Grace, it would seem, took a similar interest in her own children. When Forrest came along in 1890 and joined Grace and Fred onboard the *Belmont*, he became the focal point of her letters. In the early 1900s, Kathryn too joined them. When they took their vacation in England just after Fred retired from the sea, Kathryn was taken all over London by her "untiring" mother and shown as many sights as they could fit in. Like her father, Grace obviously thought it important that her children know something about the world around them, and she did not seem to consider their lives at sea a disadvantage to them. Grace herself had an endlessly inquiring mind that carried her through the many voyages she took with Fred. Her letters reveal on numerous occasions that she would often go out of her way to try new experiences. She seemed to fear the wasting of an opportunity far more than

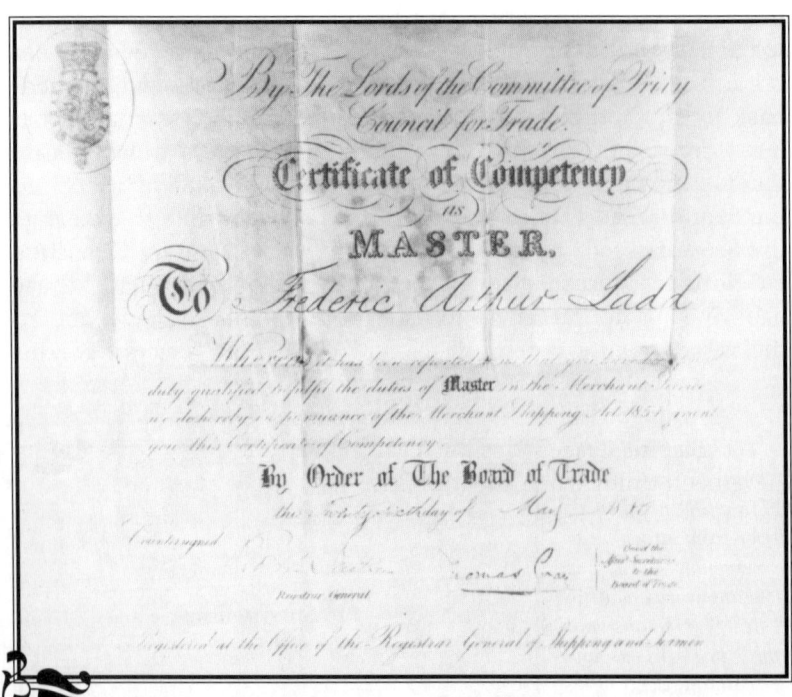

Fred Ladd's master certificate, obtained in 1880 in Liverpool. After 1850, certification was required for masters of British vessels. The regulations for such certification were incorporated into the 1854 Merchant Shipping Act.

Introduction

the experience itself. An instance of Grace's open-mindedness emerges in her letter of 1888 from Calcutta, in which she describes having witnessed a unique ritual:

Yesterday we saw where they burn their dead. It is like a large court by the side of the river. They make fires of wood on which they place the body [——]; one and another was there ready to be burned. I didn't enjoy that very much but I made Fred take me there. All these things are worth seeing.

Physically too, Grace was evidently quite active. She was obviously athletic and enjoyed exercise and sport. Her letters describe numerous adventures—from climbing mountain ranges in Cape Town to snowshoeing in Norway or horseback riding in New Zealand. When Forrest was born and began to travel with them, Grace's participation in sporting activities slowed down somewhat. But even so, a letter that Fred wrote to his brother-in-law from Tacoma in 1897 tells how the three of them rented bicycles and ventured out on a 30-mile ride.

Grace's enthusiasm for travel and learning is reflected also in the number of "curiosities" she collected. She gathered what she could from all over the world, her letters enumerating these treasures with an eagerness that again reveals her desire to discover all she can. Many of these objects (from whale's teeth to Australian weaponry) were passed down to Kathryn who then donated them to the Yarmouth County Museum. To this day, there is a corner in the museum devoted to the Ladds in which can be found a display of close to fifty objects collected by Grace throughout the years she travelled at sea. Many of the displayed objects are referred to in Grace's letters, making the museum collection a wonderful complement to them and providing a concrete link between the world of the late nineteenth century and our own.

Yet despite Grace's optimism and apparent energy, there must have been times when she found her life onboard the vessel as the captain's wife difficult and isolating. A sailing vessel was not typically an environment for women and much of the time (with the exception of one or two voyages when a stewardess was employed) Grace appeared to be the only woman present. Not only would she have felt a lack of female companionship (her obvious glee at meeting other captain's wives while at sea or in port affirms this) but she would also have been confined primarily to the after part of the ship in the captain's cabins away from the often rowdy and disreputable crew. Sailing ships were built in

The after cabin of the Belmont *was a comfortable living space. In this photo, the cabin looks cozy and lived-in, with a pillow propped on the back of the couch, and books and papers lying about. Various family photos rest on Grace's piano. The chair in front of the piano was likely made of heavy metal to keep it from moving about in rough seas. When out at sea, the carpet would have been rolled up to prevent water damage. The bright spot at the top of the photo is not caused by the lantern, but by light coming through the sky light. Directly behind this room (the photo is looking aft) was the slop chest and a food storage area.*

a manner that encouraged this separation between captain and crew. The crew lived in the forecastle (or fo'c'sle) which, by the late nineteenth century, was a raised house built on the deck toward the bow of the ship. The captain's cabins were at the other end, toward the stern. A rough diagram left behind by Kathryn gives us a sense of Grace's living space aboard the *Belmont*. This space was divided into a number of rooms. Two larger cabins (the after and forward cabins) occupied the centre of the space. Around these two cabins were a number of smaller rooms: the slop chest (where crew members could purchase supplies), a food storage area, a medicine room, a bathroom, the captain's cabin, Kathryn's cabin (after 1901), a storeroom and sail storeroom, and several small cabins for the mates and stewards (or stewardesses). The forward cabin was where the captain's family and chief officers would eat. The after cabin was a more private living space for the captain and the captain's family. Photos of the after cabin of the *Belmont* show a warm, comfortable space, not unlike a cozy parlour in a house on land. On one side is a fireplace; on the other, a piano. Touches of family life abound in the

The other side of the cabin. In the mirror above the fireplace, the top of the piano and a couple of photographs are just visible. The open door on the right provides a glimpse into the captain's cabin. The two doors on either side of the fireplace would have led into the forward cabin.

books and papers strewn on the table, the sheet music ready to play, and the family photos resting on the piano and fireplace mantle. The only thing missing are the windows one would expect to see in such a room on land. Instead, the *Belmont* cabin had a sky light in the ceiling to allow light and air to penetrate from above.

Unquestionably, Grace's accommodations were more luxurious and upscale than those of the crew. The separation then between Grace and the crew was not only one of physical space, but also of social class. In her reminiscences, Grace's daughter Kathryn does not mince any words when she refers to the sailors (or at least the majority of them) as the "scum of the earth" and the "dregs of humanity." Grace often makes judgmental comments on members of the crew too, although her comments normally focus on their lack of ability rather than on their lack of refinement or morality. And so she says of the carpenter on one voyage, "[he] does not know how to do Ships' carpentering at all" (24 Oct. 1889). Or of the steward and stewardess on another, "Of all cooks he is the worst, dirty and extravagant, and she does not know any thing, and can't learn" (25 Dec. 1891). But Grace also has her more generous moments, where her comments reflect concern and sympathy for the sailors who are forced to work in occasionally rough and cold conditions. In the same letter that contains her criticism of the carpenter, she also writes, "The poor sailors. I was sorry for them," and at another time, her comments reflect compassion for a crew member who boarded the vessel with consumption and whose health worsens throughout the long passage from New York to Shanghai: "Poor McCoy is just alive. I do not see how he can possibly last, but he has held on to life wonderfully although too weak to turn himself in bed" (31 Dec. 1894). On a later voyage, when one of the crew members falls from the rigging into the sea and drowns, Grace writes an emotional vindication of sailors in general, inspired by the courageous behavior of five of their crew members who risked their lives in an effort to save the missing man: "I do not see how some people can call sailors 'dogs.' If they could have seen the sea those brave men started out in with a small boat to try and save that man's life, I am sure they never would do so again" (21 Nov. 1897).

However, Grace's statement confirms that sailors were often called "dogs," and it remains the case that Grace was set apart from members of the crew on account of both her gender and social position. Her letters do not give much indication that she interacted with the sailors or had any relationship with them personally. On special occasions, the crew members were invited to cross the line into her world, such as Christmas in 1897 when they were invited aft to see the tree and were offered a cigar and a drink if they wanted. But the lavish descriptions of Christmas dinners shared by the captain's family and officers suggest that life in the captain's quarters was considerably more comfortable than life in the forecastle. Grace's complaint in one letter that "yesterday we were obliged to eat our Ducks without any gravy" (Christmas Day, 1892) is testimony to how great the distance was that separated her world from the world "before the mast."

One segment of ship life that Grace seemed to have participated in was the running of the galley. She certainly was given the liberty of using the facilities to cook or bake at various times for her family and perhaps for the officers, especially in preparation for holidays or when livestock was killed. On one voyage, when the cook became ill, a shuffling of responsibility took place which put the cabin boy in the galley and another crew member helping with the work aft. When the cabin boy's cooking did not meet the usual standards—"even the sailors growl[ed]"— Grace was forced to take over and "cook for aft" (26 March 1893). Moreover, she clearly had some decision-making power. After indulging in a freshly caught turtle while sailing through the Java sea, Grace (who was not overly impressed with her turtle steak) instructed the steward to "give the men the rest of it, not to cook anymore for aft" (7 May 1897). She must have had enough responsibility to feel a degree of pride, which one can sense on a number of occasions, for instance when reading her 1894 letter at the start of a passage to Shanghai; the crew was not working well but the steward and cook were doing exceptional work, prompting Grace to state (with a good deal of satisfaction), "In *my* department every thing moves smoothly" (31 Dec. 1894, emphasis mine).

In fact having Grace on board seemed to transform part of the vessel into a domestic sphere as though it truly became a home as well as a working environment. This combination of home and work created a situation quite unique, and perhaps broke down some of the usual barriers that existed between a woman's world and a man's. Grace would often perform domestic tasks aboard the vessel such as washing, cooking, and sewing. She also took part in a number of leisure activities typical for women: reading, music and, of course, writing letters. When their children were with them, Grace provided for them and educated them in the manner of a nurturing mother. But she also shared much with Fred. His tasks as captain and the business transactions he handled were never very far from Grace. There are times when she (like many wives and daughters who went to sea) would assist Fred with the navigation. By the late nineteenth century, a number of instruments and reference tools were used to calculate the ship's position: a sextant, a chronometer (providing accurate Greenwich time), a nautical Almanac and mathematical tables. A sighting of the sun (or another heavenly body) would normally be taken when the ship's chronometer registered noon. Grace would call out the exact time (referred to as "taking the time") while Fred would measure the angle of the sun (called "taking or shooting the sun") with the sextant. The sextant measurements would allow Fred to calculate latitude and estimate local time. The difference between local and Greenwich time would then provide the longitude.

Grace's participation in such routines, and in Fred's world generally, grows as time goes on and as she begins to feel more comfortable. In her early letters from the *Morning Light*, she does not speak often of other vessels, writing many of her letters from port, telling of what she does while on land. Later, she begins to write more at sea, her letters becoming chronicles of daily life, referring frequently to other vessels met and spoken. It's as though the vessel itself becomes a stronger focus for her as time goes on, perhaps indicating that she eventually finds her own place in this working environment, blending her role as wife and mother with Fred's as captain and businessman.

This integration of worlds is apparent in the ship's logs as well as in Grace's letters, and the one factor that makes a large difference is Forrest. Before the birth of his son, Fred's logs are primarily what one expects log records to be: they contain a day-to-day record of the ship's business including such details as latitudinal and longitudinal position, weather conditions, distance travelled, vessels spoken, and activity aboard the vessel such as the working of sails and general ship maintenance. A typical log entry would read something like the following for April 8, 1887: "Lat. 12.41. Long. 13.24. Baro. 30.20 & 30.25. Theo 80°. Wind first strong S.E., middle S.S.E. light, last S.E. fresh. Made N.W. 3/4 W distance 170 miles. Painting on Main deck." With Forrest's birth, however, the vessel becomes a place for family and Fred's logs begin to take on a different character. After 1891, his entries are more detailed and include stories about Forrest and Grace as well as the required technical data. His entry for March 7, 1897 (Forrest's seventh birthday), for instance, reflects a combination of work and domestic life:

Lat 9.42. Long 31.04. Baro 29.95. Theo 84°. Wind first fresh then Moderate. S.E. by E. Sky blue, cloudy 2. Cum. Sea Smooth. Lovely Weather. Made 172 Miles. This is Forrest's 7 Birth day. Grace made him a pair of long Pants & he feels quite grown up. We gave him a Small Steamer, goes with an Alcohol lamp under the Boiler. We lit it & started it in the Bath Tub. He was delighted. For dinner gave him Roast Chicken, Boiled Ham, Green Peas & Plum Pudding with Brandy poured over them set on Fire. I made & worked Molasses Candy for him. He treated All hands in the Ship. I measured him. He is 3 ft. 11 5/8 in in his Sock feet. Grace made him a Cake with raisins & Currents. Also, Some Peppermint Candy with White Sugar. Gave him one of my hard hats filled inside with Paper to keep it off his head. He feels Big. Distance Sailed to date 4,727 Miles.

Such details show Fred's enthusiasm and affection for his son, but they also indicate Fred's participation in the domestic side of his family life. Elsewhere in the logs, he details Grace's activities—washing or cooking and baking. One of the log books contains a collection of recipes at the back presumably used by Grace. In short, Fred's logs take on the character of a personal domestic journal as well as remaining a technical work record. As Grace shares his world, he shares hers, and the vessel becomes both a workplace and a place of family warmth.

For Grace, the vessel was a moving home. Throughout the period of her letters (from 1886 to 1899), she only failed to depart with Fred on two voyages, and on the first of these she joined him halfway through, taking a steamer across the Atlantic and meeting him in England. She continued to sail with him after the turn of the century until his retirement from the sea in 1915. Once retired, they settled in Yarmouth and remained active in the community for many more years. This chronicle of their lives is told as much as possible first in Grace's own words, and later in those of her daughter, Kathryn. It begins with Grace's sea letters to her father, and ends with Kathryn's recollections, as an older woman, of her parents' life at sea and her own life with them as a child aboard the *Belmont*. I have tried to fill in the gaps, providing short linking passages between letters and brief summaries of the Ladd's later years at sea and their retirement years, periods not covered by Grace's letters. I have also annotated the letters with notes that offer expansion or explanation, wherever possible, of events and circumstances mentioned by Grace. Asterisks throughout the book indicate sea terms or expressions that are explained in the glossary. As to the letters themselves, I have preserved Grace's wording, changing only punctuation when necessary for clarity, and occasionally updating the spelling (especially of geographical place names). What is clear in the end is that the sea remained for all of them a strong point of focus. Even when in her 70s, Kathryn's memories take her back to the first fifteen years of her life. She recalls those times more than any other of her experiences as though her childhood at sea left a mark on her that all her subsequent adult years failed to diminish.

The story of this particular family's life at sea began several days after Grace Brown and Fred Ladd were married. On May 22, 1886, they travelled to Boston and then to New York, leaving for Shanghai on May 29 aboard the *Morning Light*. Grace's first letter back home to her father was begun as they sailed through the south Atlantic, having just passed by Gough Island and Tristan da Cunha. Grace's introduction to the sea, which took her away from home for over a year, must have been both exhilarating and difficult, but her adaptability and sense of humour are already apparent. In her letter, she laughs at her own initial attempt to complete a load of washing with two tubs and "a wash bench with a board," but she appears to adjust easily to the motion of

Grace Ladd's carte-de-visite. *The photo was taken in Calcutta, probably in 1888 when Grace was 24 years old.*

the ship, and already her curiosity is evident when she is introduced to sharks, whales, albatross and a variety of other marine life. She is also forced into her first confrontation with a culture very different from her own. While sailing past the numerous small islands of the East Indies, they are met by natives— "savages" as Grace first calls them, in the language of her time— who are anxious to trade the fruits of their islands for western goods, and whose desire for those goods (even to the point of selling a young boy for tobacco) is something that Grace clearly finds shocking.

At the start of her letter to Charles E. Brown, Grace proudly writes the words "My first voyage." It was to be the first of many.

The Letters of Grace Ladd

My first voyage
G.F.L.
Lat. S. 39.40 Lon. W. 7.48
Ship *Morning Light*
14th August 1886

My dear Papa

No doubt by this time you think we are well around Cape of Good Hope; instead of that we have not fairly started and are about 90 miles from Gough's Island, east of it. Fred wanted to sight Tristan da Cunha but we passed it in the night. I was sorry as I have almost forgotten how land looks. We have had splendid weather ever since we came out—not one storm and only a few squalls. By splendid weather, I mean for me—poor Fred is almost discouraged. Where ever there was a calm, we have had it. Perhaps we would get a fair wind for a day, but if we did, head winds would blow for a week. However, since yesterday morning we have had strong fair winds. I think they will last. During the first week I felt dizzy whenever we would get a breeze, but since then have been perfectly well—have not had a sick day, everything seems to agree with me. The weather was awfully hot just before we crossed the equator, the thermometer standing between 80° 88° for over a week. Fred had a cover made for the After* sky light* so the sun could not get in. Then we had an awning all over the poop.* Mr. Crocker (the second mate) made me a fine canvas hammock with twine fringe all round. I used to lie in that nearly all day and read. Evenings Fred and I would walk up and down the house.* It took us about [a] quarter of an hour to walk a mile. The house is 40 ft. long. One cannot take much exercise on board a ship. I have [a] small pair of dumb-bells (about four pounds each) I try and use every day, but forget it often. Have had three wash days, the first

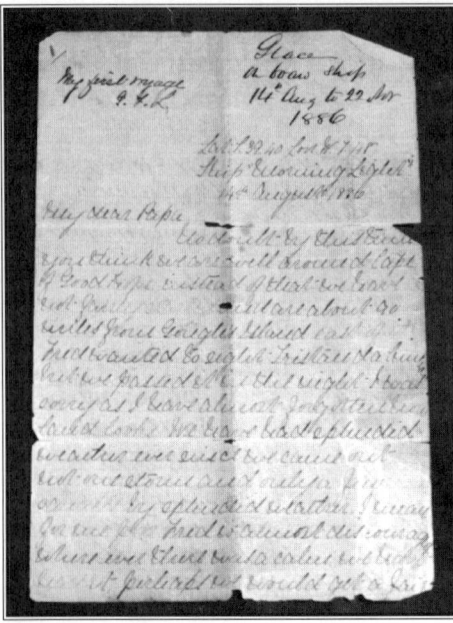

The opening page from Grace's first letter to her father with "My first voyage" inscribed proudly at the start. The writing in the top right-hand corner, "Grace on board ship, 14th Aug to 22 Nov. 1886" is in the hand of Charles E. Brown and was added later. Charles E. Brown often labelled Grace's letters, all of which he carefully saved.

time it took me all day. Everything seemed so strange. Then I had a large washing. I have two tubs, a wash bench with board. Mamma would have laughed if she could have seen me. I rinsed the clothes in the bath tub. Fred rang them all out for me and hung them up. Since then, I have managed better. Get them all washed and dry before dinner. The stewardess would do the washing for me but I like to do it. She does the sheets. We have seen a number of vessels and spoken* some. Day before yesterday six were right round us, all speaking each other and getting the different times.[4] Before that we had not seen a sail for a number of weeks. The glasses you gave Fred are splendid. We use them every day. Just after we left N.Y., we sighted a Norwegian Bark, spoke her, and found her to be the *Amelan* out two day[s] longer than we from N.Y. and bound for Shanghai too. On board her, with the glasses, I could see the sailors quite distinctly. We have caught lots of birds—catch them with a piece of pork on a hook. The steward stewed some Cape pigeons. They were very nice, very much like wild duck only the meat was much darker. One day last week we had seven Molly hawks[5] tied up under the bridge.* The steward fried the liver of three for tea but I could not make up my mind to eat them. Fred said they were splendid, could not tell the difference from bullocks liver. They are splendid looking birds, about seven feet from tip to tip. An albatross has been flying round but it wants something more tempting than pork to catch it. The sailors caught a large shark while we were in warm weather. It was too old to eat. Schools of all kinds of fish would pass us. About two weeks ago Fred called me on deck to see some whales. They passed right by us. One went off with my hat, or Fred's. I ran up in my bare head. He gave me his hat as I ran to the stern to see them better—away it went—it is the only thing we have lost yet. It was more provoking than losing a hat over the bridge. The sky light is full of plants all in blossom. Fletch gave me some seeds. They all came up, even the sunflower. It is about five inches high. It will blossom about the time we get in Shanghai. It is beginning to get dark, so will have to put this by for to-night. It is a few minutes past four. You can imagine how short the days are.

27th Aug. Have just a few minutes before dinner. Ever since I wrote last we have had fair winds. Fred was up all last night. It looked very stormy but passed off, and today is beautiful. It does not seem possible we have been out three months to-morrow, three months since I have seen land, but I expect we will see too much of it before long up among the islands.

29th Sept. Well, we are almost up among the island[s]. Early this morning Fred sighted Fly Island a small island south of

Four crew members aboard the four-masted barque, Iranian *(Captain Isaac Webster) hanging a catch of albatross. The birds were caught using a triangular piece of metal with bacon wrapped around it as bait which the bird would swallow. The bones were used for pipe stems and the skins of the feet were used for tobacco pouches. The photo was taken on a trip to Japan with a cargo of case oil in 1896/97. The captain unfortunately died just before they arrived.*

Sandalwood. After breakfast I saw Black Point on Sandalwood quite plainly, but there is not much satisfaction i[n] seeing land at the distance of 15 or 16 miles. A piece of seaweed floated by. Fred put out a draw bucket and got it for me. We have had a splendid run from Tristan da Cunha, and not one storm—squalls very light. We have sailed a long distance without seeing land, 15,216 miles. When we passed St. Paul's we had hail squalls so we could not see that. It is the island vessels try and sight to correct their chronometers, but ours was only out about 30 miles; but Fred says 120 day[s] is too long to be at sea without seeing anything. I have made me a sun bonnet out of white cotton. It is quite fine, have it all quilted. F. thought it looked so cool I had to go to work and make him a sun hat out of the same materials; however, that was not as great a success as my bonnet. The rim falls down over his eyes. I wonder how you all are to day and what you have been doing all Summer. It seems strange to realize it is getting cool home now, and every day the weather is getting so much warmer with us. I do not know what I would do if it were not for my cotton dresses. We have awnings everywhere it is possible to put one. One day, we were just sixty miles from Australia. It was perfectly calm. I was sitting at the stern of the ship reading. On looking over saw Fred rowing about having a fine time all to himself. You can imagine my surprise. They had put the boat over so quietly I had not heard the least noise of it; however, they soon got the ladder over for me and we had a splendid row for about an hour. While we were out a whale blew about a quarter of a mile from us. I enjoyed the row very much but it was not like rowing in the ponds where trees are on all sides. The Ship was the only thing we could see. Had a good view of her under full sail. Fred has been getting his fire-arms put in good order preparatory for the savages but trust we won't have occasion to use them; but will write more after we get safely through.

27th October ☙ Here we are drifting about the Pacific Ocean. Just a week since we saw the last island, and have had calms ever since. We were three weeks among the islands. Came through "Ombai Pass," passed within about 1 ½ miles of Ombai. I wish I could describe the scenery to you. It was beautiful. The land is very high. We could see the beach and the huts down along the shore. As it grew dark, saw the fires all along. We went up the Banda Sea where we got a heavy squall. Passed up by Buru I. Saw lots of canoes in near the shore and a small vessel. Supposed it was trading among the Islands. For four days while we were in

Pitt's Passage we did not make a mile. Had heavy rain squalls. Got our tanks* all filled. We have been very fortunate—have had plenty of good water since we left N.Y. One day a canoe came off from one of the Islands. We thought it was coming off to us, but it passed to another island—were disappointed as we had made up our minds to have some fruit. Going up Gillolo Pass, we drifted back and lost all we had made for two day[s]. We had currents against us all the time. I thought we would never get out of it. It was pleasant too seeing the different islands. The trees are magnificent. To get out from the islands we had to pass between Moer I. and Gebe I. It was about noon we saw what we thought were boat[s] coming off, but had been disappointed so many times. However, in about half an hour we had three canoes along side. It was worth the voyage to see them. Two out of each boat came on board. They wanted to trade, had cocoanuts, lots and lots of them, a few bananas, 2 dozen sweet potatoes, about the same lemons. Fruit must be out of season, as what they had, except the cocoanuts, was green, all kinds of shells, hats, boxes, mats, and coral, poultry and a red parrot—I got it for a handkerchief. They wanted any thing—shirts, pants (suppose they are going to reform) blankets, Tobacco, knives, iron, wire, they make fish hooks out of it. They were very friendly, shook hands with us. One called himself "Cap. Paul." He was the Captain, could speak about six English words. Another fellow was all tattooed. There was not a bare spot on him. They have long bushy hair and are darker than our Indian[s]. In one of the boats there was a little boy about the size of Hermann. They brought him on deck and let him run about. They must be used to trading with passing ships. They were like monkeys going up and down the ropes and made an awful noise all talking together, and so loud. We kept the breeze just long enough to get out of sight of land when it left us. I begin to feel anxious to get in and hear from home, but we are only 17 hundred miles from our port now. I will never complain of the heat again. Although I have stood it well, it has been terrible. I hope the next time I write will be to close this letter.

29th Oct. ~ We have had such a time today but I must begin with yesterday. A nice breeze came up yesterday morning. About four PM o'clock we sighted Anna I., a small island, about a mile in circumference. When we were about ten miles off, we saw two boats coming off. We thought they must be some ship boats which had been wrecked there, but as they came nearer we saw they were natives. We knew they must want something pretty badly because it was getting dark and looked like squalls. They came up along side. Fred let them come on board. They all came, about twenty, among them a little boy about Ron's age, perhaps older but not as large. All had long straight hair and the poor things were almost starving—didn't have a thing in their boats except mats, splendid fishing lines and shells, said they were "poor." They ate about a bushel of bread but the only thing they would take for their mats was tobacco. They seemed crazy for it. You can imagine how much they wanted it when I tell you they *sold* the *little boy* to Fred for *four pounds* of *tobacco*. One they called the king, he did the trading. Wanted to sell two more but F. would not take them. In fact I think they all would have stayed (except the king). The island must be over running with people. When they left, the little boy's father rubbed his nose four times, all the rest once. [I] sent a piece of tobacco to his mother so she would not cry. It was dark when they left us. Mr. Crocker cut Johnnie's hair, gave him a bath. He seems contented, amazed at everything. Did [not] know how to go downstairs, cannot speak a word of English, but seems bright and is a nice looking little savage. But this morning—how shall I write about it—we were surrounded, 15 canoes, 10 in each canoe. We did not know these islands were inhabited. They are so small. The name of this island is Sonsoral, about 40 miles from Anna. We saw them coming so were prepared. Sailors were all stationed along the deck, armed. They were bound to come on board. F. had the ship turned around but they came right up on us. They paddle at the rate of ten miles an hour. They screamed for "tobac tobac tobacco." F. threw them some. If a piece happened to go in the water, they jumped in for it if they had to swim half an hour to catch up with us. We were thankful for the breeze we had. They would have made short work of us if they had of got on board. They came prepared to trade. We got a large barrel of splendid sponges from them, some very beautiful shells, more lines. They would have followed us yet if we had not traded and we got a lot of their arrow heads. I do not know where I will be able to stow all of the things. We go[t] about 9 turtles. Had turtle soup and fried turtle for dinner. All they would take was tobacco. They yelled for it—"tobac tobac, tobac" was all you could hear. Johnny didn't have any thing to say to them, has been running about today with an old shirt of Fred's on. The stewardess and I are going to make him some clothes. After a time I think they got tired of paddling. They left us one at a time. We were not sorry to see the last of them. Fred had to fire two shots, not at them but off, to show them what he would do [if] they would have come up. I never want to see any more savages, but they must suffer on these islands.⁶

22nd Nov. ∽ Safe at last, anchored 14 miles from Shanghai at a place called Wusung. Fred is going to Shanghai with the tug* so I have only a few minutes to write. Just think, last Wednesday morning we were about ten miles from the Light ship.* Sailed about all day trying to get a pilot.* There was an iron ship in company with us. Spoke her, found her to be the *City of Florence* of Glasgow, the Captain in the same fix as ourselves, wanting a pilot, had two days less than we. Well towards noon it began to blow, the glass* falling fast. At night it was a fearful gale. A steamer passed us bound in. It promised to send us a pilot. We had to put way out to sea. It was something terrible, thought the masts would blow out of the ship. Sea coming over everything filled the cabin, kept the stewardess and me wiping up salt water all day. The plants were looking splendidly but they got a salt water bath. However, it lasted only twenty four hours. At noon Friday we tacked* to come back. Got back yesterday morning. Still no pilot to be seen but we had the tide with us. At eight o'clock last night, got a pilot, found him to be the only one to be had. One boat was lost in the storm and the other was waiting for a steamer. The Iron ship had not arrived, am afraid something has happened [to] her⁷. I tell Fred it does not seem right to feel glad, but we are the first of all the Ships who left just before and after we did to arrive. We have been very fortunate. Have had no sickness among the sailors and have been perfectly well ourselves. Lost nothing, had no storm except the one we had the other day. Two Chinamen are on board now with long pig tails reaching the heels. Fred will bring me my letters this afternoon. You can imagine how anxious I am to hear from home, but the time has passed quickly and pleasantly. I hope you will get this before Christmas which I hope will be a pleasant one for all. I shall write Stayley & Ron a long letter soon, will commence one to Mamma as soon as I hear from home. Have one half written to Fletch and lots more. Fred joins me in love to everyone. A kiss for Hermann. Suppose he has grown very much this summer. Am afraid you will have some trouble reading this.

Yours affectionately

Grace F. Ladd

In her letter above, Grace's shock over the selling of a boy for tobacco is obvious, but Grace's comments, including her gesture to the boy's mother (a bit of tobacco to keep her from crying), suggest a confidence in her own superiority over the people of these islands. Language was often an important measure of "civilization" whenever the Ladds encountered various native peoples. The ability (or lack thereof) to speak English was something Grace routinely mentioned as though it was some kind of measuring stick of just how developed a culture was. Fred and Grace became clearly irritated, for instance, when they attempted to talk to some Javanese natives (letter of May 7, 1897): "The Peddler tried to interpret for us. Fred was quite disgusted—they seemed so stupid." However, there were moments when friendly communication did take place and many occasions when the Ladds, along with most merchant ships, benefitted from what the natives had to trade. The term "savage" (used several times by Grace in the above letter) rings harsh on our ears with its strong negative connotations, but Grace significantly (and for reasons unknown) never uses the word again after her first letter. From this point on, when referring to aboriginal peoples, Grace uses the term "native."

It would seem that this cultural encounter, one that occurred on her first voyage at sea, stayed with Grace for many years and became something of a family legend. Kathryn Ladd quoted in her notebook the portion of her mother's letter that described acquiring the young boy, and then reminisced on a version of the story that was surely passed down to her a long time afterward by her parents. Whether or not events happened exactly as Kathryn records is questionable (there are some inconsistencies between her account and the log record), but the story of this boy (whom Kathryn calls "Albert") must have taken its place in the Ladd family history:

> He was completely uncivilized but very smart and eager to learn. My parents became very fond of him. When mother took him down stairs to the After Cabin* to find some clothes, he looked at the stairs—then proceeded to go down on his hands and knees head first. The first thing he wanted was shoes. He kept pointing to his feet which were flat with great calluses on the insides from shinnying up cocoanut trees. Mother eventually found a pair in the Slop chest*— Size twelve in to which the small boy squeezed his feet— delighted with them. She cut down a pair of dungarees and a shirt for him. ... Mother amused herself by teaching him to read and write. He caught on quickly and soon learned to speak English. One day she noticed some Chinese characters

at the top of a page in his scribbler. When asked about them, Albert said he had drawn them, that "I teachee Cooky English. He teachee me Chinese!" Unfortunately the cold weather in Shanghai in late November and early December did not agree with Albert. He caught a cold and then as they sailed back south to the Equator, he seemed to recover— until they sailed for South around the Horn when the cough returned. By the time the *Morning Light* reached New York on June 24, Albert was very ill and they took him to the Hospital. He was dying and very home sick saying to mother, "Oh Misey, if I could have a Cocoanut!" In 1887, Cocoanuts were scarce in New York. Father combed the City and eventually found one. Little Albert died with the Cocoanut in his arms.

Sometime after reading Kathryn's account of the above story, I talked to Jim Day, a grandson of Grace's sister, Florence. He told me he remembered hearing a number of stories about the Ladds at sea when he was a child. He said one story was about a native boy they picked up and took with them back west, but the boy became ill and was given a cocoanut before he died. I asked Jim if he had ever met Kathryn Ladd. He never had. So the story must have come down to him some other way.

After the Morning Light *arrived in Shanghai, the discharging of case oil* began and was completed on December 6. By the time Grace wrote her next letter, ballast had been loaded and they were ready to set out again for sea.*

Ship *Morning Light*
Shanghai 9th Dec. 1886

My dear Papa

I was much pleased to receive your letter of 29th Oct. and a *Yarmouth Herald*. I was afraid I would not get anymore letters, got so many on arriving. I think I must know almost every thing that has happened since I left home, but every time I read a letter over, find something new. We got both the *Times* and *Herald* with the Exhibition list of prizes. We are keeping all our papers to read over when we get to sea again. Don't you remember I said I did not believe Jennie Van Norden would ever marry the Washington gentleman. Wonder what the trouble was. Am afraid there is not much hope of the Ship going to San Francisco, but if we should I won't forget to call on the Van Nordens and I should like to see

Mrs Clements too. If we should go, will you send me her address? I cannot tell you how kind Mr and Mrs Yens have been.[8] We always manage to meet at the Astor House. Mrs Yens gave me a programme Mr Y. made out for us. I will send it to you. Before that we had been to a number of places with them. I think they really enjoy taking us. It is so much nicer having a native to tell where to go and go with us. I went to the Theatre. It was so funny. Of course I could not understand a word, but the dresses were elegant and the acting altogether different. All the time the play was going on, cake and tea was passed around. Miss Purple is one of the teachers. It was she we found at home the day we called at St John's College. Mr Yen's Church is altogether Chinese. The sermon is preached in Chinese and no one but Chinese attend. The Cathedral is the largest Church, that is, English speaking church, where all the aristocracy go. We went to the Government Arsenal yesterday. The ride was rather long. Then one has so much sympathy for the rickshaw boys. Mr Yens had to change his twice. Said both were opium smokers—that makes them stupid. They only charge ten cents an hour and run almost as fast as a horse. When we were going through the Arsenal, Mr Y. said he would think the men ought [to] wear their hair done up so it would not get caught in the machinery. He told us all about the ladies' little feet. His wife has small feet, but he is not going to have his little girl's feet bound; but he says his boys like the small feet best, think they are prettier. I have a pair of the little boots. It does not seem possible a human being could ever wear them. Mrs Yens speaks English very well. They have four boys and one girl. The oldest son, 19, is at the same school in America his Father was. By the "City" he mean[s] the Chinese City that is all walled in.[9] Do not think we will be able to go there until next week some day. That wedding is not the one we got the direct invitation to; this one is a Christian wedding. Of course the people are Chinese, but the ceremony is like our[s] except the man has never seen his young lady. The wedding we were

Rev. Y. K. Yen, his wife and his daughter, Julia. The Yens hosted the Ladds while they were in Shanghai. One of Mrs. Yen's "small feet" is just visible beneath her dress. The photo was taken in 1895, nine years after Grace's first visit.

 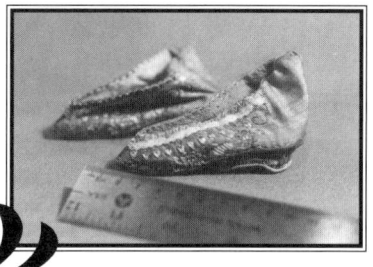

A fan given to the Ladds as a wedding gift in Shanghai, perhaps by the Yens. Known as a "hundred face fan," the fan displays 50 people on each side whose faces are made from painted ivory.

The "little boots" Grace obtained in Shanghai are part of a large collection of "curiosities" she gathered throughout her years of voyaging with Fred. Many of the items Grace collected are on display at the Yarmouth County Museum in Yarmouth, Nova Scotia.

invited to by the parents themselves comes off a week from Sunday. I am very anxious to go; if we are here we will. I wrote you a long letter and sent it by a German Steamer which we heard went ashore, but suppose the mails will be forwarded. Am sending you a Chinese paper enclosed in a Shanghai paper. They are both Shanghai papers but one is English, the other Chinese. I have not time to write Flo by this mail. She wrote me such a nice long letter that I want to write her a long one in return. I can imagine the boys and the pup. I expect Hermann is delighted. The Salvation Army is know[n] even here. The congregations are large in the other churches. It would seem strange to see them marching about Yarmouth. Poor Mr Burrill. I am sorry he is so ill. I suppose Mrs Burrill is as cool as ever. She will be sorry she did not stay with him while he was away. Is Jud doing anything yet? There does not seem to be any stones about Shanghai. It is low and marshy. The City is dyked in. I am going to get some curios. Have quite a number already. Fred often laughs at the things I get. He believes in getting nice things but I like the little things, such [as] their pipes. They are so funny—it would take a day to learn to smoke one. We are all ready for sea, are just waiting to get chartered. Things are so bad we may be here some time yet. Fred joins me in love to all. I have kept a kind of diary but what I haven't written I can remember. With much love,

Yours affectionately

Grace F. Ladd

It took another couple of weeks before Fred received orders to proceed to Manila to load sugar. Grace sent the next letter, the last from Shanghai, as they were making their way out with a pilot onboard.

Shanghai
Ship *Morning Light*
23rd Dec. 1886

My dear Papa

Was pleased to receive your letter dated 29th Oct. Was afraid you would not write again after the fare-well letter. We are on our way to Manila to load sugar for N.Y. No doubt you heard as soon as we were chartered, as Fred telegraphed to Mr. Hall.[10] I am afraid you won't get the letter I wrote you during our passage out as I sent it by a French steamer which went ashore. Am sorry, am sure I could never write such a long letter again, but if nothing happens we will be home next June or July.[11] I suppose you are all very busy preparing for Christmas. I shall think of you all tomorrow evening sitting around the dining room table, filling the stockings and marking the different parcels. I remember last Christmas Eve, Fletch and I went in town—coming back the bus broke down. We had to walk the remainder of the way through deep mud. Mr. Yen has been very kind to us. Sunday we went to a Chinese wedding with him. The ceremony is so queer. They have to go through all sorts of funny performances. I know you have read better descriptions of Chinese weddings than I could give you. I was not much surprised to hear Jennie Van Norden had broken off her engagement. I wish we could have gone to San Francisco. It is more than likely we will come right out this way again from New York. Perhaps we will get a freight* to San Francisco. Then every thing is so low here, times are very hard. One ship has been here five months. The pebbles here are such common looking ones. I suppose I could walk for miles and not see one stone. You know Shanghai is very low and marshy, but I will tell you what we have got: the most beautiful shells from the Islands. We have that trunk you had such a time locking packed full, and a large box besides; however, I will select a few pebbles. It is getting late so I must hurry. I do not suppose you will write to Manila. We have 32 days to load. I wonder if Beverly Jones is still paying attention to Maria. It would be funny if [she] settles in Yarmouth after all. We are taking to Manila two cases of beautiful Pheasants. They are very common here. I do not like them to eat. They have a peculiar taste. The pilot is about leaving us—With much love to all—

Your[s] affectionately

Grace F. Ladd

The Morning Light *arrived at Manila just after the New Year (1887). Fred's log records the cost of taking in and storing sugar at 11 cents per ton in Spanish currency, and hemp at 5 cents per ton. They loaded 1,000 tons of sugar and 49.70 bales of hemp. Loading was finished by the end of the month after which they left for New York to arrive there on May 17. Discharging began and was completed by the beginning of June.*

There is a 15-month gap between Grace's last letter and the next one in part because she spent some of this time in Yarmouth. She was pregnant and probably decided it would be better to miss Fred's next voyage and remain at home for the birth. Both Fred and Grace returned to Yarmouth in June, but Fred went back on his own to New York a couple of weeks later and sailed out again for Batavia (now Jakarta) with a load of oil. The passage across had its rough moments. The weather was stormy in September with a sea so strong the ship's dog was washed overboard. There were also a couple of injuries that Fred had to contend with. The carpenter cut his foot badly and, on another day, a crew member fell from the yard* to the deck, injuring his head. As captain, Fred had to take care of medical emergencies and would have consulted a medical reference book for help (Grace mentions such a book in her letter of Christmas Day, 1892 below). In the case of the carpenter, Fred had to stitch the cut himself. In his log, he records, "Carpenter cut his foot & layed up. Sewed the cut up with needle & thread after taking up the arterys."

While Fred was dealing with his various problems, Grace too was having a difficult time back in Yarmouth. She gave birth to a daughter on October 4 who did not survive. Her father's journal entry for that day describes the ordeal in some detail indicating that Grace had clearly experienced trouble during labour and that a cesarean had had to be performed:

Dr. Anderson came down and saw that the case was similar to poor Eth's, that extraction by instruments was necessary to save the Mother's life. He went over to Dr. Lovitt's and borrowed his instruments and relieved the suffering Mother, whether at the cost of the infant's life or not is not certain.

The doctor thought it had died between 1 & 4 AM, that he watched and listened carefully before removing it, but could see no signs of life. ... Poor Grace! It will be a great affliction when after enduring all the pains & perils of labor to lose the precious life which alone would have compensated. Rest, quiet & sleep followed, and all were thankful that the trial was so far at an end.

Fred, who arrived at Batavia on October 2, would presumably have received the sad news by telegraph. But life and the ship's business had to continue, and he also received orders at this time to proceed to Surabaya (Java) to discharge his cargo.

Early in November, the Morning Light *was loaded with sugar, and Fred left Surabaya bound for Falmouth, England. He was, however, suffering from a fever and sore throat, a "throat so bad, can scarce breathe," and was forced to go onshore at Banjuwangi to see a doctor. There, he was diagnosed with Java fever, given medication and then he set out again for England. In the meantime, Grace left from New York in a steamer,* Aurania *(of the Cunard line), in early February to arrive at Queenstown (now called Cobh), Ireland on February 19. From there she travelled to Ainsdale, England, presumably to visit her Aunt Maggie (wife of Capt. Lemuel Robbins) who lived there. Fred arrived at Falmouth in early March, caught the train immediately and was reunited with Grace in Ainsdale later the same day.*

Grace and Fred went back to Falmouth together, then left aboard the Morning Light *for Kristiansand, Norway on April 1. Grace's next letter was written from Kristiansand.*

Ship *Morning Light*
Kristiansand 9th April 1888

My dear Papa

We got our mail last eve. I received four letters from you, 29th Feb, 6th, 7th and 14th March, one from Georgie, one from Eth, and one each from Min. and Fannie, then lots of papers. They will last us for some time. We hope the ice will be out of the Sound[12] the last of this week at the latest. With a fair wind, Landskrona is hardly a day's sail from here. Kristiansand is the third place in size in Norway. Our ship is lying at Flekkeroy, three miles below the town. By water it is three miles to Kristiansand and four by land. We row up some days and drive back. We have found the people very hospitable. Several have asked us to spend the day with them.

We return the compliment. They always seem to enjoy a day on board the *Morning Light* very much. Fred feels very proud to have the ship praised and I am duly proud to have the cabin praised and we certainly are very comfortable & cozy. The Harbour Master says it is the finest ship ever in the Harbour and there is no house as nice. Fred and I have had great time[s] snow shoeing and coasting. We are about five minutes row from the shore. Any of the farmers are pleased to lend us shoes or sleds. The snow shoes are made of thin hard wood turned up at the toes, 4 feet long with a strap across the middle for the foot. They are very awkward at first. One has to take a pole to keep from slipping down the hills. However, I think we get on very well now and it is good exercise—we always come on board ship with a good appetite. We get fresh milk every morning. I tell Fred he had better fill the tanks with milk— it is so cheap, one cent a quart. They have such a funny fashion of thanking you for any hospitality you show them, but especially after eating or drinking. They shake hands, make a courtesy (the women and children) and thank you. The children thank their mothers, the gentlemen lift their hats to each other when they pass (perfect strangers), even young boy[s]. When we go on shore, we meet a lot of little girls. I get Fred to take off his hat & I bow. To see them courtesy one after the other, it looks so odd. I am so sorry for Annie Biedermann. It hardly seems possible Mr B. would dare do such a contemptible thing. What do Mrs. Caie and Clara say about it?[13] Fred says Mr. Caie had the inside track of Mr Biedermann. I can just imagine Hermann when he cut his knee. I often think of him the day I took him skating, as plucky as possible, not minding a fall a bit. I hope Stayley got his neck-tie all right. It was just like Ron's. It hardly seems a safe way of sending. One always feels a little anxious until you hear. I am much pleased with the photograph of Eth's baby.[14] It could not be better. I shall send Maggie's to her today with a letter I have written her. Fred joins me in love to all.

Yours affectionately

Grace F. Ladd

By the time Grace wrote her next letter, they had sailed down to Landskrona, Sweden to discharge the Morning Light's *cargo. From there, they proceeded to Cardiff where they loaded coal for Cape Town. While still in Scandinavia, Grace and Fred took advantage of the time to visit a number of tourist spots. Grace's next two letters, both writ-*

ten in Landskrona, provide some detail of what they saw while they had the opportunity to visit this part of the world.

Ship *Morning Light*
Landskrona 28th April 1888

My dear Papa

We arrived here safely this morning early, have had head winds and thick weather ever since we left Kristiansand. Fred has not had an hours sleep, therefore is nearly tired out but he won't take time to rest even now and is ashore busy about something. There was one letter 4th April from you awaiting us here besides a number of papers and a sketch of "The History of Yarmouth" which surprised me much. Had you an idea Uncle George thought of such a thing?[15] By this time, no doubt, you know we are chartered from Cardiff to load coal for Cape Town. It will be a pleasant voyage. Although Landskrona is only 2° farther South than Kristiansand, it is much warmer—not a bit of snow to be seen and the grass is turning green, but ice is still in the Sound drifting about with winds and currents. The Baltic is still unnavigable. From our deck we can see Copenhagen, Helsingor or Elsinore, and Helsingborg. A Steamer leaves here for Copenhagen twice a day going in one hour. I am looking forward to that trip with much pleasure. If Fred can make it possible, will stay three days. Tuesday Fred is going to Helsingborg to see about getting the ship coppered.* There is a very old Castle there which we will go through.[16] Since I commenced writing they have begun discharging cargo. By that do not suppose we will be here very long. Fred and I have planned long walks. When he can't go, I shall go alone. I will find out whether it be true, in Norway, they feed cows on

The Morning Light *at Landskrona. The letters "Yarmouth NS," its port of registry, can be seen clearly on the stern. The rigging, which is attached to the outside of the ship, gives it away as a wooden vessel.*

fish. The milk was splendid. We got fresh every morning, two quarts. At noon I used to take a large cup full of cream off. Denmark and the South of Sweden supplies the whole country with hay. It is very scarce and dear. We used to see Steamers loaded with it coming to Kristiansand, packed in bales. We also got good butter, paid 80 ore a lb. for it. It takes 100 ore to make a krona or 18 kronas to make £1 or 1 krona is equal to 27C. Fred has told me this so many times that at last I have got it into my head. We paid 9 ores a qt. for milk. Our Ship is right long side of the pier. It is much nicer than having to go ashore in a boat. I shall certainly write Grandma Brown from here.[17] I am ashamed that I have not done so long ago but my eye prevented my writing from Kristiansand during the last of our stay; but it is all well now so I must not complain. It was nothing serious, but Fred was very much worried. Tell Ron and Stayley their letters are coming by-and-by. I wonder what Stayley would like in the way of a collection. Fred has a number of stamps for Ron. I expect a letter from Hermann soon—is he going to school next term? I am sorry for poor Will Chipman. His faith was so strong that I thought perhaps he would get well. If you see him again tell him Fred says, out in Java, George Cann used to read Fred bits from Will's letters and they often used to talk about him, as Fred and I often do. I never used to mind asking little favours of Will. It was never any trouble for him to do up parcels for me or give me pieces of twine. I will finish this tomorrow—Good-night. It is time for Fred back now.

29th April. ∽ Sunday morning. This morning I got a letter from you dated 4th April which had been sent to Kristiansand and sent back from there. It must be a great improvement having the Electric Light at Milton.[18] I should imagine they were arranged nicely. Jane won't be as lonely now. I wish I could remember how many years the old gardener told us the Sequoia had been planted there, but it was not many. He said it was very hardy and grew rapidly. He called our attention to the

Grace's uncle, George Stayley Brown. His book, Yarmouth Nova Scotia: A Sequel to Campbell's History *(1888) is still a frequently consulted reference text.*

size of the trunk and I asked him [what] it was. When he told me, I asked him particularly if it need any particular care. He said "no," the soil seemed to suit it there, but they require lots of room—perhaps a pot is not large enough. Tell Fletch I planted some of the seeds she gave me. I planted them in a fig box and they are all up, all kinds mixed together. Fred got a paper with our arrival in yesterday—has ordered two more, one for his father, and I shall send one to Grandma. In it I shall enclose some seeds for Fletch. Fred got them out in Java. The gentleman who gave them to Fred said they were very choice, but Fred says he doesn't believe they are any good. Any way we planted some and they are up about an inch, look something like a bean I think. When we were out in Manila, that Miss Earnshaw you have heard me speak of gave me a plant. Now it looks like an herb, smells like worm wood. I will enclose a leaf of it. All left the ship last night except Mate and Steward. They were a happy lot of sailors—a great many of them are going right home. All are Swedes and Norwegians. They were singing "Homeward Bound"[19] as they went over the side, the first time they have been on shore for ten months. It reminded me of what Arth wrote us from Rio, only this time they were really going home. It is raining hard now. I hope it will clear off by afternoon as we were going on shore. There is a prison here, 300 years old. The monks built it for a Monastery. The prisoners are in for life. I think it will be worth going through. Fred joins me in love to all. I shall write every few days.

Yours affectionately

Grace F. Ladd

Ship *Morning Light*
Landskrona, 22nd May/88

My dear Papa

The last letter I received from you was dated 2nd May. By that mail we got a number of paper[s]—enclosed in one some May flowers, the second lot. I was pleased to get them as I had been asking several people if May flowers grew in this part of the world, but no one knew them by that name. Now they say they grow up in the Mountains in the North of Sweden. We will finish discharging tomorrow. They have been very slow. Now if we can only have a quick run to Cardiff. We will not get away before the last of the week as we have to take in ballast. The Country is looking beautiful now. Sunday we went for a long drive to a health resort, a place called Ramlosa. The mineral water there is supposed to be the best in Sweden.[20] We all drank as much as we could. It was not very pleasant tasting. The farmers are just beginning to plant their potatoes and the trees are not [———] leaved out yet. They say the Season is one month late. I have written to Stayley, Ron & Hermann. I printed Hermann's letter so that he could read it himself. Last week the Exhibition in Copenhagen opened.[21] I enjoyed [it] very much. We stayed two days. It was quite enough. I do not think I ever want to go to another exhibition, but I think I stood it better than Fred. He is lame yet, not being used to standing so much, and we did not want to waste any time by sitting down. We saw the Royal Family—the King opened the Exhibition.[22] Fred bought one of the Marches played at the opening to send to Min. Do you recognize the writing on the knife handle? What do you think of it? We cut [?] of the best signature we could find. We have had some photos taken here. Fred's are good, mine miserable, so I will not send one home. Then we had three taken with the Captain who went to Copenhagen with us. I will send one of those. I shall be glad to get in England where we can hear English spoken. Very few people speak English here. We only know four. Most all speak German. We went to a concert the other evening given by some students. They tell us the Swedish Students are renown[ed] the world over for their singing, but I think I have heard as good in Yarmouth. The poorer class of children and people wear wooden shoes. I intend getting a small pair. The women wear handkerchiefs on their head like the French home.[23] Some wear hats of course. How is Mrs Stoneman, Tom's mother? No one has ever written me about her so I suppose she is getting well. She will be sorry to have Eth move so far away. I got a long letter from Eth which I will answer today. I do not know how it is, but I can not find much time for any thing, like sewing or writing. It is surprising how long each day it take[s] to clear up the cabin and take care of the flowers. They are looking well now—four geranium in full blossom, one carnation (given me in Norway) and a rose with eight buds. We have twenty plants in the after sky light, eight in the forward.* With much love to all,

Yours affectionately

Grace F. Ladd

The Morning Light *was finally loaded with ballast on May 27, five days after Grace's last letter. They got underway and arrived at Cardiff on June 7, from where Grace wrote again.*

Ship *Morning Light*
Cardiff 8th June 1888

My dear Papa

On arriving here yesterday, found two letters from you awaiting me, dated 6th and 19th May, and one from Fletch, besides papers. It was fortunate you did not send any more letters to Landskrona as they would not have got there until the day after we sailed. By every American mail I received letters and papers from home. And yesterday we anchored in Cardiff Roads while Fred went ashore to get our orders. When he came back bringing the letters, I was as anxious to read them as though it had been weeks instead of days since I last heard from home. We had a pleasant trip coming up the English Channel—went the whole length of the Channel in 24 hours, passing by the land. It was evening when we passed Dover. It was a very pretty sight, the town all lighted up. Just back, the cliffs are very high. On the top is a Castle used for barracks. This was one flame of light. The Isle of Wight we passed the next morning. Every thing looked so fresh and green. It must be a beautiful place, I think. I though[t] I would have time to finish this letter before going to Cardiff with Fred (our Ship is at Penarth) but he tells me that he wants to catch the next ferry, so Good-bye.

9th June ∽ I spent a pleasant day yesterday with Mrs Dolf Cann[24] who is here with her husband. She is coming on board our Ship today. I got another letter from you yesterday and one from Flo. They do not lose much time going to Liverpool and it is too late to give you our address here. I do not see why I did not think of it while in Landskrona. The last letter I wrote while in Norway, before catching cold in my eye, was to Laura. Her letter has not reached me yet but suppose it is on the way. The distance from Landskrona to Copenhagen is just 13 miles, and in the Winter time it is a common thing to walk across. From Helsingor to Helsinbor[g] is 1 ½ miles, and while we were in Landskrona, a man swam across there from Sweden to Denmark which, after all, was no great swim. The passage from Landskrona to Copenhagen is a shilling— for return tickets, less. Then there are very cheap tickets sold. I do not know what takes so many people back and forth but every boat used to have a large number of women. I always though[t] they took their goods to Market. They had backets [baskets?], and looked like that. I am afraid you were disappointed in the letters I wrote after visiting Copenhagen, but really we saw so much that I could not begin to write about all. It is a beautiful city. I always felt sorry when time came to leave for Landskrona. We were there three times. Every place of any interest we visited. When we told our Landskrona friends the places we went to, they laughed, and said they should never think of going to that place—for instance, a very old Church, from the ground to the top of the Steeple, 280 ft. Around the Steeple, like a snake, stairs to go to the top. On the very top, a large ball in which is a table and chairs for seven people. Well, we attempted to go to the top, but just half way up I had to give up. It was no use. In the first place, when we started, Fred thought we had better not attempt it, but I said, "oh yes, let's," so we went; but the old man walked so fast, he did not give us a minute to breathe. Did you ever walk up a number of steps one after the other? If so, you know how tiring it is. The Norwegian Captain was as tired as I was but would not give in. Fred stood it better. However, we had a fine view. We were up 220 ft. The story [is], after it was finished, the builder found he had wound the stairs the wrong way—from the sun, instead of with it—so he went to the top and jumped off.[25] I do not think there is the slightest chance of my coming across Jennie Van Norden. No doubt she has left Eng. by this time. The only chance would be in Liverpool and I do not think we will be able to go there. We are going to Bristol. If Fred gets along with his loading all right, we hope to have a quick dispatch from here. I shall look forward to letters in Cape Town. It will be only a short voyage there, about 1/3 the distance to Shanghai. Any letters or papers that come to a Port after we leave always follow us. I received the Sequoia and Parsley seeds alright. I shall be able to exchange the Sequoia seeds in Cape Town. I will plant some too. The little envelopes are just the thing. I shall be very careful of them. We are so pleased to get all the papers. I do not think there is one paper missing from the time you commenced to send them. I have kept my Journal faithfully ever since leaving home, but am afraid it is not as interesting as it might be. I shall write Fletch and Flo the first of the week. I feel my letters are a poor return for the long nice letters I receive from all at home. Fred joins with me in love to all.

Yours affectionately

Grace F. Ladd

Unfortunately, loading took longer than expected and the "quick dispatch" Fred and Grace were hoping to have didn't happen. The Morning Light *spent more than another month in Penarth. When Grace wrote the next letter in mid-July, loading had just started.*

Ship *Morning Light*
Penarth 16th July 1888

My dear Papa,

I suppose by this time you think we are almost to the Equator, but instead of that we have just commenced to load. Came under the tip* this morning. I have packed every thing movable away, taken the carpets up—the Cabin looks bare enough. Have been hard at work all the morning. There are a great many Yarmouth Ships here now—the *County of Yarmouth* among the most important. Capt Scott has been to see us several times. Capt Nichols has been here with his wife and two daughters. You remember a little paper I gave you called the *Ocean Chronicle*? Well, he is the Captain that publishes it. They were very pleasant people. This is his last voyage. He is tired of the sea. His wife has been with him eight years without taking one holiday. They sailed for Rio on Saturday. Fred and I went up to Bristol for a day last week. We enjoyed it so much. Capt George came, met us at the Station. His Ship is going to Cape Town. We may meet there. It seems years ago they sailed out of Galveston together for a number of voyages. [While in Bristol we went to see an oculist. He examined my eyes, pronounced them sound, and not near sighted, but he says I have a very peculiar sight, one eye altogether different from the other. To make them alike I have to wear glasses. It is surprising what a difference it makes. Every thing looks so different. They are very ugly looking glasses. I feel very large and round.][26] Last Friday Fred

The County of Yarmouth, *2,154 tons, was the largest vessel registered in Yarmouth. It was launched in 1884 at Belliveau's Cove, Digby County, Nova Scotia, and sold to the Argentinian government in 1895.*

and I went on Penarth Beach for a walk. We got two ponies for half an hour and each rode pony back. I am lame yet. I complained about the pony but the boy said it was because I did not know how to ride. Capt. G. Cann came down on Saturday and stayed until this morning. Fred and he talked all night nearly. Capt Cann has not had any letters from home yet so we had lots of news for him. I finished my cotton dress. It looks very well for a first attempt. I am going to make another after we get out at sea. We hear glowing accounts of Cape Town. They tell us the climate is delightful and the people friendly. Fred has just brought me a letter from you dated 28th June, and also the Yarmouth papers. I am so sorry about Hermann. I hope he is all well now. I shall feel anxious until I hear again. That will be in Cape Town.

17th July ∞ Last night we had on board to tea [the] Swedish Captain who put the leech on my eye in Kristiansand.[27] He has bought a load of timber here from up the Baltic. Captain Stray is also here with his wife and mother. His is a new Ship and the Swedes believe if an old woman will go in the Ship for the first passage good luck will follow. You know it was Capt. Stray that we were with so much in Kristiansand. He lives there. It seems strange that we should all meet here again. I will write again before we sail. We have no idea where we will go from Cape Town. Fred joins me in love to all.

Yours affectionately

Grace F. Ladd

Grace and Fred finally set sail for Cape Town on July 26 and arrived there on October 8. Due to a judgmental error, acknowledged by Fred in his logs, they lost time on this voyage and arrived later than they should have. As Fred described it, he tacked to the east as he was approaching the equator instead of standing to the west, adding approximately seven days to the time it took him to cross the equator. Moreover, Fred realized that he didn't go far enough south before crossing 0° longitude, which added a further five days to the time it took him to reach Cape Town from the meridian "making 12 days loss" altogether. Fred's "mistakes," as he refers to them, were misjudgements of wind direction. Vessels normally steered west, almost to Brazil, before crossing the equator. And the farther south one went before crossing the meridian, the stronger the easterly winds and the quicker the voyage across to Cape Town.

It must have been a big change reaching Cape Town after spending time in Scandinavia and Wales. But Grace's next two letters written from Cape Town and Table Bay show her usual willingness to venture into and experience a strange cultural environment.

Ship *Morning Light*
Cape Town 16th Oct. 1888

My dear Papa

My hand feels rather unsteady this afternoon, but as tomorrow is mail day I am afraid to put off writing any longer. This morning Fred and I took such a long walk. First we went to the top of "Signal Hill" which is 1150 ft. high, just one third as high as Table M. We registered our names in the visitors' book and look[ed] through a very powerful spy glass. We read the signals of a Bark coming in at the distance of 13 miles. We got rested a little there, then walked along the "Lions Back" (a mountain range) on to the head, then down into the town again. We intended going to the top of the head, but while we were up there the fog came in and completely covered it. We were glad to get down as quickly as possible. We were just four hour[s] and a half from the time of leaving the Ship until we got back again. Some of the views of the country we got were splendid. Cape Town is just at the foot of the Mountains on a level. The town itself is not very pretty, but the villages around the mountain are beautiful. Saturday we took Lunch with Mr Anderson at Rose Bank. He has a beautiful place. His Father, an old gentleman, 84 years of age, took me out to lunch, after which he went for a drive with us to a friend's to see the roses. I never saw so many varieties before growing together. This was also a fine place. His hobby (the gentleman's) was trees—one, a Norfolk Pine, measured 165 ft. I have given Mr. Anderson some of the Sequoia seed to try. He was much pleased, knew all about the tree, had even seen a piece of the bark, but not the tree itself. He has promised me some seed in return. He gave me a large piece of "Paper Tree Bark." They are wonderful trees, grow very large but the bark hanging all in rags just like the piece I enclose [———] large pieces. Cape Town, boasts of a fine Botanical Garden where I saw our own white water lilies growing, a fine museum which we have not visited yet, lots of churches. Fred and I attended a Methodist Church—heard a very good sermon but rather long. After church we went out to Mr Dolman's, Mr. Anderson's cashier's, and finished the day. He lives just at the other side of the mountain. We went by train, passed close by the Royal Observatory. This Mr Dolman is a very peculiar old man. He has just a funny hobby, a workshop in which he has all the latest inventions—one turning lathe cost £200. They have no children and are a queer couple. Mrs Dolman does not like the Cape. The last time they came from England, it seems they had a very bad storm. Mr D. was much frightened, declared he would never cross the water again, but Mrs D. says if it had only had happened going home. Every day we go somewhere. The flowers are beautiful, the wild one[s] I mean, all kinds and colors, and so fragrant.

Wednesday morning Fred was up at day-light this morning to go on board a coolie Ship which came in here yesterday for fresh stores. He has been telling me all about it and I am afraid I missed something by not going with him. This Ship is taking these coolies home from Demerara where they have served their ten years and made their small fortunes. There were 667 men, women, and children on board.[28] Mr. Dolman gave me a bracelet, steel, taken from the arm of a dead Kaffir chief on the battle field.[29] I hope to get out to an Ostrich Farm before we leave. There are none very near. One gentleman has partly promised to take us. We had Rick Sheldrake spending the other evening with us. He has been in Cape Town nearly four months. He is a policeman, but intends going to sea again the first chance he gets. The Captain Stray and wife I wrote you we met in Cardiff, we met them first at their home in Kristiansand. The *Tal* [?], Capt. S's ship, was then building. They were very kind to us. I made myself quite at home at their house although Mrs Stray could not speak one word of English. The leaf enclosed is from the "Silver Leaf Tree." It grows on Table Mountain, nowhere else in the world. I will send the

Silver leaves, such as the one Grace sent back to her father from the Silver Leaf Tree grown on Table Mountain, were often painted with marine landscapes. The one above shows the N. B. Lewis, *a Yarmouth ship, against the landscape of Cape Town.*

Paper Bark in a paper. It is too clumsy to enclose. With love to all from Fred and self,

Yours affectionately

Grace F. Ladd

Ship *Morning Light*
Table Bay, 28th Oct. 1888

My dear Papa

The Captain of the Tugboat came off for Fred at six this morning so that he could settle up what he had not time for yesterday early, so I suppose we shall be away by nine. It is beginning to blow very hard. I am afraid it will be very rough outside. Capt. G. Cann was on board last evening and stayed until twelve o'clock. He is looking very well, quite fat. I was glad to get the school average—just imagine Hermann getting the only 100. Stayley also did well in spelling. How is it that Ron is ahead of them all in Arithmetic? I told you I gave Mr Anderson some Sequoia seed. In return he sent me twelve varieties of cacti. I hope they will live but I am afraid they won't. This is not much of a place for curiosities; however, we have a few small things. The principal curiosities are weapons and I think they all look alike. We saw some arrow heads up in the Museum, just like you used to find in the garden.[30] In your letter you said I ought to receive it on the 26th Oct. and on that day, I received it. Any letters or papers that come after we leave will be forwarded to us. Our address will be c/o Ralli Bros. Calcutta. I hope by the time this reaches you we will be almost to our destination. I am glad we are going to India. I believe Calcutta is a fine City, but I never expect to be in a place I like better than Cape Town (except home). I weigh 116 lbs., four more lbs. than when in Norway. My eyes are quite strong now. I can read, write, or sew in the evening as well as any one with them, but I seldom use them in the day time—never, unless I am doing fine work . My sight is like this, \ /, when it should be straight. It is a new discovery. Dr. Stone told us it was very common, but for years had been treated in the wrong way.[31] When I go home Georgie will try my glasses. They may just suit her—then we could get them for her in Boston or New York. In the mean time she must not strain her eyes. One of my glasses is very much thicker than the other. I am sorry to say I have neglected my

Journal since coming here. You know any time for writing I have when in Port I feel I want to write letters. Fred had never heard the story of the "Minister and the Sailors." I told it to Capt. G. Cann last night and he had never heard it. I think the Silver leaf much prettier than the Manila leaf, don't you? This is my last letter from Cape Town. We have been here 20 days today. I must pack all movables away now. With much love from Fred and self,

Yours affectionately

Grace F. Ladd

Fred and Grace left Cape Town and sailed to Calcutta, arriving on December 17. Once again, Fred made a judgmental error which cost him time. In his logs he acknowledged that if he had kept to the east and crossed the equator at 95° E. longitude instead of 88° as he did, he would have saved 10 days "as all the Ships who did this had good runs." Moreover, the Morning Light *ran into some heavy weather about a week after crossing the equator, just as they were entering the Bay of Bengal. On arriving, Fred learned they had been on "the north side of a Hurricane going to West." Grace's next letter indicates that despite everything, they had a good passage over, but she also allows that they were lucky to have escaped the worst of the weather. They remained in Calcutta, from where Grace wrote her next letter, until the end of January—Grace's second letter while there, from Diamond Harbour, was written just before their departure.*

Ship *Morning Light*
Calcutta 27th Dec. 1888

My dear Papa

Today, I received the first letters from home, a long letter from Fletch and one from Hermann, and one for Fred from Arth, besides a number of papers from you but no letter; however, Fletch said you had told me all about Belle Farish's wedding so I know there is one not far away.[32] I wonder if you were expecting to hear of our arrival so soon. We had a nice passage, beautiful weather until we reached the Bay of Bengal where we had it stormy enough to make up for the rest—nothing but heavy squalls, one after another, and we just escaped a hurricane. The glass was very low and we took down our royal yards, but we only had the tail end of it, quite enough for me. We were 14 days beating* about in the Bay. I am much disappointed in Calcutta. Although there is much to see, it does not come up to my expectations. We have visited some of the Temples. Today we went to one called "Kalighat"; they would not allow us to go near the "Goddess" who has a tongue about half a yard long of gold. In the place they were offering up sacrifices, kids, pools of blood were about everywhere.³³ Then we saw some horrible looking men. The Hindus believe them very good. They leave home and friends, and are continually praying. The[y] cover themselves in ashes, their hair is all matted and long, they are frightful looking. Yesterday we saw where they burn their dead. It is like a large court by the side of the river. They make fires of wood on which they place the body [———]; one and another was there ready to be burned. I didn't enjoy that very much but I made Fred take me there. All these things are worth seeing. Chinese curios are as cheap here as they are in China. I am so glad we are going to Boston. I shall expect all the family to come over and pay us a visit. We can stow away as many as can come. I want you to see how we live. Mamma has promised so I depend on her. Sunday evening we went to hear Bishop Shoburn preach, a Methodist and generally liked, but I do not think Missionaries have done much good in Calcutta. Christmas Day was very different from the one I spent last year. I thought of you all. I could imagine what you were all doing. Christmas morning with us was Christmas eve with you so I had to think back. It was the first Christmas Day Fred has spent in port for some years. I am sure he enjoyed it. I made the pudding for dinner which was very good. We could not get any celery which I missed and we had green peas which did not seem in keeping. Squash is a vegetable unknown. There are a large number of fine ships here, a great many four masted. Tell Mamma I have got an ivory rod for that banner of hers. I shall try

The Morning Light *is evidently empty in this photo judging by the amount of copper plating showing above the water line. The top gallant masts have also been lowered in order to prevent the ship from being too top heavy, which could result in capsizing. Two crew members work on the side of the hull, probably painting the vessel.*

and have longer and more interesting letters to send by next mail, but I can't take the time to settle down to letter writing yet. We will send some papers. Fred joins in love to all.

Yours affectionately

Grace F. Ladd

Diamond Harbour
Ship *Morning Light* 26/1/89

My dear Papa

I have several letters from you to answer. The last one enclosed in Georgie's to Fred, I was very glad to get—was much afraid I would not hear before leaving that the boys were better, but now I sail with my mind at ease. I think you have given us rather too short a time to reach Boston. To the 15th May counting from tomorrow would only be 99 days. You must at least allow us 105, the same as from Manila.[34] The Bay of Bengal is a trying place for Captains, so many calms and very light winds at this time of year. Before I forget I must tell you about the Paper Tree bark. When I went to enclose it, found it would make too bulky a parcel, so decided not to send it but to wait and take it myself. I have some of the foliage also. I have quite a collection for you but nothing but a leaf of the Banyan Tree from Calcutta. Fred & I were weighed the other day—Fred, 192 lbs and I, 120 lbs. I feel quite proud that I have gained 5 lbs since leaving Cape Town. I do not think I ever weighed as much before. I am much surprised at Capt. D. Cann and family settling down in Yarmouth. I saw a great deal of Mrs Cann in England, first at Ainsdale then in Cardiff. We became great friends. I imagine the trouble was this: Dolf took his wife and children to Rio with him without asking Brad's permission. Brad has always been as disagreeable as possible, not allowing Capt. C. any comforts at all. I always thought before Brad was something of a man, but he's not. I wrote Minnie Pratt by the last mail. I have never written her before since she was married.[35] I kept putting it off from day to day. I hope Capt. Perry will come on to look after the Ship. I am sure Fred won't ask him. I wonder what the weather is at home to-night. Here it is delightful. We keep all our doors and windows open and are just comfortable. I hope you will send Mr Anderson some proper Sequoia seeds. They are very nice people, the first family at the Cape or Cape Town, and it will be too bad if the seeds do not turn out well. Freights are very low here. Now you can imagine how happy Captains feel. You lose a $9.00 charter by arriving two or three days too late. The weather is beginning to be very warm. It is feared there will be a great deal of sickness. Fred joins in love to all.

Yours affectionately

Grace F. Ladd

P.S. We heard out here that Lem had bought in an iron ship intending to sail her himself. If so, I am afraid Maggie will remain in England.[36] G.F.L.

Grace and Fred left the next day for Boston. As they approached, the crew spent a great deal of time painting and cleaning the vessel, getting her ready for port. They arrived on May 15, exactly as Grace's father had predicted.

A week later, Grace went home to Yarmouth followed by Fred who left Boston at the beginning of June. They spent a month at home and then both returned to Boston to depart for Dunedin, New Zealand on July 11. It was a difficult and unpleasant passage. Grace speaks about the cold and storms in her next letter, and Fred's logs confirm that the rain, hail, cold and gales that started as they rounded the Cape of Good Hope did not stop until they were about a week away from Dunedin. On August 27 Fred wrote, "ice froze in buckets on deck one inch thick, heavy snow & hail, heavy sea." Finally, they enjoyed some pleasant weather until they were a day or so away from port when they were forced to endure yet one more gale.

Grace wrote her next letter just after their arrival at Dunedin. They had been at sea 104 days.

Ship *Morning Light*
Dunedin 24th Oct. 1889

My dear Papa

After a very rough & stormy passage, we arrived safely yesterday morning. On account of the tide were obliged to anchor at Carey Bay, about eight miles from Dunedin, where we remained until this afternoon. It is now 4 PM and we are all fast at Dunedin wharf. I think I wrote you I intended writing a little every Sunday so that I would have a long letter for you all ready to send on arriving. The first few Sunday[s] I did, but the letter was so monotonous I gave it up. I do not think our Lat. & Long., Theo., Baro., and the distance would be interesting to you. We had a very good run to the Equator—crossed it 55 days out on the second of Aug. We passed a Ship homeward bound very near. Fred kept off* to speak him. We supposed the Captain thought we wanted something as he kept off too. Wasn't that contemptible? However, we hoisted our number. He must have been able to read it but did not answer and we were not sorry to lose sight of him. We signalized* one other vessel—a Bark bound to the river Plata. We have sighted lots of sails way in the distance, looked about like flies on the horizon. The days have all passed smoothly away, the crew peaceable and willing. The first mate, Mr Vickery, and steward, first class men—the others passable, except the Carpenter who was never on board a Ship before and does not know how to do Ships' carpentering at all. We used the last of our potatoes the day we entered the Indian Ocean. I often thought of the nice vegetables you were all enjoying. Our stormy weather commenced about the 8th Sept in Lat. 37.1. Long. 23.45. From that time until we passed the Lat. of Tasmania, we had a gale of wind every 24 hours. It was terrible and frightfully cold, the salt water freezing 2 in. [in] the buckets. The poor sailors. I was sorry for them. One good thing—we are very light so the decks were not wet. The cabin fire was kept burning night and day[37]. I hope we will never come on this voyage again. Fred says he won't, but he will forget all about it I am afraid. On the 25th Sept., we passed about four miles to the Northward of the Apostle Island of the Crozet Group, Lat. 45.56 S. Long. 50.21 E. I made Fred promise to call me as soon as they were visible, which he did about five o'clock in the morning, but it was so cold I saw all I wanted to of them through the window. On these Islands, provisions are placed in a cave for Ship wrecked crews, but it is a dreary looking place low on the Mountains and nothing growing except a few shrubs.[38] We sighted the first land of New Zealand about four o'clock Saturday afternoon, 19th Oct., Penpegut Point. Sunday morning at eight we were through Foveaux Straits. I sat up all night. It was delightful, not a cloud in the sky and the stars shining so brightly. Towards morning some old friends came up.[39] In some parts of the Straits it was very narrow. Until daylight I could not see very well except the high Mountains on both sides. At five o'clock we passed the Bluffs where we signalized. By this time it was quite light. The country looked brown and cold. We had a fine breeze all day. At four o'clock, were within thirty miles of Dunedin when it commenced to blow. At six, were oblige[d] to lay-to.* The gale lasted thirty hours. It was heart breaking, the sea and current carrying to the northward two or three miles an hour. On Monday, a heavy sea struck us on the Port* Beam* carrying away 50 ft of rail* and 28 stanchions.* It swept over the whole Ship. I thought she had struck a rock and was so thankful it was what it was, I could not feel very sorry; but it was too bad after sailing so far without losing even a rope, that should happen. We got within twelve miles of our Port when I went to bed on Tuesday evening. At 1 AM Fred came down to tell me he saw a light. He thought it was a pilot coming off. I was up and dressed in a few minutes, and [on] deck just as the welcome pilot was coming up the ladder. This pilot lives at the Head and is supposed to board ships at all times and in all kinds of weather. He sighted the M.L. before dark and sent word to Dunedin for a Tug to be down at daylight in the morning. From the Mouth of the River to Dunedin is eighteen miles by the channel which is about a mile across, Mountains raising on both sides. The trees seem small. Of course it is Spring here now. We reached Carey Bay at eight o'clock. Our mail met us there, a nice large one—one letter from you dated 12th Aug., one from Fletch, one from Eth, Grandma, Laura, and Minnie. Fred got one from his father. We got the Photo in good order and papers as late as 4th Sept. I was so glad to hear such a good health report. I hope Fletch and Arth won't get careless. I think Fletch's first walk was too long altogether. The St. Helena seeds came safely. I won't forget to get native seeds—both trees and flowers. The tow up from Carey Bay was pleasant. Dunedin is built on the side of a Hill and extends about four miles. It looks quite a City. I am surprised to see it so large. I have not seen a single native yet. The pilot says there are not more than a dozen pure breeds in Dunedin. Since they have adopted the foreign food and habits, are fast dying out in this island. We passed a small native village on our way up but the houses were all wooden, and a little church (Presbyterian) standing in the midst. Some of the place had small gardens laid out nicely. The people are nearly all Scotch. In a few week[s] a large exhibition will open in celebration of the Jubilee. To look at Dunedin one cannot realize that fifty years ago, there was not a European here.[40] The chief of these Maoris, who is a member of Parliament, can remember eating a piece of white man.

25th Oct ∽ Today has been very unpleasant. I didn't go on shore on account of the wind and dust which was blinding. Late yesterday afternoon I took a walk with Fred about town a little and we went to [the] Theatre with one of Fred's acquaintances in the evening. All of the Spring vegetables are just coming in—rhubarb, asparagus, lettuce etc. Oysters are cheap and very nice here. We get very nice milk from a farmer who supplies us with vegetabl[es], so I am going to have some oyster stews. Just now there is a heavy hail squall passing. My flowers never looked better in the skylight. I have watered them with warm water and the Cabin has always been warm. Mamma would not recognize the geraniums. The plant Ron gave me is thrifty enough but not in blossom and the leaves seem to be growing smaller. I shall put it in a larger pot. The ivy is just getting settled. I notice fresh shoots coming out all over. I wish you could see a rose I have. It has been on board the Ship two years. Fred got it in Java. It is a large tree now and very healthy with one full blown rose, three large buds, and two green ones—and another bush I have has only one leaf on it. There is only one other sailing Ship here, the *Clan McCleod*, a Bark. All of the letters and papers came via San Francisco. There is not another mail for three weeks. We will then, I hope, be in our next Port. I shall be able to tell you more about New Zealand when I write again. I think Flo did well to get a C. There is a large Salvation Army here; we heard them last night. I shouldn't have been much surprised to have seen Georgie or Emma Allan. Fred joins in love to all.

Yours affectionately

Grace F. Ladd

The next couple of months were spent in New Zealand. On November 7, the Morning Light *sailed from Dunedin to Lyttelton, then departed Lyttelton for Auckland on November 25. The Ladds remained there throughout most of December, once again exploring the surrounding areas and taking pleasure in the opportunity they had to be tourists. They spent Christmas onshore at Wellington, an unusual warm and green Christmas for Nova Scotians used to the cold.*

Wellington N.Z.
25th Dec. 1889

My dear Papa

It has seemed so little like Christmas day to me that I actually just asked Fred the date. We left Auckland Monday afternoon taking a Steamer at Onehuga which is twelve miles from Auckland and on the West Coast, and arrived here last evening. We walked about the town looking in the Shop Windows which were prettily lighted and decorated, the fruit shops gay with Strawberries, cherries, plums, and all our Summer fruit; the green grocers, green peas, beans, & new potatoes, while the people were all thinly dressed. It was hard to believe it was Christmas eve. This morning Fred went off to the *Tongariro* with one of the clerks from the N.Z. Shipping Office. I have a very nice room all to myself. I see by the papers we are due in London on the 6th Feb. We are likely to go through the Straits of Magellan, call at Rio and Madeira. This afternoon Fred & I were driving all about the town but there is not much to see in Wellington and people seeing only Dunedin and Wellington would carry away a bad idea of New Zealand. Now I must tell you about the four pleasantiest days I have spent for a long time. While in Lyttelton we were very friendly with a Capt. Galbraith and family, Scotch people—and Capt. Galbraith was delighted with the photo I have of Grandfather McKinnon, so he wrote to these friends of his in Auckland that we were coming, and that I was of Scotch descent, etc.[41] We had been about two days in when Mr. Crawford put in his appearance with the intention of taking me home with him to stay while the Ship was in Port. His home, Wairia South, is about thirty miles from Auckland by train, then nine miles to ride or drive. I got out of going back with him by promising to go on the Saturday and stay until Tuesday, which we did. Mr & Mrs Crawford are a very old couple, were almost the very first settlers in these parts. The old gentleman is 82, his wife, 74, their children all married and on farms of their own except their son, Dan (our friend) who is a bachelor. The poor old couple could not do enough for us. The old man asked a blessing in Gaelic. I wish you could have seen me eating my steaming soup plate full of porridge and milk without any sugar every morning as though I enjoyed it. Sunday morning, and every other morning, we had our breakfast before six, in bed before eight. 28 cows to be milked twice a day, the old lady still taking her turn at milking. The farm was immense. All the land the old man had bought from the Maoris about whom he can tell some fine stories. A great many relics they have picked up on their farm they gave us: several axes and a valuable green stone. One Sunday we—Fred, Mr Dan C. & I—went for a long ride. We left the house at 10 AM—did not get back until 8 PM. We had to ride through thick bush and up very steep Mountains, through a river. I shall never think I cannot ride again. I only intended going a short distance then turning back leaving Mr C. and Fred to go alone to the Wairua Falls, but it was so pleasant that I thought I would go too. I had a good horse and a comfortable old fashion[ed] saddle, one of Mrs C.'s full tweed skirts on. On the top of one Mountain called Sky High we had a fine view of the surrounding country, Wairoa beneath us looking so pretty with its lovely farm and surrounding Mountains. The bits of scenery we passed I shall never forget—tree ferns, little brooks & falls and all kinds of N.Z. foliage. Sometimes there would not be even a foot path. Then the horses would break their own way through the bush. The joke was Fred's horse had a little colt. Every little while this colt would get lost—horse and Fred would suddenly vanish, the horse going to look up her colt. When we crossed the river the colt did not want to come & poor Fred had a time coaxing them both over. Horses are so cheap here, horses bringing from $[—] to $50. I expected to be quite stiff on Monday but I was not a bit. That day the old Lady took Fred & me visiting with her. We left on Tuesday coming home in a little Steamer. From Wairoa to the mouth of the River is about 9 miles and so pretty, weeping willows on both sides.—By the last mail I got two letters from you, 12th Oct. & 2nd Nov., besides a large number of papers with full accounts of the exhibition. I expect two of Ron's prize Turkeys are in the oven now as it is 8 o'clock PM with us. Fred is reading one of E.P. Roe's books[42]. We are at a very quiet hotel. I have some splendid specimens of Kaurie Gum[43]. We are taking a lot in the cargo. I don't believe one could even buy a Moa's egg. They are very scarce.[44] I am sending you a few seeds from China given me by a gentleman to whom I gave some seeds. With kind love from Fred and self to all, with all good wishes for the coming year.

Yours affectionately

Grace F. Ladd

Grace's horseback ride through the bush of New Zealand would certainly have been physically demanding, but what Grace did not talk about in her letter was that she was approximately six months pregnant at this time! She did refer briefly to the visit Fred made to the Tongariro *and mentioned the "very nice room" she will have to herself. The* Tongariro *was a steamer heading to England, and Fred was making arrangements for Grace to be onboard, presumably because she was too close to giving birth to accompany Fred on a long voyage on the* Morning Light. *Grace left for England aboard the steamer the day after the previous letter was written and arrived at London on*

February 7, travelling the next day to Ainsdale to stay with her Aunt Maggie. In the meantime, Fred remained in Auckland until early January, presumably looking after the vessel's business, then set sail for London himself.

Forrest Arthur Ladd was born in Ainsdale on March 7, 1890. At this point, Fred was approaching the equator, somewhere off the coast of Brazil. There is a note in his log on March 8 that reads, "On the night of the 7th, or AM of the eighth between 2 & 4 AM had a Queer dream," so perhaps he had some sort of premonition of his son's birth. He does not arrive in London until April 22, and his log entries show his impatience with the slowness of this trip: "Calm, calm, calm," he writes on March 27; and then on March 28, "Calm all through. We haven't made a mile."

There were other changes at this time in the lives of Grace and Fred. After a number of years aboard the vessel, Fred was granted power of attorney by the shareholders to sell the Morning Light shortly after his arrival in England. His logs record, "sold the Ship to the Norwegians for £6250. Thus ends the Morning Light. I took charge of this ship on Dec. 1st, 1883. Sold her 20th May. Delivered her June 1st, 1890. Time in this ship, 6 years & six months." The ship remained under the Norwegian flag until 1908, at which time it was sold to Greece. Its final fate is unknown.

Grace and Fred spent part of the summer in Scotland and returned home to Yarmouth at the end of July. It appears they then stayed home for awhile, not sailing again until April 1891. While in Yarmouth Fred Ladd, along with other Yarmouth citizens listed as William Law, Bowman B. Law, Arthur W. Brown (Grace's brother), Benjamin Davis, Robert Caie, Hannah L. Burrell, Charles A Webster, and Willard M. Kelley, plus two citizens of Boston, Herbert C. Hall and Eugene P. Carver, formed a corporation under the name of "The Belmont Shipping Co. Ltd.," which would hold the shares for Fred's next vessel.[45] In April, Fred and Grace left for New York, leaving the one-year-old Forrest behind, and boarded the Teutonic, a passenger steamer of the White Star line bound for Liverpool, England. They spent April to June in England and Scotland during which time Fred began what would be a long command of the newly constructed Belmont. Built at Port Glasgow, Scotland, by Russell & Company, the Belmont was a 1,415-ton barque made entirely of steel, 260 feet in length. Fred records that he took delivery of her on May 20 and then sailed to Cardiff. On June 13, after they finished loading 2,417 tons of coal "plus 20 tons for ship's use," they left Cardiff for Rio de Janeiro, arriving in early August and remaining for 49 days. They left Rio in mid-September for Portland, Oregon, with 600 tons of ballast.

Grace's next letter was written on Christmas day 1891, exactly two

The Letters of Grace Ladd

The Belmont, *with its anchor ready to drop. The masts of a four-masted schooner are visible behind.*

years after her last one. At the time of this letter, the Ladds were slowly making their way to Portland, but were thwarted by strong headwinds that delayed their arrival. Grace was obviously anxious to reach shore, where she could receive word of her young son whom she must have missed terribly having been away from him for about eight months. But there was sorrowful news awaiting her as well. Grace addresses the following letter to her mother, but Mrs. Azuba Brown died on September 19, 1891, over three months before Grace wrote, and just five days after they left Rio for Portland. Once they were at sea, there would have been no way for Grace to receive word of the loss. The death of Mrs. Brown, unknown to Grace, fills the following letter with many moments of sad irony. At the end of her letter, Grace looks forward to obtaining their mail at Astoria. Unfortunately, she must have discovered upon their arrival that her letter to her mother was several months too late.

Barque *Belmont*
136.40 W. Long. 37.30 N. Lat.
25th Dec. 1891

My dear Mamma

I suppose you are wondering how we are and where the *Belmont* is today. 10 days ago we had our distance down, so that 114 miles a day would have taken us to Portland yesterday, and today we were going to wire you of our arrival and wish you a "Merry Christmas." But "The best-laid schemes o'mice and men, Gang aft agley"; a strong wind came straight from the north east, our course—and until yesterday, in fact, we have had nothing but light winds. When they have been strong, they have been ahead and calm "wherever there has been a calm for the last forty years," Fred says. Tell Arth how I wonder at him allowing his sister to come round "Cape Horn" without one word of warning. We were off there three weeks and the *Belmont* proved herself a "duck." I shall never feel a bit afraid in her after such a test. I often used to think of Arth when I would see the men pulling on the frozen braces* and thrashing their arms to keep warm. Our grate burned splendidly all through the cold weather; a stove in each fore-castle* kept the sailors warm.[46] Mr Mollar, our chief officer, is worse than no one. I hope he will take his discharge in Portland off the Cape. Where Walter's[47] good qualities came to the fore he, Mr Mollar, was no where. He seemed afraid and to crawl into a shell, which he has never come out of. The steward and stewardess, we will discharge whether or no. Of all cooks he is the worst, dirty and extravagant, and she does not know any thing, and can't learn.[48] For the last week we have had John (the stowaway) in the cabin, and I have been teaching him. He is as smart as a "steel trap." As he was Cabin Boy a passage in a Norwegian Barque, he already knows how to do a great many things. Last Monday we sighted a Brig. Fred had the boat put out and Mr Mollar went on board. She was a coaster,* the Captain a Dane. He sent us a bundle of San Francisco paper[s], none later than Oct. He is bound to a Port 6 miles up the coast from the Columbia River, and said the head wind we were having was very unusual here. Yesterday I made a pudding for today and invited Mr Davis to take dinner and tea with us. Our bills of fare for the day have been, Breakfast—Steamed Boston brown bread, fried bacon, tea and coffee; dinner—Mulligatawny Soup, beef steak pie with cranberry sauce, boiled ham, stewed canned corn, ginger bread pudding, orange sauce, lime juice, tea, maccaroni and cheese, cream biscuit, Guava jelly—Potatoes were gone before we got around "Cape Horn." I fortunately had saved a net of onions, so we still have a taste once in awhile of something green. There were five in the net this morning when I went to get two for the pie (which I made). I told Fred it was hard to realize 5 onions could ever make any one feel so happy. It is the last voyage we will ever make without plenty of onions and potatoes. Both will keep in *nets* and *I have made 24 nets*. 4 will hold a bushel. The sail maker made two for me and since I have found how well vegetables keep in them, I got Fred to make me a needle and I have made the rest. I do hope we will get in next week. I am so anxious to get home news. I suppose Forrest is trotting about everywhere now and talking also. We have a fair strong wind now and were 750 miles from our port at noon. The little Brig, we have left behind us. He has seemed like a friend all this week. Every morning and night, the first and last thing, we would take a peep at him through our glasses. Today at dinner I said "Prayers have been offered up for us this morning in church" and they are already being answered; Fred said "Yes, the reason we have had such bad luck this passage is because Mr. Teasdale has left Yarmouth and no one prays for us now Sunday mornings." I said perhaps Mr. Langille does. He said then, "The prayers of the wicked availeth naught"[49]—We have been fortunate since leaving Rio not to have had any sickness, except the Carpenter; he is still in bed with Congestion of the lung, Typhus or some Liver disease, it is hard to tell what the matter is. Anyway, he has been doctored for all three and is now getting a little better. This morning I had a fire lighted in the Grate but it was too warm, was glad to let it go out again as we were just in the Latitude of San Francisco at noon. If you see the Davises before they hear from Walter tell them he is well and looks well and is growing a mustache. Well Mamma, I have spent a very pleasant evening with you but, as usual, I have done all the talking. With love to each one in which Fred joins.

Yours affectionately

Grace F. Ladd

P.S. Fred will mail this at Astoria at the Mouth of the River where he has to enter the Ship. From there we take a tug up to Portland about 150 miles. Our mail may be at Astoria   G.F.L.

It was to be almost another two weeks before the Belmont *would finally arrive at Portland, Oregon, on January 6. On February 15, Grace and Fred left again for Queenstown, Ireland, with 2,419 tons of wheat. They arrived there, 168 days later, on the first of August "after a long passage & a tedious one too," in Fred's words. Their next stop was Bristol, England, where Grace left Fred with the* Belmont, *travelled on her own to Liverpool, and sailed from there in the* Teutonic *back to St. John's, Newfoundland, and then to Halifax (arriving on August 28). The next day she was home with Forrest (it had now been over a year since she had seen him), hoping the* Belmont *would get sent back to New York in which case she would wait for Fred in Yarmouth and take pleasure in a long visit with friends and family. But she was home for less than a week when she received a telegram from Fred telling her to "Come quickly" as the* Belmont *had been unexpectantly chartered to Cape Town. Grace then left with Forrest on the Saturday after receiving Fred's cable, "thus not even spending a single Sabbath at home," noted her father, regretfully, in his journal. Mother and son sailed back to England aboard the* Teutonic, *where they rejoined Fred. On*

September 22, the three of them left from Cardiff, Wales, aboard the Belmont, *destined for Cape Town.*

This was two-year-old Forrest's first voyage. The experience of a home in constant motion must have been strange and exciting for him, as suggested by one of Fred's log entries (dated October 8): "Forrest says while laying in the Hammock looking up at the sky, 'See Mama, the skylight is moving.'" Likewise, Grace also went through a period of adjustment. Her next letter hints from time to time of her own unfamiliarity with her son. Having been away from him for so long, she is just beginning to know him herself, to observe his habits, and take delight in his reactions and enjoyments. Much of Grace's next letter is filled with descriptions of Forrest.

Grace begins the following letter when they are about halfway from Cardiff to Cape Town. The letter ends with their arrival.

Barque *Belmont*
Lat. N. 16.12. Long. 26.26 W
16th Oct. 1892

Dear Papa

We are having such warm weather. When evening comes, one is glad to sit still or lie in the hammock and enjoy the cool—even the breeze is warm. We are having light trades and Fred has again given up all hope of making a quick passage to the Cape. Today we spoke a "Norwegian Barque," out four days longer than we from Cardiff. We have sighted a number of sails, but this is the first we have been near enough to signalize. We passed her when she was astern a long way—we were amused to hear Forrest call out "Good-bye Ship, Good-bye Ship." He has kept as well as possible. When we left Cardiff we all had colds, but a few days in the sea air and they were gone. The first day out after eating a hearty breakfast Forrest came and asked me to rock him, which I did. He was quite sick for about half an hour, but has never had the least symptoms since. Ralph and Tom, Ralph's room mate, were sick for several days and R— was homesick as well. At the end of four days Ralph looked pretty slim, but that is all over now and he has to take his salt meat and hard bread with the rest.[50] Forrest seems as happy as can be. One would not think he had ever known any other life.

27th Oct. ∽ Lat. S. 4. Long. W. 28.35 We crossed the equator Tuesday evening. Today is Thursday. Have done well since I last wrote. Neptune paid us a visit. He had six to initiate. Ralph tried to hide, but he was soon found. It is a rough performance but lots of fun for the sailors.[51] Forrest celebrated the day by having a bilious attack.[52] I was much alarmed until I saw what it was. I wonder if he ever had them at home. He is as well as ever again now. Today we had a visitor—a Windsor captain took dinner with us. We spoke this schooner early this morning, the *Moskwa*. Fred put our boat out—the wind was very light—and went over and brought the captain back to dinner, then took him home this afternoon. We were able to supply him with potatoes and exchange a few books. We got a lot of *N.Y. Heralds* from him. We still have a good stock of all kinds of vegetables, enough potatoes and onions to last us all the time we are in Cape Town. Our Hens are a failure. We have two dozen and they have never laid an egg. Forrest runs about all day long. He takes a nap for about an hour after dinner, then I put him to bed about seven. He sleeps well and eats well. In the morning Fred dresses him; then he goes straight to find the cook. We hear him saying "Good morning cook." The carpenter has made him a go-cart. He has romps with Tom who pulls him about the decks in it. Fred has made him some wind mills. It is surprising how they have amused him. He soon found which way to put them to make them go. He seems to understand so much. He knows the chronometer, compass, and sextant. I always take the time for Fred when he takes the sun. Forrest will go up on the Poop and call out "Mamma ready, time 20.22" or something of the kind. Tonight while I was undressing him he was saying M.F.G.L. and other letters. He heard Fred calling them out when we were signaling.[53] We spoke another vessel this afternoon, a coolie Ship, the *Rhine*. We asked him to report us.*

8th Nov. ∽ Lat S. 33.5. Long W 16.50. The *Belmont* has not wasted a minute since I last wrote, and we are looking forward to Cape Town in a few days. I have been making Forrest some little suits since I wrote last, white pique with kilted skirts and sailor's waists, buttoned collars and cuffs. They look very nice. Tonight I dressed him up in one and told him he would "mash" all the ladies in Cape Town. He said, "Mamma, we mash all the ladies in Cape Town, mash Aunt Georgie."[54] The other day I asked him if he wanted to go to Church in Cape Town. He said "go to Church, see Grandpa, see Aunt Georgie." When ever I put on something in the way of clothes, something he has not seen since he left home, he will ask, "Where is Aunt Eve?" He remembers everyone. Fred and I were talking of Hermann the other day; he said, "Papa talk about Hermann." Fred and he take a nap after dinner. It is laughable to see Forrest following Fred up stairs, each with a pillow and pipe, Forrest's pipe filled with red paper. He says "Forrest" and speaks as plainly as I do. He calls his mouth organ his "band." He has enjoyed that more than any thing else he has. My plants are looking well. I gave them new earth after leaving Cardiff and cut them down. —

19th Nov. Cape Town Harbor or Table Bay. 57 days—after all, a good passage. Since last night at twelve o'clock we have come 200 miles. The *Belmont* has proved, with plenty of wind, she can sail. One day we made 330 miles, the biggest run ever made by the *Belmont*, and she did it so easily. Well, you can imagine when that day I made four pies and was sewing all the afternoon, my machine on the table. Nothing of any interest has happened since I last wrote, up to last Thursday 14th. We sighted a Whaler, laying under short sail* right ahead, with her number up. Fred hoisted our flags, telling him to send his boat and we would give him some papers. Almost as soon as the flags were up, his boat was in the water. He had hard work to catch us although we backed the

The Belmont *at Table Bay, Cape Town. Two crew members are in the masts, one standing on the lower topsail yard and one on the foot rope of the upper topsail yard. Two more crew members are climbing up the foremast rigging. The mountain range in the background is the Lion's Head (left peak) and the Lion's Rump (right peak). In her letter of October 16, 1888, Grace reports that she and Fred "walked along the 'Lion's back' on to the head" while they were in Cape Town.*

main-yards.* The mate with four men came, a hard looking lot. The vessel was the *Canton* of New Bedford, out *21 months*, in to St. Helena 2 months ago. He had plenty of potatoes. He was delighted to get a good supply of papers and few books. We had a great many N.Y. papers given us by Capt. Ellis of the *Moskwa*. I gave him every newspaper I could find, even to the little "Yarmouth News," knowing how every bit of reading is of interest after a few months at sea. It is wonderful what dry books one can read and really be interested. Fred gave them some tobacco of which they were short. In return, he gave Fred a splendid Harpoon, the best steel, and all ready to use. He also gave me three teeth, one a very large one of a sperm whale, the other two, small. Last Monday they caught a whale and were then busy trying out the oil.* He said they had done splendidly and hoped to be home next March or June. Forrest is much interested in the teeth, wants to know if they are for Grandpa every time he sees them. He seems delighted to be in port. It has been blowing a South Easter so Fred could not go on shore, but the butcher managed to get off, the same one we had before. He knew what Ship it was, and the Captain. He bought us some fine Strawberries and oranges. Strawberries are just coming in Season. Forrest was overjoyed to see Strawberries and said "look! Mamma! Strawberries, strawberries," but did not touch them until I told him he could. Our second mate's name is Sullivan, a young man, a very good fellow, I mean smart. Forrest and he are great friends. The mail does not leave until Wednesday.—

21st Nov. We are still in the Bay and the South Easter is still blowing. Fred managed to get ashore this morning to attend to business but I have not seen any friends yet. Fred called in at Anderson's. They were all glad to see him and Mr. A—is coming

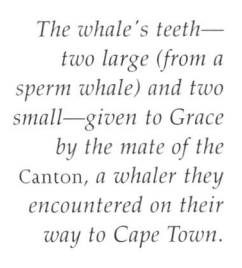

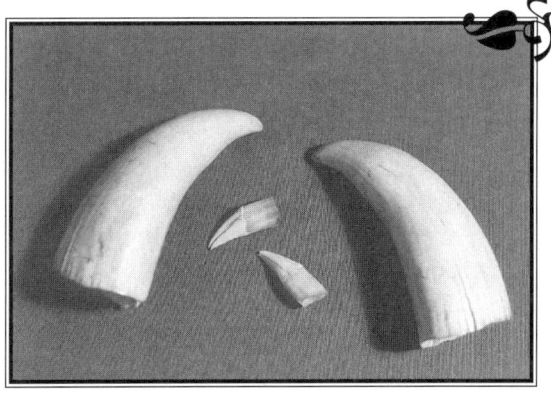

The whale's teeth—two large (from a sperm whale) and two small—given to Grace by the mate of the Canton, *a whaler they encountered on their way to Cape Town.*

to see me as soon as he can get on board, but if possible, I am going on shore to-morrow. It seems strange to see this scenery again. The Mountain, it seems to me, has grown. The town I believe is much improved. We are looking for letters from home by the next mail. Fred only got one written a long time ago from Hall. Ralph got one from Maggie. You have heard by this time of our arrival. It is nice to have made a good passage. Fred is "beaming." He looks younger again. I hope to hear good news from home. Fred joins in love to each one.

Yours affectionately

Grace F. Ladd

Fred began discharging his cargo a few days after this letter and finished ten days later, on December 7th. He then took in ballast and the Belmont departed Cape Town on December 10, destined for Adelaide, Australia. Grace's next letter describes another Christmas spent at sea, but this time Forrest's presence adds more colour and warmth to the holiday.

Christmas Day
Barque *Belmont*
Lat. S. 43.40. Lon. E. 65.30

My dear Papa

I suppose you will celebrate Christmas to-morrow, but we have had ours today. I wanted Fred to keep to-morrow, but he said he could not afford an extra holiday for the men. Forrest hung up his stocking last night at the foot of his bed. He says, "Santa is a fine old fellow," and this morning his face was a picture—he sat up in bed, all he could say was, "Mamma! Santa Claus! Look!" He has spent a very happy day. Fortunately it has not been very rough although last night was very stormy. The ship tosses about so in ballast, but she is doing good days work so we do not complain. Today Fred kept the ship off before the sea* while we were at dinner so we could take it with comfort. Our turkey was delicious (it came on splendidly, did not mind the rough weather at all). We had a ham, boiled vegetable marrow (Cape Town), nice potatoes (from England), and a pudding made by our home receipt, wine jelly, nuts, etc. Ralph took dinner with us. I am always so thankful our boys are not going to be sailors—such a miserable life

Some samples of the silverware used aboard the Belmont *for dinners such as those held at Christmas.*

A close-up of the napkin rings shows the engraved initials of Grace (G.F.L.) and Fred (F.A.L.).

until one is Captain—even then it is full of hardships. Ever since we left Cape Town, the weather has been very unsettled, cold with rain squalls, and Fred has to be on deck. Today the Ther. is 45° on deck and 70° in the Cabin. The grate makes the Cabin look so cheerful. To-night, after Forrest was ready to go into bed he said to me, "Mamma, let me burn my feet," meaning warm them, but it was only an excuse for a few minutes longer up as they were quite warm. He calls blowing out the candle "cooling the candle." Did I ever tell you about the day we took him to Church in Cape Town? The first Sunday morning we were there, after dressing, I gave him a pocket handkerchief. It was warm walking to church. After getting nicely seated Forrest asked me out loud for his handkerchief. I said, "Shu, shu." He called out as loud as he could, "I'll throw Mamma right over board." I don't think there was a straight face in church but mine. I made up my mind master Forrest would be a few years older before I took him to church again; however, I whispered to him to "look at the people, they were not talking. No one talks in Church." He looked around and was as good as possible the rest of the time. When we got home he asked me, "what's that man talking?"

2nd Jan. 1893. I hope this will be a happy year for you all at home. As for us, we are very thankful to have come safely through a very bad gale of wind which lasted 56 hours and has left us in Lat. S. 41°.30. Long E. 167°. The gale was S. W. so we had to run off* to the E. N. E. You will see the distance we have made since I wrote last eight days ago. Yesterday was the most miserable New Year's day I ever spent. Poor little Forrest was perfectly happy throughout it all. You can imagine when the Ship would give a sudden roll and almost throw us bodily out of our chairs. Forrest

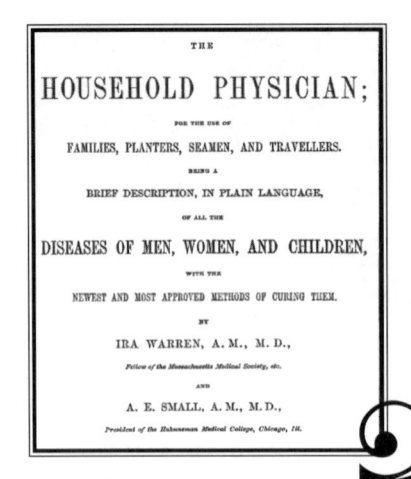

The frontispiece and title page of Ira Warren's Household Physician, *the medical text used by Captain Ladd aboard the* Belmont.

The young Forrest believes the portrait of Ira Warren is his grandpa Ladd.

would look up [at] me and laugh. I would laugh back at him, feeling very little like it. At the table he said, "I don't like this rolling. I am going to throw this Ship right over board." I amused him these last few days by cutting animals out of paper. He always wants a Billy and a Bell.[55] He likes to be read to and for me to tell him stories about Grace[56] and Uncle Hermann. He has all the little boys and girls in his books named. The other day Fred was looking for something in "Dr. Warren's." Forrest said the portrait in the front was "Grandpa."—we supposed he meant Mr Ladd.[57] Yesterday we were obliged to eat our Ducks without any gravy. I could not help but wish I had the old Stewardess out of the Caspian down here yesterday. I shall write Arth but send the letter to you as I have not his address.

Lat S. 41° 35. Long E. 115°.25 I shall finish this letter at once as I begin to feel like tearing it up. We are now under the shelter of the Australian coast and today has been lovely—balmy with a nice breeze. This morning, about seven, Yarmouth was under our feet. I am trying to answer all of my letters before reaching Port, have written seven all ready, Miss Smith and Miss Shaw among them. I received another letter from Miss Smith. She was just returning from school in Eng., a nice plain girl. While in Cape Town I got from a Norwegian Barque a few very pretty shells of curious jelly fish. They came from the Island of Keeling, Lat S. 12°5' Long

96.°54 E. You will find about it in your Gazetteer. The account is very interesting. Fred joins in love to all.

Yours affectionately

Grace F. Ladd

In his log account for Christmas day, Fred gives a more detailed description of Forrest's excitement: "Forrest woke at 7.30 AM, looked in Amazement at his Stocking hanging at the foot of his bed with a Boy doll looking out the top. He was delighted & called out 'Mama, look! Santa Claus has come.' He had a train, Cow on wheels, Pig, Sheep, Elephant, Two dolls (girl & boy), Two Rubber Balls & Candy. He has Amused himself All day, hardly took time to eat. He says, when we aide or Correct him, 'Forrest don't love Papa. Going to leave Papa. Will throw Papa right overboard.' He is growing fast."

The Belmont *arrived at Adelaide on January 13. Fred received orders to discharge ballast and load wheat at Wallaroo, which they left on March 7 for Queenstown, Ireland. They were to have a long passage ahead of them as shown in Grace's next letter, which she wrote over a period of several months at sea. The end of the letter gives some evidence of the effect such extended voyages had on Forrest's perception of the world. As they approached the green fields of the Irish shore, Forrest couldn't believe they were real. "Who painted them?" Grace records Forrest as asking—then Grace's comment: "he wants to know if the land will go away." An article published in* The New York Times *on December 22, 1889, entitled "Children on Blue Water" describes the typical reactions of a child at sea to the unusual appearance of land:*

> The first vague impressions of the world which the seagoing child forms seem peculiar to folks ashore at first sight. The child does not realize that there exist such things as hills, woods, and fields, or long blocks of city streets and parks. …To a child who is reared upon the ocean the deep-sea swell becomes as homelike a sight as the old familiar streets or the fields of the old farm to the child reared upon land.

And so with Forrest it was possible that after such a long period at sea and after having lived for such a short time overall, he would find that he was familiar with the landscape of the ocean more so than of land. The sudden appearance of hills, trees, and green grass must have seemed truly artificial to him, especially when approached from a distance—and the concept of a fixed place that did not move, a difficult one for him to grasp.

Grace began the following letter as they were passing to the south of New Zealand, heading toward Cape Horn.

Barque *Belmont*, Lat 49° S., Lon. 173°E
26th March, 1893.

Dear Papa

I do not suppose we will have another day like this one has been until we get around the Horn. The weather is keeping wonderfully warm, not cold enough for fires, although we have one in the forward Cabin. It looks cheerful. A fire in the grate makes our bedroom too warm. Since we left Port we have done fairly well. Two days ago we passed the Snares, small islands south of New Zealand. We have had rough seas, a great deal of water on deck, but today it has been perfectly dry, and Forrest has enjoyed his freedom. He calls the sailmaker and Carpenter, "Sails" and "Chips." He has never heard either Fred or me call them so, but he has picked it up.[58] Our sailmaker is a Yarmouth man—he looks like a Frenchman—John Maloney from the S. End, age 53. He signed on the articles as 38. He has a wife in Cardiff. I have put Forrest in pants, got a pattern in Wallaroo, and the first day out, made him a pair and put them on him. He said good-bye to skirts; he gets about so much better and I think is warmer. I knit him long-sleeved under shirts and made him under drawers out of old ones of Fred's. I have commenced teaching him his letters, but he is very frivolous. He knows nearly all of Mother Goose rhymes and Little Drops of Water.[59] He commits to memory very quickly. I was only a few minutes one afternoon teaching him the four lines of Little Drops of Water, and the next day he had not forgotten it. Our old cook makes such nice bread out of ground wheat; we grind it in a coffee mill. Forrest does enjoy it. We also have it for breakfast, boiled, in place of oatmeal. His breakfast is a large plate of it. I have learned to eat it to please him. He seems quite distressed if I do not eat some of whatever he has. As soon as breakfast is over, he goes on deck, no matter what the weather is like, and stays until dinner time. Then he has a nap, two or three hours, after which I usually show him pictures and read to him, then tea, then on deck for an hour or so. I do not put him to bed early as he does not go to sleep. After his long nap, before he goes, he has a piece of bread and a cup of cocoa which we all indulge in. Forrest thinks it great fun, going about with me on tip toe, making the cocoa, so as not to awaken the cook and John. Fred has written a number of letters. He hopes to have a chance of giving them to some vessel near her port to mail for him. Our fowls are not laying at all. I am disappointed, not having eggs for Easter. Last year we had plenty; however, we shall have hot cross buns on Good Friday. This year has passed so quickly. Yesterday I came across a lock of Hermann's hair, cut off before I was married. I put it along side of Forrest's, hardly a shade's difference, Hermann's a little the darkest. We measured Forrest again on the 16th of this month. He has grown one inch, measures now 3 ft 2 ½ inches. I could hardly believe it although I thought by his clothes he had grown tall. He is growing to his head. Do you remember you used to think his arms were like [——]? We will weigh him before I write again. He is still very fat. He lost some in port, but is gaining again. Good-night.—

Sunday 16th April ∞ Lat 49° S. Long. 119°W. We have drifted the last 700 miles. For eleven days we have had little or no wind; most discouraging here to lose time where one expects to average 200 miles a day.[60] It has been like tropical weather. I always expect nothing but strong, cold winds and high seas in these Southern Latitudes. Does it not seem strange when so many ships must be crossing here that we do not see one? We crossed the 180 meridian on a Tuesday, so that week we had two Tuesdays. The old cook could not understand it at all, said "it was no proper fashion," and for two or three days with him, every thing was upside down. To-night Forrest climbed up in Fred['s] lap and said, "Papa! tell me about when you were a boy," and Fred can tell some very interesting stories. We have a new moon tonight so probably we shall have a change. I do hope we will get a start and get safely around the much dreaded "Horn," although my experience has not been bad. I can remember, when very young, pitying any one who had to go round "Cape Horn." It seems so ridiculous now—the wind blows with the same force every where, and Fred says he has seen much higher seas in the North Atlantic. I have not —

May 21st ∞ Lat 27°.54' S. Lon. 29° W. It is nice to be in fine weather. We have had a very poor chance, head easterly gales all the time. We passed Cape Horn 27th April—did not sight any land, but saw a Ship westward bound, felt sorry for those on board thinking of the siege he had before him judging from our own experience last year, but before 24 hours had passed, the wind changed and we have had gale after gale until the 15th of this month. Passed within 20 miles of Falkland Islands to the Eastward. Tom, Forrest's friend, has an uncle living at Port Stanley, a baker; four of his children were in England for five years at school. That is about all Tom can tell us. I have asked him all sorts of questions about him, but it is always, "I don't know Ma'm." Forrest has stood the weather well. I do not think we have had more than two days he has not been on the poop for an hour or two. He thinks it great fun to get a spray over him, so that he has to come down and get changed, "like Papa." One day it was very stormy. We were under topsails wearing Ship*; the men were all on the main deck, Forrest and I in the chart room* looking out of the window. Fred saw the men were half afraid, so he ran down off the Poop and along the deck making a great splashing as the deck was full of water. Forrest looked up and said, "Isn't Papa a clever old fellow?" The tone of his voice was too much, so full of pride. Yesterday was the anniversary of our wedding so we celebrated it to day, Eth's birthday, by having a good dinner—a pair of chickens (they were so nice, as fat as could be); a part of a ham, boiled; the remains of a trombone, a vegetable which is very much like a squash, the same flavor; red currant jelly; and other vegetables; a good steamed pudding. I do hope, now we are in warm weather, our hens will lay; last year we had as many eggs as we wanted. I sent a dozen to the [—]field. I do not know whether I wrote to you or not, we bought a goat in Wallaroo, price 2/6, but this thing was such a nuisance and made such a noise, the cook said, "very good, all the same mutton,"—we decided to kill it and give it to the

A helmsman at the wheel onboard the Belmont. *He is standing on the grating to raise himself up.*

men, but after it was dressed, Fred thought he could eat some and Mr Vickery thought he could, so the goat was eaten in the Cabin as well as forecastle. Forrest was helped twice, said "Please give me some more Billy goat, Papa." I did not taste it but Fred said it was good. We still have plenty potatoes and onions. They keep well in nets. Ralph is the best helmsman* we have. He learned to steer very quickly. I used to pity him in the Stormy weather. It is a miserable Life; I do hope Fred won't always have to go to sea. I have worked you a pair of slippers. I commenced them after we left Cape Town and finished them the day we passed the Falklands, so you see they were worked in Southern seas. Of course I only worked on them when I felt in the mood. I am going to send them home parcel post from Queenstown—Good-night.

Sunday 28th May ∽ 18.°20' S 27.°25' W. Calm and has been for three days. This has been rather an eventful week. In the first place the cook has been sick since Wednesday. John, the cabin boy, had to go in the galley.* Tom has, with my help, done the work aft. John's cooking is not up to much, even the sailors growl, so that I have had to cook for aft. I am quite proud of my bread and rolls. It is the first time I have made bread since I have been married, and never yeast before, but I have the home receipts. Fred says he will give me a dollar a week to make the bread from here home, but it is too little so I refuse. It is amusing to hear Forrest ask, "Is it John's bread Mother?" On Thursday evening we sighted a Ship, Friday morning were within half a mile of her. Fred was up and the *J. W. Marr* had her signals flying at day light. After the usual questions Fred put up, "Can you exchange books?" As he could, our boat was put out and four men with Fred and Forrest went over. They stayed to breakfast. The Captain's wife with four children were on board. Forrest was delighted. They were short of coal and were coming on board of us to see if we could let them have some, which we could do. When Fred came back he brought the captain and three children with him; and our boat came of course, and we gave them a good supply of potatoes and a net of onions, also one fine fat chicken as they had no fowl. Every morning, Forrest has a salt water bath on deck. He is up at six o'clock and goes himself with his towel and clothes, and either Mr Vickery or Sullivan, whose ever watch* it is on deck, bathes and dresses him.[61] Today a young whale has been playing about the Ship all day, some times not five yards away from us. Forrest says, "Don't sit on the rail Papa!" He was half afraid. His back had about a dozen barnacles on it. I didn't tell you the *J. W. Marr* is a wooden American Ship from Tacoma, out 97 days. She is still in sight but too far away to visit. I was sorry not to have met the Captain's wife, Mrs Carter, but she had a young baby which she could not leave; and it was so early when Fred started, I did not think of going, but I should have gone if I had known the Captain's wife was on board. We may meet in Cardiff. We are having such lovely nights; to-night is perfect, all but the calm. The moon fulls to-morrow; the moon brings us either head winds or calm.

Sunday, June 18th ∽ Lat 13.° N. Long. 29.38 W. Since I last wrote we have cleaned and almost finished painting ship. It seems too bad—in a few weeks she will probably be filled with coal. We have sighted a lot of steamers, all bound South, and only one near enough to signalize. Crossed the Equator 7th June; on the 13th, spoke two vessels, both outward bound, one a very large wooden ship showing K.H.C.T., not registered in our book. Fred says it is one of Sewell's of Bath, he thinks the famous *Shenandoah*, from New York for San Francisco[62]—the other an English Iron Barque, *Lorton* of Liverpool. Last Thursday our dog, "Ponto," went mad. He had been tied all day forward. After tea someone untied him. In a few minutes he was racing about mad. Some of the sailors were actually up in the fore top,* and for a short time the dog had full charge. Fred, Forrest, Mr Vickery and I were on the bridge; the first thing I knew, Forrest and I were in the chart house* with the door shut. I have a dim recollection of Fred's calling out for me to climb up in the rigging.* Fred managed to get along on top of the forward house* with his revolver from where he shot the poor dog. Forrest and Ponto were great friends, and he had been calling him to come up on the poop only a few minutes before. To-night we have strong N.E. trades, a ship in sight, bound the same way. We have been weighed, Forrest and I—Forrest the same, 48, but I, 131, three more lbs than I weighed just a year ago.

Wednesday, 28 June ∽ Long 39.°15 Lat. 27°32 This evening I have been looking over and reading some of my old letters. The *Belmont* is certainly unfortunate in her homeward passages. We lost the N.E. trades in Lat. 22° and for four days had it almost calm. On the 23rd, sighted our old friend again, the *J.W. Marr*—were in company four days. The 24th (last Saturday) after dinner, we put our boat out and went onboard. Such a shouting from the children and clapping of hands. Mrs Carter is very nice, looks like

Mrs Is. Lovitt, about 35, I should think. This is her last voyage. She is going out home this time and settle down with her children. I took her another chicken—should like to have taken some potatoes—but could not spare them as we will have only enough for our own use; but if we had known, they were short of a great many things which we have plenty of. They were to come and spend Sunday with us, but on Sunday, we were just in sight of each other like flies on the horizon, but dead calm. We have sighted a number of sails, but all a long way off. Yesterday we spoke an "Austrian." After signalizing we put up "Thanks" and he put up "As much as." It was such a strange hoist. Once Fred spoke a Norwegian. He wanted his Long. and he put up "Tanks," of course meaning "Thanks." The Austrian was from N.Z., 83 days, bound to Falmouth. He has beaten us greatly and yet we sail much better. Forrest has been amused lately with gulf weed, picking the little crabs out of it, and jelly fish, and putting them in bottles; all of these treasures are for "Aunt Maggie." The other day he went in the bath room while Fred was brushing his teeth and said, "Papa I want to sharpen my teeth too." The last week two of my hens have commenced laying. Forrest does enjoy the eggs. We have had about ten eggs. Forrest has never had a sick moment since we left Cape Town. The other day Fred and I were speaking of Georgie. Forrest said to me, "Mother! what did Aunt Georgie do?" I said "I don't know I am sure, what did she do?"—ans. "She spanked me, and my Mother was come home," and he remembered what for. I think this wonderful, but he wants to go home and see Aunt Georgie and then come back to *Belmont*. He asks questions by the dozen, such as "Where is Aunt Eve? What she doing? She love me? What she love me for?" etc. Uncle Tom and Ron are always connected with horses. We have had a good breeze since Monday which has brought us to Lat 27.°32. Long. 39.°15 but the moon fulls tomorrow, so I expect another calm—Good-night.

Sunday Evening 9th July ∽ Lat 35° N. Long. 38.°12 You will see we have done very little since I last wrote, nothing but calms and light winds; however, since Friday afternoon we have had a breeze and I hope it will not leave us until we are safely anchored in Queenstown. No doubt you are growing anxious about us, and all the time we are as happy as possible. This has been rather an eventful week. Last Sunday we fell in with the ship *Haddon Hall* of Liverpool, Capt. Dixon. We met last year in Rio, now out just the same time as we from "Port Augusta," not far from "Wallaroo." He ran up his signals asking us if he could come on board. Of course we were pleased. In a few minutes he was alongside in a small boat. He was very pleasant. He has had frightful weather—gales we did not mind at all, he had to heave to* in. His ship is 26 years old. We crossed the Equator six days ahead of him. He caught us in the calms. On Sunday he stayed to tea. We supplied him with sugar, beans and peas. I think it disgraceful the way English owners send their ships to sea. Every owner ought to make one long voyage. On Monday, Capt. Dixon came and spent the day, our ships just steering. On Tuesday, Fred, Forrest and I (with four men in the boat, Ralph among them) went on board the *Haddon Hall* and stayed to tea. He gave me two fine albatross heads and a whole bird—nicely cured, but not stuffed—a small fish he caught in Baleia and cured, also a good collection of Australian weapons.[63] On Wednesday, the Capt. came here to dinner but went home early as it looked like a breeze. About ten o'clock in the evening a Brig passed close by us on the other tack. Fred called out to him from our poop, "What vessel is that?"—ans. "A Norwegian." "Where from?" "River Plate.[64]" "How many days?"—ans. "70 days." You cannot imagine how weird this sounded coming from the dark. He asked us to report him, but we did not have his name so Fred called out, "What name?"—but we could not understand his long Norwegian name. I felt sorry for the poor fellow and felt like calling out to him myself and tell him to "cheer up." He never asked us a question. Fred wished him, "Good luck." Dolefully came back, "Tank you." By this time he was a long way off. On Thursday we only exchanged signals with the *Haddon Hall*, on Friday the Captain on board here to breakfast and dinner, then we said Good-bye until we me[e]t in "Queenstown."[65] It has been fortunate. The few hens I have left are all laying and we are getting a good supply of eggs, so can indulge in Cottage puddings and muffins, also cake. The *Belmont* is all cleaned. She looks well. The sailors have nothing to do now but sit with folded hands and admire their work. To night the *Haddon Hall* is out of sight astern. There are three sail in sight, one Barque. We exchanged Signals just before dark, but only got his name. Perhaps to-morrow we shall be near. "Forrest" takes great interest in Signalizing, knows the color of the flags and does all the hoisting of the one and two flag hoists.

Sunday 25th July. ∽ Lat. 49.° N. Long. 16° W. You see we are nearly at the end of the long passage, 300 miles from Cape Clear. We have had it very foggy for the last two days, but to night is perfect with a good moon and a strong breeze. I should like to write this letter over but dare not or you might complain again of the shortness. Last Sunday we spoke the Ship *Cleomene*, 124 from Rangoon. The Captain asked Fred if he has his wife, with flags of course; then put up, "I have mine." It was so funny—he evidently is not used to taking her with him—but it was strange. He might have asked 20 Ships and not one Captain would have had his wife. We spoke a steamer on Wednesday going East. He answered our signals so Maggie's winds will be easy to morrow—

25th July ∾ We got our "Pilot" early this morning, are now in tow, the same tug boat and Captain that towed us to Bristol last year. Forrest has been so excited all day. Fred said to him, "look at those green fields Forrest,"—he, "Who painted them?" He wants to know if the land will go away. When he is cross he says, "I will jump out of England. I don't like it." Tomorrow morning you will hear of our arrival. Fred joins in love to each one, with a kiss from Forrest,

Yours affectionately

Grace F. Ladd

One thing Grace neglected to mention in the above letter (perhaps for fear of worrying her father) was a fire aboard the vessel at the end of April. In his log entry for April 30, Fred described the incident: "Smelt smoke having been to Sleep in Chart Room & Grace thought it was from washing up the tiles. I lifted tiles & the Smoke poured up, then I raised Lazaret* Hatch. Found the place full of Smoke and Flame. Stopped all ventilation. Got Hose aft & Fore ... Then I took a large Bath Towel—Soaked it in Water and wrapped it around my head & turned on the hose. I got the flame under. When we took turns with the wet towel & a rope about the Men & hauled all the sails out, found some burned bad. Took everything out. At 7 PM, fire all out but it was a close call."

At the end of July, Fred and Grace arrived in Queenstown, where Fred got orders for Dunkirk (or Dunkerque), France. While in France, they visited Paris before leaving in early September for New York, arriving there on October 4. They returned home to Yarmouth for a couple of weeks, then left again (with Forrest) for New York, where they loaded 60,100 cases of oil for Anjer, Java.

Quite A Curiosity

Grace's next letter was written after they'd been at sea for several weeks. They experienced some bad weather to begin with, making the trip uncomfortable and causing Grace to express feelings of homesickness—a rare occurrence.

Barque *Belmont*
North Atlantic Lat. N. 26° Long. W. 37
30th Nov. 1893

Dear Papa

It does seem too bad we cannot get a chance of making a good passage in this Ship. For eight days leaving New York we had head winds and blowing hard all the time. It was wretched enough, and the twinges of homesickness reminded me of those I used to have once in a while when I was a child at the Manchester's. Even Forrest "wanted the Ship to turn right around and go back to the dock," but things are moving smoothly along now and we have a fair wind which make[s] a great difference on board Ship with one's disposition. We have a Ship in company with us a long way off, but there is the hope that in the morning she will be near enough to signalize and that she has been out longer than we. Last Sunday we cut Forrest['s] hair off, six little locks; he looks so different, older, but as the weather is getting warm I think it is best. He is looking forward to "Santa Claus," has a chat with him every day up the chimney. It is very amusing. I have given our steward a blank book and he is writing down all of my receipts in Chinese. He is not a good cook, but I hope will learn. We miss our old Jap. This book I think will be quite a curiosity—

13th Dec. ⁓ Lat. N. 1°40' Long. W. 27.° 20. We have been fortunate in crossing this calm belt with out a calm. The wind gradually hauled from the N.E. into the S.E. On the 8th Dec we spoke a four-masted Barque, *Curzon*, bound home. He came close by to ask our Longitude—so near Fred called out and asked him to report us—and on the 9th we spoke a French Steamer bound home, so probably one of them will report us. We have seen such a number of vessels bound with us, but all a long way off. Today we spoke an iron barque, French, the *Les Adelphes*. He left N.Y. 5 days after we. He asked how many cases of oil we carried. After Fred answered, he ran up "You are too more greater than we bear," meaning you are larger than we. Of course his code is French and ours English. When we left N.Y. we put a dozen oranges in pitch, first covered them with paper then poured hot pitch over them. Today we opened one. It was perfectly good. It is the first time we have tried this way of keeping them, are sorry now we did not do more. The days have been very warm, but I expect cool compared with what Java will be. The stop at Anjer will be pleasant with letters and papers to follow. Forrest says he is a "Nova Scotian" and "he has a house in Yarmouth, a horse, and lots of cows and cats in a barn. His horse is Uncle Ron's too, and you can put your hand right on the cows and they won't bite." The other day he put two pieces of card board up to his eyes and said, "Billy wears things like these."[66] Charlie left his cloth brush with us. I have put it away so some day he shall have it again.

25th Dec. Lat. S. 27.° Long. W. 29.° The thermometer today has been 83° in the shade. I wonder what it has been with you. It has been almost calm for two days, but a breeze is coming now. Last evening Fred dressed Ralph up as Santa Claus—filled him out, and with a manila wig and long beard, he made a splendid

Taken in the back parlour of the Charles E. Brown house, this photograph shows, from left, Azuba Davis Brown (Grace's mother), Arthur ("Arth") Brown, Mary Fletcher ("Fletch") Brown, Florence ("Flo") Brown, Thomas Stoneman, Grace Muriel Stoneman (in white), Ethel ("Eth") Charlotte (Brown) Stoneman, Charles E. Brown, Charles F. Brown, Georgina ("Georgie") Brown, Capt. Fred Ladd, Grace Ladd. The children on the floor are Ronald Brown, Stayley Brown and Hermann Brown. On the back of this circa-1890 photo is written, "A Happy Christmas. With love, from Grace."

one. Forrest was so excited. We had prepared for his coming by making doughnuts, etc. and had some ginger beer ready for him. Forrest asked Santa "where he had left his rein-bow?" This morning he was awake at half past five, his delight at seeing his stocking full and a large basket trimmed in popcorn (which Willie and he had popped and strung) also full, you can imagine. He has spent a happy day I think. It was so hot we could not enjoy our dinner. Chickens took the place of turkey; a very nice ham, well sugared and browned; squash and potatoes with jelly and a pudding; nuts, etc.; plenty of ginger beer was enjoyed more than any thing, which we have made every Friday since we came into hot weather. I hope the girls will try this beer. It is so easily made and refreshing. The principal thing is corking the bottles tight. Use new corks, before using the first time pouring boiling water over them. The same corks can be used again if not broken. Tie down with twine.[67] Ralph and Mr. Anderson took dinner with us. The sailors also enjoyed a good dinner. They all came aft and wished us a Merry Christmas. I do wish we all could spend a Christmas at home. It is not the same any where else to me. Fred has not spent a Christmas at home since 1873. He left Y— Christmas Eve '74, you remember, and the last Christmas evening in Yarmouth he spent at our house. I can remember we had a fine tree in the back office in the old house. In the evening all the Ladds came up. In our track there is an Island called "Tristan da Cunha" Lat S. 37° Long W. 12° 15. Every time we have come this way, we have always tried but have never sighted it, as it is generally thick weather, but we have often talked with Captains who have. They, the natives, are very anxious to board Ship and want medicines and reading matter in exchange for sheep, fowl, eggs, and all kinds of vegetables. I have a large bundle of papers for them. I hope I shall not be disappointed.

Grace's letter continues, but her thoughts of home on Christmas day were answered by her father's thoughts of her, Fred and Forrest. While Grace wrote the above words to her father at home, Charles E. Brown took some time himself to write to Grace on behalf of family and friends back in Yarmouth. The letter he wrote Christmas day 1893 was found stashed within a file of other family papers in the Yarmouth County Museum Archives. Below is the Christmas letter written to Grace from her father, which fills her in on various bits of news about family and acquaintances back home in Yarmouth:

3.30 PM
Yarmouth, Nova Scotia
25th Dec. 1893

Dear Grace,

We wish you and Fred and Forrest, A merry Christmas and a Happy New Year.

> Charles E. Brown
> M. Fletcher Brown
> C. Ethel Stoneman
> Thos. W. Stoneman
> Grace Muriel Stoneman
> Arthur W. Brown
> Chas. F. Brown
> Florence I. Brown
> Georgie E. Brown
> Stayley Brown
> Ronald L. Brown
> Hermann H. Brown
> Frederick Coulson
> C. A. Webster
> Frances L. Allan
> Alice M. Allan
> Effie Putman
> Nellie L. Crowell[68]

We only needed you three to bring us all together today, and as you see by above, our thoughts went out to you over the wash of water with the hope that you may be sufficient unto yourselves for this time. I wrote to you on the 6th Nov. to your Anjer address, sending papers then & since. This is the first to Batavia address with papers. Arthur came with Mr. Coulson (Fred) on Saturday—proposing to stay only a week but may remain a few days longer. Arthur never looked better. In June he will complete his 2 yr course and it is very uncertain where he may be another year, as he will probably accept the best offer in any Y. M. C. A. Inst., independent of locality.[69] Cousin Henry I. Brown was married in Chicago to Anna F. Lenz on 28th Nov. Sent all his Y. friends notice of his marriage, to be at home after 1st Jany, at Lakeside [——], a suburb of Chicago. His mother saw the fiancée when in Chic. in Oct, but although he told Arthur he was to be married he did not take him to see the expected wife. I am not sure whether I told you in my last that Bert sent a very grateful letter for your parcel.

Bertie Lovitt is still here and may live until spring, although steadily failing with the progress of the disease. Her father sent for Dr. McLaren of St. John to visit her, and his statement that she might live, to get out again in the spring, although not to regain robust health, encouraged Bertie so much that she rallied at once from the state of extreme prostration in which she had been for some days.

You would be sorry to hear of the death of the Lt. Gov. of New Brunswick, our old friend, John Boyd.[70] After his death, there was but one expression from press and public, that few men in public life had done so much for the Province, nor had any so well merited the distinction which crowned only the last few weeks of his life. Mr. Manchester wrote to me a very sympathetic letter to say that although they had at one time been estranged and scarcely spoke to each other on account of political differences, this had for some years passed away & they were good friends again. On Saturday evg. Mr. & Mrs M. were staying with the Allisons. Gov. & Mrs Boyd went out to see them & they spent a delightful evg. remaining until nearly 12 o'clock. Within less than 24 hours, he was dead. Mr. & Mrs. M. are going South for the winter. Mr. Coulson brought me from his Father a collection of Photos of Flowers, Plants, Park, Fountains, etc. his own work. The most valued plant in their possession is a Strelitzia reginae[71] grown from seed I gave him from Cape Town. Tell us all about Forrest, your voyage, where next, etc. etc.

26/27

Arthur & Coulson have gone duckering down to Sluice Point. Ron & Hermann are skating on the Alarcon [?] where the ice is in fine condition. Girls all well. With love,

Yours affectionately

Charles E. Brown

27th Dec. 3.30 PM Arthur & Coulson have just returned "in high feather." Shot eleven ducks, gave to friends/outfitters, [——] four pairs & have three for ourselves. Coulson sends his remembrances, Arthur his love.

C. E. B.

The Letters of Grace Ladd

Grace's long letter resumes in January, taking up where she left off with mention of Tristan da Cunha and her disappointment at not being able to get close enough to see it.

14th Jan. 1894. ⁓ Lat. S. 43°.45'. Long E. 19°.30'. I have nothing to tell you about "Tristan da Cunha" as we passed about 15° to the South of it. We had calms and head winds up to the 6th since when we have done well with fine weather and a strong breeze. Tell Flo my sewing is almost done. I made two white dresses. They fit and look very well. Forrest is really learning his letters at last, also to count. Fred has promised Willie a parrot and a monkey if he will teach him them before we reach Java. Fred says he thinks every school teacher ought to have a pension. Today we have seen five very large ice bergs.[72] We are steering more to the Northward again. The day has been perfect—bright and warm. It seems hardly possible ice is around. I am glad the nights are so short and we have a moon. I hope this will be a Happy Year to you all —

29th Jan. ⁓ Lat. 38.°37'S. Long. 78.°35'E. We have come this long distance without a single gale, a steady breeze which has brought us quickly along; as you see we have done well. We did not see any more bergs although for two days had it quite cold, so supposed they were not far off. Since yesterday we have been in Company with an American Ship, the *El Capitan*, from N.Y for Shanghai, out 78 days. As we have both been steering off the island of St. Paul's, were near each other today when we passed it—had a long chat. We had a fine opportunity of getting a good view of St. Paul's. We were within about 2 miles of it at 6 AM and passed along the South side about 1 mile off. This island is one of the natural curiosities of the world being an extinct crater. It is 2 3/4 miles long and 1 ½ miles broad, 860 ft above the sea. I made a little Sketch of it which I will enclose, but after opening out the point on the right hand side of the sketch, we came in sight of the Crater which opens towards the sea around this basin. The cliffs rise to 700 or 800 ft. "Findlay" gives a good description. He says there are several boiling springs which will cook fish and the water when cold is drinkable.[73] Once a few Frenchmen live[d] here for 6 years, catching and salting fish for the Island of Bourbon. Imagine the loneliness of those 6 years. Fred could see to the North, Amsterdam Island outlined. It is 51 miles from St. Paul's. I hope we will keep this breeze for a few days until we get the Trades. Forrest doesn't want a monkey or a Parrot. He wants a Camel.

19th Feb. ∽ Lat. S. 8.° Long. E. 103.° We made splendid time up to the 6th Feb. when we were in Lat. 21° Long. 100. Here we had safely crossed the track of [a] cyclone which we had been preparing for for three days by sending down royal yards and battening all the doors. I shall never forget that experience and I never before watched the glass so anxiously. I am sure we only escaped by carrying sail.* Fred hardly left the deck all that time. Both sky and sea looked wicked and at times every thing seemed to echo. It passed to the South of us. The result is the Trade winds have been broken up and we have averaged only 60 miles a day for 13 days. However, we are now 170 miles from Java head and we have a light breeze. The heat has been intense, 90° in the Cabin. I am writing this on deck under the awning—we have a little one for sea use. The sun is just setting, the moon well up. It fulls tonight. I am still gaining in weight, was weighed on the 8th Feb. and weighed 137 lbs. Fred tells me if I keep on, by the time I am 35 I will [weigh] 200. Forrest weighed 46 lbs, Fred 202. Forrest does not mind this hot weather a bit. I do not see how he stands it, running about as he does. Yesterday we caught two sharks and drove a harpoon through another. Have saved the back bones. The Cook and Steward kept the tails and fins. Forrest told us, "Cook gave him some shark fin soup, but it was no good."

Straits of Sunda 23rd Feby. ∽ We are now just five miles off Anjer, 2 PM. Have had a feast of letters and papers today. Scott's boat brought them off to us this morning.[74] Fred sent the boat right back with a cable and a letter to Scott to get our orders if possible, as it seems impossible to beat in to the place against the current. Six sail in company. It was so nice of Scott, sending the letters. The time has flown today. Several native boats have been off and Forrest is the happy possessor of a Monkey and a cage of Java sparrows. The former and he are friends all ready. He was much interested in the letters and said he did not get any. I only got two letters: one from you and one from Maggie, but lots of papers. Fred got Charlie's letter and one from his Father & Mother, besides others. Sorry to hear of Troop failure. Fred is congratulating him self that he did not leave any money in J.W. Parker's hands, but paid his own bills before leaving although they made a great fuss about it and said Captains always left it for them to pay their bills; but Fred told them he always made a practice of paying his own bills.[75] I am sending Hermann a few Stamps and an Envelope which the Steward has given me. It was forwarded from London here in an English envelope. I think it quite a curiosity. We are all well and hope to get a load of sugar back to N.Y. or Boston. Fred and Forrest send love to all, with Yours affectionately

Grace F. Ladd

P.S. I want to look at the land all the time and do not feel like writing. The wind is blowing paper every way. Shall write Fletch after we get orders. G.F.L.

After reaching Anjer, Fred received orders to go to Semarang. They arrived there on March 5 and started discharging cases of oil, a task that took over a month to complete. While at port, Fred and Grace were very rarely alone. Other vessels came and went, forming a community of captains and their families that would meet and share time together, some already knowing one another from back home or from other voyages. Such opportunities for contact with others after weeks or months at sea must have been much desired, and, for Grace especially, a welcome chance to encounter other captains' wives and children and to pass some time in their company.

Fred's log entries for the time they spent in Semarang give us a sense of a community that may have been temporary but strong. Amidst his description of successive social activities with others whose vessels were docked, one can almost sense the relief felt by both Fred and Grace that they were able, for a time, to share experiences and to spend a number of days in a fixed place. The following sampling from the log books, which covers the days spent in Semarang, gives us some insight into how Fred and Grace occupied their time in port while they were waiting for the discharging of cargo to be completed:

March 12—Grace, Forrest & Self onshore. Had lunch at Jansens Hotel & back at 4 PM. Capt. Thompson of BK *Cashmere* took tea & Spent the Evening with us.

March 17—The American Bark *Mary S. Ames* & Austrian Bark *Stipan* came in today. Capt Thompson & I called onboard when we came off. Saw the Captain's Wife.

March 18—Captain & Mrs Knowles came over & Spent day with us. Capt. Griffith of ship *Carnedd Llewelyn* and Capt. Thompson to Tea & Capt. Jones of *Cambrian Princess* After Tea.

March 21—Went onboard the *Mary S. Ames* at 11 AM & back at 8:30.

March 23—Good Friday, a holiday. Went visiting about the Bay to the different ships.

March 27—Went onshore at 10 AM with Grace and Forrest. Got Lunch at Mrs Ralphs. Grace not taken with the place. Too many flies. They did not get back from shopping expedition in time. We got caught at the Boom in Rain Shower. Could not go onboard, so went back to the Pavillion Hotel & put up for the night. Capt. Knowles' Wife & Child, also the Austrian Captain, with us.

March 29—Onboard until 3 PM. Went onboard Ship *Carnedd Llewelyn* with Grace, Forrest & Mrs Knowles. We Staid for Tea & left at 6 PM.

   ...and so on, until their cargo was discharged and their next cargo (458 tons of sugar and 200 tons of sand ballast) was loaded and they were ready to go.
   Their next destination was Singapore. Fred left Semarang battling a fever which he had a hard time shaking for the next couple of months, in part because his duties as Captain allowed him very little rest. Grace expresses her concern for him in her next letter which was written just before they arrived at Singapore.

Barque *Belmont*
China Sea
9th May 1894

Dear Papa

Three weeks tonight since we left Semarang. I did not write on leaving as I was busy and anxious about Fred who was ill with fever. I also thought I should catch the first mail from Singapore as the distance is so little, but I forgot the calms, currents, and head winds. Fever did not put in an appearance on board the *Belmont* until the last week of our stay in Semarang. One man we left in the hospital and have only had two cases among the crew besides, and the Cook and Fred. Fred has been very sick and, of course, as he has been obliged to look after the navigation, and we have had such a tedious time, is not yet quite well. I have done nothing but mix quinine, make gruel and soup since we left, but all are well now and I hope shall go into Singapore with a clean bill of health. Forrest and I have escaped and are looking forward to Singapore and the [——]. We are talking about home every day and Forrest is very anxious Grandpa shall know of all the commendable things he does. Yesterday Fred and Forrest were on the poop, Mr Vickery standing near. Forrest had a pair of scissors, and turning to Mr V— asked him, "if I should stick these in you what would it do?" Mr V., "It would kill me Forrest." "Ah, then I would be mate. Would you like that Fred?" One day he asked me "if in heaven they sang 'When Jack comes home'?" one of his favorite songs[76]. We went up to the coffee plantation at Ouorang [?][77] but Fred was taken sick the day we left and was sick all the time up there, so he did not enjoy it at all. Forrest had a lovely time riding about on a pony all the time with a coolie leading. We went up on Saturday and came down Monday morning. The plantation is 2,000 ft. above the sea on the side of a Mountain. After the heat of Semarang the change was delightful. The whole process of coffee was explained to me and I saw it in all of its changes. I should like to have bought a few pounds but did not like to suggest it as they only sell it in large quantities. I got a few beans. While we were in Semarang, Capt. George Hatfield was in Batavia in the Ship *Lancing*.[78] He sails her under the Norwegian flag. I wonder if you read that letter from Captain Trefry in one of Burrill's ships. There are no Pirates here now—too many steamers go up and down these straits. The wrappers they had on were their "sarongs" (the native dress) worn by both the men and the women.[79] In Sunda Strait, natives come off from Sumatra as well as Java to passing ships to trade. We were at anchor in these straits some days and every day had three or four boats along side with sweet potatoes, limes, pumpkins, cocoanuts, monkeys, cockatoos, Java sparrows, etc. In every boat one man could speak a few English words. I don't know whether I have acknowledge[d] Fletch's letter or not, but think not as it was the last I received. I have assorted my home papers—such a lot— by and by, shall read all the advertisements. Singapore is only thirty miles off but I dare not say we shall arrive to-morrow. Fred and Forrest join in love to all.

Yours affectionately

Grace F. Ladd

Fred and Grace were lucky after all and did indeed arrive in Singapore the next day. They remained until June 16, and left again for New York, making their way back through the Java sea. Grace wrote the next brief letter knowing she would have an opportunity to get it in the mail before they set off into the open ocean.

Barque *Belmont*
Java Sea. 30th June 1894

Dear Papa

I may have a chance of sending this on shore to-morrow at Anjer. No doubt you will wonder how we are. All are well. Fred says he feels better than since we were in Java, but wants sleep greatly as it has been a hard beat down from Singapore with strong head winds.[80] We just managed to slip through Gaspar Straits last night and are now about forty miles from Anjer. Nothing has happened to write about. Every day has been the same, except one night we anchored about four miles off the coast of Borneo to see if we could find out about the currents. After waiting about five hours in constant dread of hearing the dip of paddles and being surrounded by the "Wild Men," Fred thought tacking was better. So "up anchor" and away.

Sunday 6 PM Off Anjer light. Scott's boat in sight. Fred and Forrest join in love to all. Forrest is anxious to know if we will be in Yarmouth next week. The *Belmont* sails well so we hope to go home in 100 days.

With love, Yours affectionately

Grace F. Ladd

P.S. I hope Arth. will be somewhere near when we arrive

G.F.L.

Grace's next letter was written almost two months later while they were still making their way back to New York across the Atlantic. In it, she describes an unpleasant problem common to sailing vessels: the presence of rats. Her letter reminds us that even a captain's wife did not live a life of total comfort—and that rats made their way into the captain's cabin as readily as into the forecastle.

By the end of the letter, Grace and Fred have arrived at St. Helena, a small British island in the South Atlantic. Forrest was evidently anticipating the visit. In his log book, Fred copied a prayer that Forrest invented himself and recited: "Oh Jesus don't let me dream bad dreams. I am going onshore at St. Helena in the Life Boat & get some Apples & Grapes & all the Birds of the air fell sobbing & crying When they heard the bell toll far from Cock Robbin. Ahmen."

Barque *Belmont*
South Atlantic Lat. S 18°50. Long. W. 3°
24th Aug 1894

Dear Papa

If we have a quick passage, I might possibly be at home before this reaches you. So far we have done the average and have had the finest passage I ever made. The weather has been lovely, only one little hard blow off the Cape for 24 hours. The Ther. has never been below 60° and it was mid-Winter when we came round the Cape of Good Hope. We have been and are over run with rats. On leaving Singapore we had two cats but they both died, we thought from eating too many rats. I don't know what we shall do if we can't get a cat at St. Helena. I am afraid to go to sleep now. We caught two the other night in the Piano— killed them both. I read somewhere Cayenne Pepper scattered around would keep them away. I tried that but the draughts kept it in the air, and we nearly all strangled with coughing. Last Monday we spoke and passed the four masted ship *Andromeda* from Iloilo for Delaware, out 97 day[s]. He passed Anjer 15 day[s] ahead of us. This Ship belongs to St. John. I waved my handkerchief to the Captain's wife. We have spoken several Ships. At noon we were 230 miles from St. Helena. Although the trades are light, we hope to get up to the Island in time to go on shore for a few hours. The *Belmont* is rolling very much— one of her accomplishments.

Sunday afternoon, St. Helena ∽ We are just on shore for a few minutes, but such a lot of letters and papers we find awaiting us. I shall be kept busy all the way home reading.

With much love, Yours affectionately

Grace F. Ladd

Fred's logs provide us with a bit more detail about the St. Helena visit.

Before collecting the many letters awaiting them, Fred had to pay the postmaster to open the office on a Sunday. The hotel was also closed on Sunday, so the postmaster, a Mr. Young, took Fred, Grace and Forrest home to dinner. Fred adds, "he gave me a cane made from Whale Bone with the Handle of Whale's tooth & gave Forrest 2 pigeons."

Grace's next letter was written as they were finally approaching New York, but the journey had been longer than expected.

Barque *Belmont*
75 miles from New York
12th Oct. 1894

My dear Papa

I am so glad I sent you those few lines from St. Helena. I almost did not—we were so sure of arriving before the letter could, but this North Atlantic is an unlucky ocean for the *Belmont*. We have simply drifted from the Equator to the Gulf Stream since when, last Monday, we commenced to get a breeze, and I have quite made up my mind again that it can blow, hasn't forgotten how, by any means. On Wednesday last at 5 in the afternoon we passed an abandoned three-masted schooner. It was a sad sight. As we sailed away from her, it seemed like leaving a living thing to perish. It was blowing very hard with a tremendous Sea. We did not see a sign of life; if we had, of course, would have stayed by her until we could send our boat. But the rigging was all cut away and some hanging over the bow. It looked desolate. It has made me quite nervous. Forrest is so excited with the idea of getting in and seeing you all again, poor little mortal, he is looking forward to so much. I do hope Scarlet Fever is not in Yarmouth still. We are all well except the Cook who has been sick for three days with a bad cold, but he is not much good, and we are getting on better with a boy in the Galley. Our Steward is a treasure, but he is going to leave in N.Y. I am very sorry. He wants to go home. Mr Vickery is also going to leave. He wants to go in steam. Old Anderson, Fred would take again if he would go for nothing. The *Belmont* looked so nice before we got these gales. It is disheartening, all the labour of weeks destroyed. This morning, off of one Port (the glass), I got a good saltspoon full of salt. The rigging [w]as white like snow. For the last three or four weeks we have had dozens of birds fly onboard tired out, land birds. We have thought probably it was blowing somewhere, but the sea was like glass with us. I shall stay in New York a few days before going home. If you think of coming we shall be delighted. I should like for you to see the *Belmont*, but the Ship won't be long in Port— only about five weeks— so come at once. Fred and Forrest join in love to all,

Yours affectionately

Grace F. Ladd

P.S. I hope all are well. Thank you for the letters and Papers at St. H.

The next day, Fred and Grace finally arrived at New York. There's no information to confirm whether or not Charles Brown made it down to New York to see the Belmont *as Grace wanted him to, but Grace returned home to Yarmouth about a week after their arrival, and Fred followed her several weeks later on November 10. Near the end of the month, the three of them left again for New York, and for the next voyage, Grace's younger brother Stayley was part of the crew. He would have been 18 years old at the time.*

The ship was in port for longer than the five weeks that Grace predicted in her last letter. The next cargo was case oil for Shanghai and they were not ready to go until December 6. The voyage began rather unsatisfactorily with an inexperienced crew. In her next letter, Grace complains about their inability to function, an irritation that is echoed in Fred's log entry of December 8, just after they started out: "find I have a Miserable crew of Men. Six have never been aboard a Ship before & the other seven are the O.S. and four A.B.'s, only four that we can trust at the wheel. A fine lot for a trip like this, 21,000 Miles Ahead of us." The A.B.'s (able-bodied seamen) were more experienced than the O.S. (ordinary seamen), making the number of sailors that Fred could truly rely on small indeed!

Grace began her next letter at the end of December and continued writing it until they arrived at Shanghai in May. Fortunately, as Grace notes, the crew improved as the voyage went on.

Barque *Belmont*
Lat. N. 24° 53' Long. W. 37°05
31st Dec. 1894

Dear Papa

Shanghai looks a long way off to night. Fred says we are all "Jonahs" this voyage[81]—We have the most miserable crew a Ship ever left port with. I do not see how they could possibly be any worse. You can imagine; five of them do not know the Bow of the *Belmont* from the Stern; two more cannot speak a word of English; one, a Scotch boy of eighteen is in consumption— he is only able to do very light work about, sleeps in all night. I hope he will get better but am afraid not. We only have four men who can steer, two each watch. The weather has been very bad ever since we crossed the Gulf Stream. Every time we tack Ship all hands are called, and when ever we shorten sail, it makes it very hard on all. Stayley has concluded one voyage will be enough for him. There is nothing but the actual life to knock the romance out of "going to sea." Do not know whether I wrote you or not, we got our old Steward again. It has been such a comfort having him and we have a splendid cook, the best we have ever had. In my department every thing moves smoothly. Christmas Eve, Santa Claus payed us a visit. It was such a rough day that I thought I would have to give up making Doughnuts, but Forrest seemed so disappointed I made the effort and between the seas Forrest and I [went] to the galley with our dough to superintend the frying, the cook balancing the lard on the stove while I rolled out the cakes and put them in the kettle. When they were done Forrest said "they were good but Aunt Eth's were good too." I had kept the wig and beard of last year, so as Ralph represented Santa again, Forrest thought it was the same old fellow. Just before he came the mate threw a flare up forward and Santa blew the fog horn. Forrest was very much excited. We treated him to ginger beer, apples & doughnuts. Forrest went to bed early and happy, woke up about five o'clock and saw the basket which he had trimmed with popcorn filled with things. He had a double share of presents. Fred & I bought him toys the same day, I not knowing Fred was going to. He had what pleased him most—a cast iron train, a good size fire engine with horses to come off and on and a bell, also a street car with horses, several books,—boxes of blocks and Brownies in all shapes—brownie nine pins, brownie lamps, brownie blocks, and a brownie book.[82] All of Stayley's things, when put together filled quite a basket. I called him in after breakfast and gave them to him. He was very much surprised and pleased, but it was almost too much for him. He felt homesick no doubt on that day. I gave him a pair of shirts and Ralph "Cook's Voyages" with nuts, raisins & candy. We all had dinner together, eight at table—Ox-tail soup, Turkey, boiled ham, mashed potatoes, boiled onions, tinned peas, currant jelly, chutney, Christmas pudding, German sauce, Nuts, Apples, Ginger Beer. It was the stormiest Christmas I ever spent at Sea, but not much sea until after dinner. The sailors had an extra dinner also. Tomorrow we have our last Turkey. Mr Durkee, the Mate, is a very nice man. Fred likes him very much. He is quite young, 25. The second mate has been a good man, but is useless through rheumatism. Today I did my first big washing. I am always glad when it is done. We never keep New Years day at sea so I shall iron. I hope it will be a Happy Year to you all—Good-night.

6th Feb. 1895 ∽ Lat. S. 27° Long W. 24° We are all glad to be in cool weather again, and as this is the Summer season we expect fine weather running our Eastern down.* Crossed the Equator 21st Jan. Neptune payed us a visit and initiated eight of our men (they needed it—all took the fun in good part.) Sidney Jones paid his footing.[83] The sick boy, McCoy, has been laid up for some weeks. Seems to be slowly growing worse. I have nine hens and a roaster (pig). They have commenced laying. Forrest has had some more doughnuts. Dennis the Pig is growing.[84] We intend killing him off Tasmania. The day we crossed the Equator we spoke a steamer bound North and on the 1st of this month, the Ship *Trafalgar* from Sydney for London 56 days out. So you will see by the reports [how] slowly we are getting along. Our men have improved wonderfully. Can nearly all steer now and know all the ropes. Can tack ship with one watch. Stayley thinks there is too much drudgery about a Sailor's life for him. He is well and seems happy enough.

30th March. ∽ Lat S. 34.04 Long. E. 158.55. Stayley and I remembered your birthday and wished you many happy returns. We are now 113 days out (about 75 miles from "Lord Howe's Island.") We had hoped to pass close by this Island as the natives board ships and supply them with potatoes etc., and ours are getting low although we have still some left and a few onions. I am putting by eggs also for Easter Sunday. But the wind is light and ahead. We passed about four miles off Tristan da Cunha on the 8th Feb., but it was foggy and we could see nothing. The *Gleneida* was in company with us bound to Algoa Bay, the Captain a Yarmouth man (Corning) in her. Fred knew him and we had quite a talk with flags. Two days before this, in putting out our life boat for practice, two men who were standing on the boat skid* pushing the boat, as she swung out, fell, one into the sea, the other on deck. In a minute or much less a life buoy was thrown to the man who was fortunately a good swimmer. Sydney Jones went aloft to keep the buoy in sight. By this time the Ship was up in the Wind, Main yard aback,* and the boat in the Water. The man in the buoy began yelling out as soon as he saw the boat coming. The second mate stood up in the boat and waved his hat to let the fellow see they saw him. When they all got safely on board again, the fellow said, "the second Mate looked just like an Angel when he stood up in the boat." He also thanked Fred for taking so much trouble stopping the ship etc., this one of our A.B.'s, a German, never been on board of a ship before—a well-educated man, about twenty, [he] is helping Ralph & Stayley with their arithmetic. The man who fell on deck fared much worse. He was insensible for some time and was laid up for a day or two then, and has been off and on ever since, this one of our best men; however, it was good *practice*. We spoke two ships in the Indian Ocean running our Eastern down. Forrest also had his fifth birthday. I had a box of blocks and transparent slate for him. He could not see where I got them. The next Monday, commenced learning to read and count. Killed Dennis on the 15th March and we did enjoy fresh pork for one week. I made sausage meat and head cheese. Last Sunday we rounded Tasmania in company with a German Bark, *Triesburg*, from Cardiff for Nagasaki out 4 days less than we although we have beat him from the Equator 11 days. Sighted the land South Tasmania 40 days from Tristan da Cunha. This is good work and we have had beautiful weather—no more accidents. All hands well except McCoy who keep[s] about the same. Fred and Sydney made a room for him in the carpenter's shop where he has been comfortable. He comes out every day for a little while. On the 26th this Month, we were all weighed—Fred 202 lbs, Sydney 136, Stayley *163*, Ralph 165, Forrest 50, Grace 144. Last night a good sized flying fish flew onboard. Forrest had it for his breakfast. Fred caught a Porpoise one day, tried out the fat and got me a nice bottle full out of the head.[85] Ralph and Stayley have been oiling their boots. One week running across* we made 1495, one day [March 3rd], 308, the biggest days' sail the *Belmont* has ever done.

1st April. ∞ Lat. S. 37.° Long. E. 159.° After 113 days at sea it was a most agreeable surprise this morning to be awakened by the hauling of yards,* and on asking Fred through the speaking tube* what was up, he told the wind had broken us off,* and we were standing straight in* for Lord Howe's Island which was about 10 miles off. I got on deck just in time to see the sun rise back of the land, a lovely sight. This island is five miles long, in some places very narrow, taking just five minutes to walk across (as we found out later). Ball's Pyramid, 1800 ft., bears S.E. about 15 miles—a strange looking rock coming straight out of the sea almost perpendicular, appearance of the "Goddess of Liberty." We all thought the highest point of the island is 2600 ft. We were too far off to distinguish objects, but at daylight hoisted our ensign. The breeze was very light; we seemed to make little headway. I went on the forecastle head and made a little sketch of the land which I will send you. About ten o'clock we could see a few houses on the low part of the island and a flag staff, the signals flying. We were much surprised as we were expecting boats, not signals, but they read, "What assistance can I render you?" We ran up "Vegetables." In a little while they answered they would send a boat, so we waited patiently watching the shore. In about 1 ½ hours saw a whale boat coming. [At] 1.50 was along side, with five men who all came on board. They were very glad of a lunch which the Steward had ready for them. They had brought us only a few things as they said they did not know what we wanted, and all their men and boys were off gathering "palm seeds," so they thought they would come off to us and then return for what we wanted. However, they had 7 bunches of Bananas, 1 bushel of Irish potatoes, 14 squash or pumpkins, a Tropical vegetable between the two / a good supply of small onions and 4 doz. lemons. The boats' crew consisted of an old man who was formerly a whaler named Thompson, a native of New Bedford Mass., age 73. [He] has been now living on the island 35 years with his wife, a Fiji; (his son) William Thompson, unmarried; Mr Baron an Adventist Missionary, only 3 months on the Island, a son-in-law of Mr Thompson; and two others. After a little talk and assuring us they had plenty of potatoes on shore, fowl, sheep etc., Fred decided to send our boat, Mr Durkee taking her with four men, Sydney, Forrest, and I as passenger[s], Mr Thompson pilot. They only wanted Tobacco in trade, but would take any thing. As we had plenty of tobacco, gave them that with a few extras. They asked for liquor, but we could only spare one bottle of whiskey, McCoy has used so much. We were just *three* hours rowing ashore. The reef runs across the little bay, at the neck of which is the settlement. I never saw coral before in its native state. Forrest and I were interested in looking over the boat's side. The water was very clear, beautiful green and white coral, all kinds, fine comb and sponge, and what looked like large jaws. The trees are quite distinct this time, fine Palms, not cocoanuts (although we did not know before, cocoanuts did not grow to bear fruit out of the Tropics), Banyan and Norfolk pines. We landed on a fine sand beach. Mrs.

Baron and William, with several children and the crew of the whale boat, welcomed us. We were glad enough to feel ground under our feet again, "dirt" as Forrest calls land now. We followed the path up towards the houses which were almost hidden among the trees. Mrs Thompson, the first Fiji Islander I have ever seen, was introduced to me by her daughter, Mrs Williams. She was in the kitchen and diningroom, a separate building. There were an abundance of dishes and a large table, some rude kind of fire place. I did not take it half in as before leaving the Ship Fred had warned us to leave before dark and it was already five o'clock. We just for a minute looked into the building across the Path, a nice room with an organ, table, chairs, and pictures on the Walls of all the famous Americans, a few nic nacs and papers about. Every thing was beautifully clean. Mrs Baron then took me to see a little of the Island and to another house where she thought I might get a few curios— seeds, shells, etc. Our sailors were by this time enjoying plenty of good milk and looking well payed for their hard row. I felt sorry Stayley was not one of them, but his rowing could not be depended on and the *Belmont* is short handed enough with our poor crew. It was so delightfully cool and fragrant, no insects, neither flies nor mosquitos. Was not very successful get[ting] seeds. I got a few Palm, also two growing in pots, also two Norfolk Pines with 150 oranges and a pr. of game cocks. I had much rather have had a good pair for eating but had no choice in the matter except as to color. She was very anxious to know which I had rather have, white or black. After some indecision I decided on one of each. We saw lots of cows in good condition. Everything seemed very tame, the fowl would run right about our feet. The women seemed nice and intelligent, dressed well, shirt waists and woolen skirts, women above the average height and fine looking. We all agreed there. The men on the island have been sailors but one, and he is an Australian, Mr Wilks. Our second mate says it is his "Snug Harbour."[86] A steamer calls once in three months and a schooner calls often for fruit. By the time we got back to Mrs Thompson, I found Mr Durkee there in great distress anxious to get away. I felt reluctant to go. Poor Mr Durkee had had a hard time. On asking where the Potatoes were Mr T. asked him if he was going to dig them. He said yes, to give him a hoe and show him the place, so he took Ralph and another man and they went to work cutting the vines away and trying to find roots, but could not. When Mr Durkee told Mr T. he could not find any potatoes, he was shown another place, but without much better success. Then Mr T. said, "Oh well, I don't know much about it. The old woman digs all the Potatoes." However he managed to get about a bushel and with several bunches of Bananas, 150 oranges, 6 chickens, 8 ducks, 1 sheep, 1.5 weeks old Pig (Little Lord Howe), sugar cane, ears of corn, a bag of cabbage shells, and my plants, we rowed back to the ship after promising to call again next year. In the mean time Fred had sailed in close and was throwing off rockets giving the Islanders a little display of fireworks, and burning torches, we thought for us, but found on getting along side, the water was alive with fish and they were trying to catch some, without success. Tea had been kept waiting and we did enjoy it, after which we looked over our collection and through some of the Sydney Papers, the latest only a month old. Are sorry to know the war is not yet over.[87] It has been a delightful day. Good night.

13th May. ∽ We are on the last thousand miles of our journey with a breeze now. It will not be long before we are in. Yesterday, Sunday, the sailors were giving their chests a final clear up. Poor McCoy is just alive. I do not see how he can possibly last, but he has held on to life wonderfully although too weak to turn himself in bed. Yesterday he got the man who waits on him to get him out a shirt collar and necktie to wear ashore, also asked him to try and press the creases out of his pants. It reminded me of taking Forrest home from Halifax gotten up in his very stiffest dress and bonnet. We have had a great deal of rain and light winds. Passed to the eastward of Soloman Islands, sighted two islands of the Caroline group, also two of the Ladrone group. Are now sailing towards the Loo Choo. Have sighted two ships in the distance; both passed us. The *Belmont* is in Port trim.* Stayley has had a taste of holy-stoning.* He is well and looking forward to home news, as we all are.

22nd May. ∽ At anchor in the Yang tse Kiang. We got our Pilot this morning and were surprised to hear not one of the fleet of ships due had arrived. Fred was so sure the *Burrill* would be discharged and away.[88] Have had dreadful weather since I last wrote.

Forrest Arthur Ladd. The photo was taken in Shanghai, circa 1895.

Put back the night of the 18th to escape the centre of a Typhoon. We got all but the centre and only lost one sail. I sat up all night, one of the few nights since I have been going to sea. It was a wretched night. I never want to experience another like it. Lights would not burn in the binnacles.* Haply it only lasted a few hours. Forrest has grown a little and has made a beginning with his lessons. The other day he asked me if Shanghai was as large as New York. I told him almost and asked him if he liked New York. He said "Yes, I like all land." He asked the Pilot tonight "if he ate Pilot fish?" Stayley is writing a long letter to you. Poor McCoy is still alive. Forrest sends a kiss to each one. Fred joins in love.

Yours affectionately

Grace F. Ladd

On the voyage to Shanghai, Fred had to put his skills as the ship's "physician" to work once more on a number of occasions. One was the case of McCoy whom Grace writes about several times in the above letter. Fred notes in his log entry for January 11, "McCoy, O.S., laid up since 6th Jany. Giving him Medicine and food to keep up his Strength but Am afraid he has consumption. He came onboard with a bad cough." The other medical problem was a consequence of the boat accident Grace describes, especially for the sailor who fell and struck his head on the deck. At one point, Fred was occupied with both McCoy and the sailor at the same time:

March 8—The Seaman, Jack Blake, fainted at the Wheel at 2 AM caused by the Fall he had some weeks ago.

March 9—Blake out of his head. Gave him hot Mustard foot Bath for an hour with cold Applications to his head which brought him to.

March 12—McCoy about the same. Blake slowly improving.

Grace and Fred arrived at Shanghai just after Grace's last letter was completed and began the long process of discharging cases of oil. On June 7 they took in 350 tons of ballast and then loaded 2,244 bales of wool and 1,359 bales of straw braid. At the end of June, they left for Hong Kong and arrived there on July 25. Grace's next letter was written from Hong Kong and records her initial impressions of the city.

The Letters of Grace Ladd

Bark *Belmont*
Hong Kong
27 July, 1895

Dear Papa

We arrived here on the 25th, all well. Had a long run down, calms and head winds all the way but fine weather. Find on arriving three typhoons have passed up the China Sea since we left Shanghai and we escaped them all, only seeing the fast flying clouds and having the heavy swell with a low glass. Does the vessel not seem lucky in that way? We were in sight of land all the way down, either Formosa or China. Forrest was quite sick for the first two weeks, lost such a lot of flesh, but it is all coming on him again now. Hong Kong is very different from Shanghai in every way. Shanghai is much the finest, cleanest, and largest City, but Hong Kong is a beautiful place from the Harbour which is land locked. We have hills all around us, very green but treeless. I do not understand that. I should expect to see lots of bananas every where and cocoanuts, but not so. The only trees are trees which have been planted about the residences. There are a large number of Ships here and lots of Steamers going and coming every day. I have only been on shore a few minutes, yet did not see much of the place; but up the Mountain there are two good Hotels, so if it gets very warm we are going up there. Canton, also, I want to see. We received a lot of papers from you on arrival with four letters, two for Stayley and two for myself. Forrest was much interested in Billie's escapade. I have had to read it to him two or three times, that part of your letter. Georgie has faired poorly with Billie, both riding and driving. The girls will remember Hattie Hibbert. I did not know she was in this part of the world and was greatly surprised, the evening we arrived, to receive a call from her and her husband Capt Brown.[89] I knew her as soon as she took her hat off, but until then thought it was an American lady we expected to meet here (she called today). I was so astonished to see this familiar face. I said, "Why, where did you come from? How did you get here?" etc. We laughed and talked. She can, she is just my age. Her husband has a good position here, is much respected. They do not live on the Island of Hong Kong but across, about five minutes in a ferry which goes every fifteen. Forrest and I took lunch with her yesterday. She has a beautiful home which is found, house and furniture, by the people [he] works for—also their gardens, both flower and vegetable. I shall give them some of the Sweet Briar seeds. Stayley is well—will probably write to-morrow. Forrest and Fred join in love.

Yours affectionately,

Grace F. Ladd

Fred and Grace spent about a month in Hong Kong, some of which (especially their visit to Canton, or Kwangchow) is described in Grace's next letter. They left at the end of August for New York with 430 tons ballast and 2,999 tons "several cargo."

Fred was forced into the role of "ship doctor" yet again on the next passage, but this time his patient was Forrest who cut his head severely enough to require stitches when he fell down the steps leading to the after cabin. Grace mentions the incident in her next letter, stressing Forrest's pride at having stoically survived the injury and the treatment. Fred, who had to stitch the cut himself, describes it in his log, clearly taking a great deal of pride in Forrest himself: "Forrest fell down stairs, cut his head open so the skull was exposed. Stitched it up with needle and thread & he stood it like a little Man. Dressed it with iodoform. Shaved off the hair & used sticky plaster."

Grace wrote the following letter as they were making their way through the Java sea among the Indonesian islands, heading toward Anjer where they would stop and pick up their mail.

Bark *Belmont*
Java Sea 18th Sept. 1895

Dear Papa

Our troubles are about over. We are out of the China Sea. Came through Gaspar Straits last night, anchored for a few hours waiting for the tide to turn, about a mile off Shoal Water light. Such a pretty little island. I was hoping a boat would come off to us. I should think people in such a lonely place would be glad of a chance of seeing somebody from the world. We have passed a number of islands on our way down. Quite near shore to the North of Borneo, could see houses and cuttings, but no boats. We are looking forward to Anjer. Hope to be there tomorrow. Will anchor for a few hours. Captain Hemeon who was in Hong Kong with us said he would forward any letters or paper[s] which came after our leaving. Capt. Hemeon's wife is a sister to George and a daughter of Steven Churchill—his ship, an American, *George W.*

Homer.⁹⁰ I am writing this on deck under the awning. Looking forward I can see the door of Stayley's room which faces this way. It is his Watch below*; seven bells* has just gone. Stayley has just come out on deck, taken a look around, gone back into his room, filled his pipe and is sitting on the sill of his door smoking, a sailor's trick. He says he won't write from Anjer. All hands have been kept pretty busy hauling yards and I do not [think many of] them feel like letter writing. Lord Howe has grown well, is now larger than Dennis was when we killed him. By the time you receive this we ought to be off Cape of Good Hope enjoying fresh pork. Forrest is very anxious I shall tell you he fell down our after steps leading to the Cabin one day just after we left Hong Kong, cut the back of his head against the corner of the door. Fred had to shave his head, and put a stitch in the cut. It must have hurt badly, but he did not murmur. My finest needle was number eight and my white silk embroidery. It is all well now and will not leave a scar. He has been dreaming bad dreams lately—this morning he told me he prayed twice not to dream bad dreams, and he did not. He has lost faith in one prayer. I do not think I have ever told any of you about our trip to Canton which we all enjoyed except Forrest who says, "it was too much for him," meaning noise, dirt, etc. We left Hong Kong one Sunday evening in a fine large Steamer with 600 Chinese passengers. We were the only Saloon* passengers so had lots of attention from the Waiters on the look out for fees. The Captain, an Irishman, told us just how to see the most of Canton in a day. We anchored for two hours in the river on our way up so as not to reach Canton before day light. There are no lights on River, except the lights of a few stray junks.* We had Dinner at eight o'clock, went to bed soon after, so as to be ready for a long day. These Steamers all carry an armed guard, Portugese. At daylight we were surrounded by hundreds of boats, all kinds. The [——] boat, famous for its swiftness, goes always five miles an hour—Flower boats, beautifully decorated with all kinds of flowers; Sampans,* all anxious for passengers from the steamer. While I was watching the boats, Fred had engaged a guide, and we were at anchor just outside of the wall over which we could see the tiled roofs. About fifty policemen were on the wharf on the look out for thieves. Such a noise I never heard before of tongues. We got our breakfast on the boat and had a lunch put up so as not to lose time by having to come back for it. Our guide looked out for this and engaged our chairs,⁹¹ four, Forrest and I using one, with four coolies— Fred one, Sydney one, the guide one— the chairs were comfortable, and the little trot the coolies kept up rather pleasant. Passing through the narrow streets, one could see everything in all the shops as they have no front petition [partition?]. In a very few minutes without a guide we should have been lost—the building[s] are so close together with so many turning[s], and all look alike, no paint, not white, just dark gray. Every now and then, we would pass a stone building with high walls and a large doorway, always resembling something in a Chinaman's mind, an orange, a leaf, a pineapple, etc. We visited several of manufactories. The most interesting thing to me was the scene from which the willow pattern is taken,[92] the willow still thriving, an immense tree, now sacred. The bridge has been removed but the stone arch is still there. Quite a number of lotus plants grow in the water. The pagoda at the back still is a pretty picture. The English Willow pattern is copied from the Chinese, so that platter on the back of the side board in our dining room must be Chinese. If so, is valuable as it is not made now. The art is lost, so the story goes. I could not buy a piece in Canton. Should have been satisfied with a very small piece just as a memento. We got quite a number of very curious bits of crockery.—We saw the Water Clock still in order and agreed with our time. This clock was invented a great many years ago to give the time to Canton. Three Copper Jars of different sizes arranged one above the other—every morning the top one is filled with water; from this into the next one, the water drops, and from it into the bottom one in which is placed a bit of wood with an upright copper rod with the hours and half hours marked on it. As the jar fills this rod comes through a cover. So the time was told. For many years, it was the only time piece in China. From this tower we looked right over the house tops which had rows of stone jars filled with water in case of fire. We took our lunch in the top of a five story Pagoda. While there, the wife of a Chinese officer came to offer thanks to the God of War. She had the smallest feet I ever saw, could hardly walk, had a servant on either side of her. This pagoda was built on a hill about 600 feet above Canton. We got a fine view of the country outside the wall. While there had a chat with our Guide who was very intelligent—said ex Mayor Harrison of Chicago and H. J. Stockard had both gone through Canton with him.[93] He had their letters recommending him. I offered to buy these, but he would not sell at my price. The execution grounds are use[d] for drying their stores when not in use. This is the shape [rough sketch included in original]. The jars on one side are filled with skulls. I wanted one of these too, but could not get it. Visited the Viceroy's Palace. When we got back to the Steamer, had been just seven hours away, had not seen a single European. The steamer reached Hong Kong about three in the morning. Our Sampan was waiting for us. We were glad to get back to the *Belmont*. Fred and Forrest join in love to all.

Yours affectionately

Grace F. Ladd

28th. ∽ [Log dates this as 23rd] Have just arrived. Scott's boat along side with our mail. Papers and letters: one for Stayley, one for me. 16th July dated. Shall enjoy reading them in a few minutes. All well, fair wind.

Grace

Almost eighteen months pass before another letter from Grace. After the stop at Anjer, the Belmont *continued on its way to New York and Fred's logs tell us the passage went well, giving us also some indication of how Grace and Forrest spent their time as the vessel crossed the Atlantic. With his usual sense of humour, Fred recounts a number of incidents involving Grace and Forrest:*

> Nov. 19—Caught 5 Bonito. Grace caught one using her umbrella as a fishing rod. She was more surprised than the fish.
>
> Nov. 6—Forrest was on top Fore house & poured a Tin full water down the Skylight on the cook, Meaning it for Stayley. Grace took him to task for it. Asked why he did it, Forrest said, "I asked him the time. He said '4 o'clock,' & [I] thought he wanted me to make it a little cool down there, so I poured down the water."
>
> Dec. 7—Forrest put a letter to Santa Claus in the Grate. I lowered a string down the stove pipe & tied [it] to the letter while he was out of the cabin. When he came in & went to see if it was still there, I hauled it up the stove Pipe & if ever a boy was convinced that Santa had his letter, Forrest was.

The Belmont *arrived at New York just before Christmas and the Ladds spent the holiday at Montclair, one of their rare Christmases on solid ground. After this, they likely went back home to Yarmouth where Fred* left Grace and Forrest, returning himself to New York at the beginning of February, 1896, and departing on his own for Sydney, Australia. He arrived at Sydney at the end of April, loaded 806 tons coal and 80 tons ballast, and departed for Honolulu. He left Honolulu at the beginning of August to return to New York, arriving on December 7, five days too late to send a telegram to Grace for her birthday, but he notes that he and his mate, Mr. Durkee, "drank her health and wished her Many happy returns."

Having been away from Grace and Forrest for almost a year, Fred spent some time at home with them after this last voyage. It appears they were all in Yarmouth for Christmas and in Yarmouth also to attend the wedding of Grace's brother Charles F. Brown to Maria Tilley on December 21. A letter from Fred in January to his brother-in-law, Charles Pratt who was living in New Jersey, describes some of his time spent in Yarmouth: "...have had a fine time. Forrest & I go Skating every chance I get. I got word from N.Y. this AM that they were in no hurry to load the Belmont—So I have postponed leaving until next Saturday. This will bring me in N.Y. Tuesday as I want Monday in Boston." In the end, Fred, Grace and Forrest departed on the Belmont at the end of January from New York for Shanghai with a load of oil. Grace's younger brother, Ronald Brown, came with them on this voyage, apparently as part of the crew; Fred also took aboard a passenger bound for Shanghai—Selwyn Hatfield, of Yarmouth. It would appear from Grace's letters that Ron and Selwyn spent a great deal of time together on the passage out.

It is difficult to say why there are no letters from Grace during the opening months of this voyage. Perhaps she wrote but the letters did not survive. From time to time, Fred wrote about Grace in his log record, such as on the date of Forrest's seventh birthday in March (quoted in the introduction) where Fred recorded that Grace made Forrest a pair of long pants. The log books also reveal that Grace was quite ill for a period of time in April with some sort of digestive distress and fever. The condition persisted for about two weeks, her progress documented day by day in Fred's records along with his own efforts to care for her:

April 3—Grace Sick terrible. Cutting pains in the Stomach. Some Fever. Tem 101. Giving the Fever Mixture & Barley Water diet....

April 5—Grace up on the sofa for an hour. A little better. Tem 100....

April 8—Grace up from 10 AM to Noon. Feeling Better. Tem 100. Still on Barley Water....

April 10—Grace up for a short time. Tem 99. Living altogether on Barley Water. Everything else distresses her....

Finally on the 14th, Fred optimistically notes, "Grace improving fast." At the beginning of May, the Belmont *stopped at Anjer, just after which there is finally another letter from Grace.*

Straits Sunda
Bark *Belmont* 7 May /97

Dear Papa

This morning we were all awake at daybreak. It seemed so strange to be at anchor, every thing so quiet, not a sound on board ship as all hands did not turn to until six o'clock when they had breakfast. Anyway, all they will do now will be to work ship* as the weather is terribly hot, the Ther. 88° in our bedroom all night. I slept in the hammock on deck under the awning, Forrest sleeping in his little canvas bed, under the skylight. We had two or three bumboats* along side. Got a good supply of yam sweet potatoes, bananas, cocoanuts, and pomelos.[94] Forrest got a young monkey. Selwyn and Ron were much interested in the boats. Selwyn expected to see Java merchants I think, but these natives, with their mixture of dress, were a great curiosity, consisting of two pieces pants and shirt, or Sarong, and Kambaia, as the native dress is called, but they seem to like to get on an European pants and shirt no matter what kind. We left the ship at sharp seven, Ron, Ritchie Otto (a man who was with Fred last voyage) and another sailor rowing. We had anchored to the South of the Light and just ahead was anchored "Ross's" Yacht with what we thought Scott's boat along side, so we rowed over. Found the new agent with our big mail on his way down to us, but willing to go on shore, taking the Captain of the "yacht" with him. Mr Sem, the Agent, is a Norwegian, unmarried, about 35. He intends buying all of Scott's property at Anjer.[95] Mrs Scott and her daughter still live in the old house which has been much improved. We went to see them. They are Javanese, the daughter an intelligent girl about sixteen. The yacht belonged to the Glasgow Yacht Club. We did not get her name, could not understand what they said—will get it on our way down. She did not have a cargo as I thought, but was going to Batavia for stores for Christmas Island and the Keeling. She is 47 tons register, yawl* rig* and steel, a very pretty thing. Her Captain and Mate are Norwegians. We asked if they had any shells or sea eggs on board—they had not. Remembered the *Rosalie*. We did not go on board—just waited along side. I found out all about Christmas Island. We sighted it, did I write you? There are 30 people living there belonging to Ross[96] (who is half Malay, born on the "Keeling"; his wife is pure Malay. They live at Batavia.) On the Keeling Island nothing grows except cocoanuts—no vegetables—they get everything from Batavia, but on Christmas Island everything grows—Oranges, lemons and all kind of fruit trees have been planted. The coffee is not grown yet, has been planted too short a time. It takes four years before it is ready for market. Until a few years ago no landing had been found, but Ross found a very small place 2 miles from the N.E. point and applied for possession. Got the right from the British. While we were on shore, Forrest, Selwyn, and I went up in the Light house. Got a fine view of the Straits and the country which is very mountainous. As a little breeze came about 9 AM, we started for the Ship. I felt anxious to read my letters, had just taken a peep to see that all was well and to tell Ron although he had a chance to read his. We got lots of papers too. All day have been sailing up the coast with just an air. At 5 PM, found the tide was against us. Anchored about 1/4 mile off shore about 12 miles above Anjer as the sea breeze does not come in until noon. Perhaps we will go on shore here to-morrow.

8th May ∽ This morning when I woke up, could hear the birds twittering and singing on shore quite plainly. It was lovely—the sun not up, the sky such lovely colors, and the sea like glass, smoke from small fires along the shore. Had breakfast 6.30. Taking the same men in the boat, started for the shore. We took a large bag of bread for trade, landed on the beach where there were a number of fishermen. We tried to talk with them but they only laughed. Couldn't get any satisfaction so we started across a grassy piece of land where there were lots of buffaloes feeding, tied, Selwyn said, to a clump of grass, so you can imagine how safe we felt. But they only stretched out their necks at us. Every one did that. We walked towards a lot of banana trees where we thought was one house, instead of which we found a Javanese village. We did not go far in. Several natives came towards us, among them a peddler who had combs to sell. You know men, as well a[s] women, have long hair in Java. The Peddler tried to interpret for us. Fred was quite disgusted—they seemed so stupid—and turned back. I was trying to buy a goat for Forrest. There were lots of them of all ages. Ron had the bag of bread. They took some of that all right. Would give in exchange nothing. Fred said he would like to have had a snap shot of us—Selwyn, Ron, and I among those natives. We walked back by the road which had trees planted on each side. The roads are good all over Java as each native has to do so much road wor[k]. Forrest had stayed behind with the men, found them all having a swim. They had got a lot of pumice and shells off the shore. On our way to the ship, we rowed along side a fishing boat to watch them pull in a net. It pulled heavy. To their surprise as well as ours, they had a large turtle. At once we all felt glad we had not left the bag of bread behind. In a very short time we had the turtle and they had the bread, both pleased with the bargain. We will have turtle steak for dinner to-morrow. It weighs about 75 lbs. As soon as we got on board, got underway again. Passed out of the Straits of Sunda at 2 PM into the Java Sea. Spoke the Ship *Sierra Ventana* from Saigon for Falmouth. Reports light winds and calms, no monsoon yet. I expect we are going to have a bad time of it, but I will write every day or two, just to let you know what beating up to Shanghai is. I felt sorry not to have sent from Anjer a longer letter, but each day is the same and to you everything is an old story.

9th May Sunday ∽ Last night we had very little wind, just managed to hold our own; but with a current and a light fair wind are about 70 miles up the Java Sea. It is not as hot as it was in the Straits. Fred is not sure yet which passage he will take. All depends on the winds. For dinner today we had the Turtle steak. Although well-cooked, broiled with lots of butter, we all used plenty of Worster sauce to cover up the taste of fish it had. The sailors had it as well. I asked one man how he liked it. He said he "wanted to eat it because of the big name it had," but he liked Albatross much better. I never tasted Albatross, but I had rather have tough steak. I told the Steward to give the men the rest of it, not to cook anymore for Aft. We are enjoying all the fresh things we got at Anjer. The cocoanuts are green, nearly all milk, each one holding two good glasses. It is very amusing to watch Forrest and the monkey. He thinks he is going to train it. We have an old soldier among the crew. He has made a cap and dress for it—we have passed a number of small islands in the distance.

11th May. ∽ Still in the Java Sea with a light head wind today.

We have seen three native vessels and one steamer, all a long way off. I made some cocoanut candy and preserved some pumpkin. The Java pumpkins are more like our squash. Ron invested in a parrakeet. We have three monkeys, 1 pig, 1 doz duck[s], a mongoose, [——], and a musk *cat* (if there is such an animal)[97]—quite a menagerie. Have read all of the letters and papers two or three times. I felt sorry to hear of Mrs Anderson's death. Some way or other, no one seemed to have any sympathy for her.[98]

13th May. ⁓ At anchor again just at the entrance of Gaspar Straits. We hope to get up the Macclesfield Channel to-morrow. All day yesterday and today, have little better than stemmed the current and when the wind died out this PM, the current was carrying us right on a reef. Forrest asked if "ever Fred was in such trouble before?" and suggested we put the boat out and put a board up with "Reef" on it so people would know just where it was. This was his own idea. All we do these days is to keep as cool as possible. The men are at work painting ship. Forrest has a line on bottom trying to catch fish. I do not see why we cannot catch a nice fish in 10 fathoms of water, but we are unlucky fishermen. Not a sail of any kind in sight or smoke from a Steamer. Just a week now since we anchored at Anjer, but I suppose every day means a better monsoon in the China Sea.

14th May ⁓ Got under way again at 6 AM. Have sailed all day, only made 12 miles. It was very hot all night, dead calm today. The ther. 90° in the cabin. About 2 PM, sighted a boat coming off from the Island of Jelaka. These men had rowed 9 miles, left the Island at 10 o'clock, 7 natives, Malays, much better looking than the Javanese but not so much civilized. On our left we have the Island of Lepar off the East end of Bangka and a number of other small Islands in sight. Both Jelaka and Lepar have Light houses, and as there is good anchorage, this is a fine channel. The wind died out and we anchored again in 12 fathoms of water having made only 12 miles today. We got from the Natives, cocoanuts, bananas, and shells—the very large scollops. They brought off seven pair. I got two pair, the men got the rest. Otto got a turtle. We have all had enough turtle Aft. These men have beautiful teeth. One fellow opened his mouth to show us his, every one perfect, a complete set not in the least discolored. The front upper six were filed off even with the others. He said it took ten moons to do this and he used sand to clean them. We tried to catch fish again without success. Aft, one of the sailors caught four fine one[s]. Another boat came off, but only had a few coconuts and bananas. These fellows beg more than trade, but it is nice to have them come off. Their canoes are very rough with bamboo sails. At Anjer all have cotton cloth sails. Macclesfield is one of the channels of "Gaspar Straits"; Stolze Channel to the eastward, divided from this by Lepar, we have always come before, but there is no anchorage.

15th May ∽ Last night about 2 AM the current changed and we up[ped] anchor and again are now about 1 ½ miles east Gaspar Island, an island 812 ft. high covered in trees, about 1 mile long, ½ mile wide. Just to the N.W. of this is the Ismir Reef, famous to us as discovered by George Cann.[99] We have had a good breeze today, so it has been comfortable out of the sun. Fred has a bad head ache, I think from taking bearings and not keeping under the awning. There is a sail in sight from Aloft beating up. Perhaps we will overtake him by to-morrow.

16th May Sunday ∽ Fine breeze from N.E. We have come up on the ship a lot. Can now see her from the deck. Make out wooden full-rigged Ship. Borneo is away to the East of us. Our course is right up the middle of the sea. This afternoon, have had rain squall[s] enough to make everything cool. Forrest was pleased with his letters from you and Maria, says he is going to answer them, but never seems ready to begin, and it is too hot to bother much with him.

17th May ∽ At noon were on the Equator, the Ship *St. John* about ½ mile off. She left New York 11 days ahead of us and passed Anjer a day ahead of us. She is bound to Japan. Several small islands in sight. Made 75 miles, but there is hardly a breath of air today. Very hot, again.

25th May. ∽ It does not seem possible it is more than a week since I wrote last. Since then we have come 488 miles, are now in 7° 50 L. North 107° 58 Lon E. On the evening of the 17th, Fred had the small boat put out. He, with Selwyn and Forrest, rowed over to the *St. John*. The Captain said he didn't believe there was going to be any monsoon this year. I begin to think he is right. We are keeping on the West of the sea[100] but the little air we have now is from the N.E. when it should be from the S.W. Fred is teaching Ron navigation. He is learning without any trouble. We do not have much music now. It is too hot in the Cabin, but the sailors do their share. Yesterday, the 24th, Forrest and I both talked about a year ago, what a good time we had that day.[101] Well yesterday, it was perfectly calm and I never saw so many fish before swimming around. We tried every way to catch them but not a bite. There is too much good eating for them, I expect. The first shark we have seen this voyage was around yesterday. Forrest put a sweet potato in a bottle some time ago. Now it is all growing, he is perfectly delighted. He wishes he was home now "to have a swim in the pond" although he has two or three baths a day and we have plenty of rain squalls, so fresh water is plentiful too. But Forrest likes salt water baths best. While we were at Anjer, I saw a Maritime Register of 2nd April. The *Ancona* had not arrived there. I do hope she arrived soon after that, but what a time to be at sea.[102]

30th May ∾ Lat. 10.00 Long. 110.05 We are still having calms and light airs. Have sailed 1137 miles from Anjer. Have not made that much in a straight course. Two ships are in sight. We have been in company with them for several day[s], one a German bound to Nagasaki; the other English, to Hong Kong. Have sighted a number of steamers bound all ways. It is still very hot, the Ther 90° in the cabin. Have finished painting Ship this week. Will holy-stone decks.

6th June ∾ Lat N. 20.10 Long 115.45. Last Monday we got the first of the Monsoon, so this week have had a little breeze making it much more bearable. On Friday the English Ship *Bidston H[ill]*, after being all the morning only about two miles from us, altered her course and at night was out of sight to the Westward, but the German is still with us. He is going up the Formosa Channel so will be with us for some time yet. We hope to get in Shanghai this week. It seems so long since we passed Anjer, I suppose because the weather has been so hot. The *Belmont* is all cleaned and looks very nice again.

13th June ∾ Lat. 24.57. Long 119.48 We still have 412 miles to go before we reach Shanghai, but now we have a 7 knot breeze. I should think we have had our share of calms and head winds so perhaps this will last us. It is so cool too. To have it cool is almost as great a treat as to get in Port. Last Thursday i[t] was perfectly calm. Selwyn has been anxious to have a swim all the voyage, but Fred has discouraged him on account of sharks; however, this day we had been watching the water to see the dolphins. We counted over 40 in one school, caught 4. They were very small. About 4 PM, Fred put a canvas belt around Forrest, made a small line fast to it, and let him swim around. Selwyn was over also with a line to him. Forrest will soon learn to swim, is not a bit afraid as long as he knows the line is tied tight. To day we almost ran down a fishing junk. They were drift net fishing. Did not see them until they were right under our bow. Passed close long side. I expect they were pretty well frightened. The German has altered her course for Japan. Have been in company three weeks.

20th June ~ Sunday. Mouth of Yangtse River. About twelve o'clock last Sunday night the wind hauled right around and came down from the North. Since, we have had light winds always ahead and rain four days. We neither saw sun, moon, nor Stars. We will probably go up the river this evening. It is a beautiful day, lots of fishing junks around and every body seems happy. It is nice to reach Port after a long voyage. We feel sure of not getting a Typhoon for the next two or three weeks any way. I have written nearly all of this on deck under the awning which will account a little for the writing and a blot now and then.

21st June ~ We did not get our Pilot until evening. Have been all day getting up the River. Are now at Anchor. Tow up to Shanghai early to-morrow morning. Fred and Forrest join in love,

Yours affectionately

Grace F. Ladd

As Fred notes in his log, the Belmont *arrived just in time for Queen Victoria's diamond jubilee celebrations. Grace and Fred were in Shanghai until the middle of July at which time they left for Port Townsend, Washington, probably in ballast judging by Grace's reference to the vessel being "high out of water." The next letter from Grace was written just after their departure from Shanghai.*

Bark *Belmont*
18th July 1897

Dear Papa

We have averaged over ten miles an hour since leaving Shanghai. The *Belmont* looked so high out of water I was afraid she would roll dreadfully, but she goes along as easily as possible. Besides Cook and Steward, we only have one new man; the second Mate we paid off* and took one of our sailors in his place. Today have been reading over our papers; we got a fine lot. I wonder if Ralph and Oscar will make a living in the Paper business. It seems such a funny thing for them to go into. Last night we passed through the Loo Choo Islands to the south of Japan. We have only one more group of islands in our way then a clear sail across the Pacific. The last evening in Shanghai Selwyn took dinner with us at the Astor House. After we said Good-bye, when we had been on board about ten minutes, who should come but Selwyn. He said he could not bear to have us go. He stayed until nearly one o'clock. I expect Ron will miss him very much as all of R's spare time they were to-gether. I hope he will be able to stand the climate. Shanghai is a very unhealthy place. We were fortunate not to have sickness on board.

Thursday 5th Aug. 178.40 East. Tomorrow we will be in West Longitude, so it will be Thursday again—the old cook says "me savey this moon got two Thursdays." I hope if you are having a wet foggy Summer, you are not thinking Yarmouth is the foggiest place in the world as we have not seen sun, moon, nor stars since we passed Japan—thick fog and rain all the time. I look back to last Summer as all sunshine—was surprised to see in "Whitaker's Almanac" it was the wettest season in Nova Scotia for a number of years. We have had very smooth sailing. The *Belmont* does not roll at all. Have seen such a lot of whales. It is so wet, I suppose they still think they are under water. This morning we found Selwyn's valise in the store room—can not imagine how he came to leave it—we were not on board when he packed, and the storeroom it was in is one not much used, so we did not see it before. I shall take it home to his Mother some time if we do not hear from him to the contrary. Forrest has been answering his letters, is going to leave yours until the last so it will be the best. He says "I don't think Shayne Evan will feel very good when he gets my letter written with ink." He is very persevering, but it wants lots of patience to teach him. I shall be glad when he can read.

Wednesday 18th Aug. "Puget Sound." Last night at six o'clock we were 150 miles from here in a dead calm. It had been a beautiful day, the sea like glass. About 12 midnight a little breeze came with thick fog, but we sailed straight on and this afternoon about 5 the fog lifted and we had the land all around us with a Tug boat not far off. 33 days from Shanghai, a very quick passage. Captain Ferguson in the *Brodick Castle* arrived on Saturday so we have beaten him 20 days, and another Ship which left the day after the *Brodick Castle* has not yet arrived. We are all delighted. Fred is sending you a Pilot Chart* with our track on it marked in red ink. I hope there will be at least one letter awaiting us. With much love to all—

Yours affectionately

Grace F. Ladd

19th Aug. ∽ Thursday. We are on shore. No letters yet. Suppose you thought we were going to make a long passage.

G.F.L.

In another letter to his brother-in-law, Fred boasts that the Belmont's *voyage from Shanghai (33 days) was "a record breaking passage for a Sailing Ship," so Grace may be right when she guesses they arrived before their mail from home had a chance to reach them. They spent over a month in the Puget Sound area, and Fred's letter speaks with delight of the "splendid time" they had there: "We visited Seattle twice & haven't decided which we like best, here [Tacoma] or there. I have met a number of old acquaintances here & the time has passed very quick. Forrest has learned to ride the Bicycle since we came here & on Sunday we went out & took a thirty mile ride & Forrest Stood it like a brick. None of us have a wheel—all hired ones."*

They left Tacoma on September 23 with lumber for Buenos Aires. Grace's next letter in November was begun just after they passed Pitcairn Island in the Pacific Ocean, heading south to round Cape Horn. Her letter reflects the usual anxiety that was felt when vessels approached the Horn; but unknown to Grace when she began the letter, they were indeed to experience an unfortunate loss.

Bark *Belmont*
Lat. S. 35°11' Long W. 126°
21st Nov. 1897

Dear Papa

59 days out and until we got in the Lat. of Pitcairn Island, the weather had been perfect. Except two days good rain just before crossing the Equator, had not even a squall. We hoped to sight Pitcairn Island last Sunday the 14th, but on Friday night it com-

menced to blow. Saturday at 4 PM we were under goose winged* lower top-sails, main and fore, blowing a hurricane. It seemed to me I had never seen a worse storm, but I suppose the disappointment of having to give up a chat with the Islanders was half. One tremendous sea came over, sweeping fore and aft. Forrest and I, sitting in the Cabin under the after skylight, were drenched. The sea raised the weather* sky light and came down full force putting out light, etc. On deck they fared worse. It took all the rails off the bridge and threw one life boat to leeward,* tore the chalks* away, not hurting the boat. However, three men washed against the rail (Ron, one of them). I do not believe one of them got even a scratch. All day Saturday, Sunday, and Monday, it blew with a heavy sea running. We used oil during the worst of it, and all the time the sailors were bending* good sails.* We did not think to get such a storm there. We were still in the S.E. Trades. Have only seen one sail and that a long way off, bound with us. We are all well. After leaving the Sound, Ron was laid up for a few days with a bad sore throat. We applied linseed meal poultices which relieved him at once.[103] Since then he has been perfectly well.

Sunday 28th. ∽ Lat. S. 45°30' Long. W. 108° Fine weather all the week. Today has been beautiful. Tuesday we sighted the Ship Erby of Liverpool from Victoria B.C. with a load of salmon for London. Yesterday we killed our pig, dressed it. [It] weighed 180 lbs., the largest one we have ever had. To day, had a fine spare rib for dinner. We had apple sauce, but squash had to take the place of turnips. The squash have kept well; we still have three. Tomorrow I am going to make sausage meat and head cheese. We are sugar curing one 15 lb. ham, more to experiment than any thing else. If it is good we will cook it for Christmas. We were all weighed yesterday while the scales were aft. Fred, 207 lbs.; Mr. Durkee, 176 ½; Ron, 178 ½; Forrest, 60; and myself, 138. I think we are all in good condition to go around the Horn. There is a new moon. This is a perfect night.

Thursday 2nd Dec. ∽ Lat S. 50°1' Long. W. 97°. Today is my 33rd birthday. I cannot realize it. The weather is still fine. Ron said tonight "if this is Cape Horn, I would like to be down here all the time." I told him he had better say it easy, a gale can come up so quickly, but the sky looks fine and the barometer is high. I had good luck with my sausage meat and head cheese—have also made mince meat and prepared the fruit for the Christmas pudding. I use tinned apple and steak for mince meat, and when I make the pies, put little pieces of butter in to take the place of suet, so you see I have been busy this week. Forrest has his lessons regularly, is getting on pretty well. He likes to talk about when we go home again just as he use[d] to about meeting Fred at the boat. He has written a letter to Santa Claus. When Santa came to get the letter he dropped his mitten in the grate.

Sunday 5th. ∽ Lat. S. 54°30' Long. W. 84° Weather still fine with a strong westerly breeze, quite a sea running. Forrest thought he would commence a letter to Grace today but it was too rough for him. Yesterday I had to read all of his letters over to him. He can almost read them himself. We have two fires going. The grate keeps the after Cabin very comfortable in this weather but in N.Y. last Winter Fred had to get a stove. Forrest is getting ready to go to bed. He does not see much fun in going to bed in broad day light. Last night there was day light in the sky all night long. The sun rises in the morning at 3.30, sets at 8.30.

Wednesday 8th ∽ Lat. S. 56.°20. Long. W. 68.°15' Die Ramirez Island[104] bears S.W. by W. about 20 miles. Passed 3 miles on the North side of it at 7 PM. We could see the land also to the North with the snow with the setting sun shining on it, a fine sight, but we have not the heart to enjoy any thing, such a sad accident has happened. Poor Charlie Ritchie is gone.[105] Fred was of course on deck at the time, and I am going to just copy what he has written in his journal: "Monday 6th Dec. Lat. S. 55°40' Long 78.°34' W. At 6 PM blowing hard. As the Starboard Watch came on deck, we hauled the Mainsail up. All hands went aloft to make it fast. This sail clews up* at the Yard arm. They had furled* the sail, all but the clews.* Charlie Ritchie was the outside man. He was down on the foot rope* (sitting down) and passing a turn of the Gasket* around the clew, and passing the same to the man inside of him who was holding the sail on the yard. Somehow, he lost his balance and slipped forward of the foot rope and came down. He held on the Gasket, but it was a small rope, 1 3/4 in. It slipped through his hands and he fell into the sea. As I saw him fall, I rushed Aft calling to the man at the wheel (Chris) to put the wheel hard down.* In the mean time I had thrown the life buoy to him. It fell about 10 ft. from him. He clutched the log* line; this slipped through his fingers. When he came to the log he held it for a moment and this towed him under. As he let go, the life buoy was close by him—a few strokes and he got it. When I called out "put the wheel down," I also said "let go top gallant halliards* and topsail halliards." I sent the boy Ali Chang, also Otto Anderson, aloft to watch him. We did not try to take in any sail but tore the covers off the Gig,* off gripes,* and carried the boat over the deck load* to the lee side,* and threw her over the rail with a single line in each end (the gig is a splendid boat, 22 ft. long. They never could have pulled the Life boat against the sea, or I would have sent it). Mr. Durkee and four men, John Donnelly, Charles Anderson, Dan Lynch, and Phillip Thomas, started from the Ship. I gave them a tin of oil. The sea was very heavy and breaking badly. The boat would stand almost on end. After half an hour we lost sight of the boat. I wore Ship at once. We had clewed top gallant sails up, and clewed down the upper fore topsail. In the mean time I let her wear round on her heel, hauled main yards aback, clewed up the Foresail which was badly torn in the slatting* as we had no time to clew it up, hauled down the jibs, and clewed up weather side of lower Fore topsail, and hauled out the foot of the Spanker. She was now making a dead drift, not going ahead a bit as I wished to keep the boat to Windward to give them a square run before the sea* coming back. Rain squalls had shut in blowing hard. Soon as I wore ship, I set the ensign, the signal agreed upon to recall the boat, but for one hour and a quarter we saw no sign of her. I had given her up. One must go through this experience to realize how horrible is the feeling. Charles Collins was in the Main cross trees* all this time trying to see the boat. At last saw her right to windward as the squall cleared, steering for the Ship. As they kept her right before the sea, the boat would run as much as ten feet of herself out of water. They got under the lee of the ship and pulled along side, the boat half full of water, but no Charlie. He was gone, poor fellow. Twice the water had been up to the athwarts* as the sea broke over them. Had she filled, they were gone. The oil saved them. It smoothed the water, kept the sea from breaking. One man saw an empty life buoy on the top of a sea. They went until they lost sight

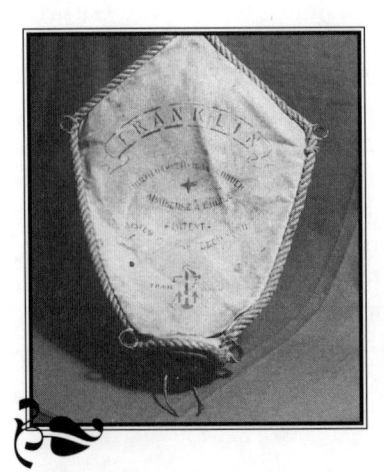

An oil bag from which oil was thrown over the surface of the sea to keep the waves from breaking during rough weather. Fred speaks of giving his crew a tin of oil when they went out in the boat to search for Charlie Ritchie.

of the Ship in the squalls and then started back. Poor Mr. Durkee. He said it was the hardest thing he ever had to do, to come back without him, and he did not think it possible they could save them selves. The last the man aloft saw of Charlie, he was on the weather quarter with the life buoy around him. Several seas had broken over him. He could not last long as the water was ice cold. Ali Chang had also thrown a life buoy. When the men got back they were most exhausted. They were gone two hours. Never again would I risk a boat's crew in such a sea. It was Providence that saved them.[106] We lay until 9.30, then wore Ship and started. At the time of the accident we were going ten miles an hour with the wind N. by W., fresh to strong gale, steering E.S.E., carrying whole Topsails, whole Foresail, reefed* Fore and Main top gallant sails." F.A.L.

I do not see how some people can call sailors "dogs." If they could have seen the sea those brave men started out in with a small boat to try and save that man's life, I am sure they never would do so again. I did not go on deck until Fred said we have lost sight of the boat, but had hot fires and lots of hot water and blankets ready. When I did go I felt sure she was lost too. It seemed so terrible—the sea was dreadful. We have had nothing like it since we left except in the hurricane, and not since. Have had exceptionally fine weather.

11th Dec. ∞ Fred's birthday, 39 years old. We feel such a change in the climate, so much warmer. We are now in Lat. 53° S. and Long 59°.5' W. Can see plainly a small island called Beauchêne 30 miles south of the Falklands. Thursday at 2 AM (broad day light), passed 8 miles South Cape Horn. Spoke the English Ship *Travancore* from San Francisco for Queenstown, out 60 days. On the 9th we had 6 Ships in sight, all coming East. Yesterday, the 10th, at 3 AM, Mr. Durkee called Fred saying "4 masted ship astern showing flags." We knew he wanted something, or a friend, to signalize at that time. It was the Ship *Corinnea*, sailed from Tacoma 5 days after we. He asked us if we would take letters for him.[107] Of course we were pleased to do so. It was a lovely morning. We were just 30 miles South Staten Island.[108] almost calm, 9 ships in sight, 2 going West. At 6 AM, Captain MacMillan and his passenger, Mr. McGrady, were along side. It was pleasant meeting them again. They stayed with us about an hour, would not wait for breakfast, so we gave them some hot chocolate. They brought us a piece of spare rib and were so disappointed when they found we had just killed a pig. Their steward had not made any sausage meat

Quite A Curiosity

so I gave them about 2 lbs., also some mince meat and books. Capt. MacMillan said they had spoken a great many ships: the *Pendeere*, one of the Ships in sight, 70 days from Frisco; and one ship, 80 day[s] from Frisco. Three weeks ago sighted the *Brodick Castle* too far off to signalize. She was sailing very slowly he said. Soon after he left us we got a breeze and separated as we wanted to go West of Falkland, but the wind headed us so we had to come East. I am glad we are bound to the River as we would make a very long passage home. Forrest has written a letter to Grace today.

Christmas evening ~ Lat. S. 40°.30' Long. W. 55°.20. We have thought of you all at home today and hoped you were having a very happy Christmas. Notwithstanding head winds and rain squalls, we have all enjoyed ourselves although we have almost given up ever getting in. We are in a trap here. We have a strong current against us running 3 miles an hour as that is all the *Belmont* can sail now, she is so dirty.[109] The outlook is poor. This last week have only neared our Port 94 miles. I just heard the man at the wheel say she would not steer[110] so probably before tomorrow we will lose some of that. Last evening Ron represented Santa Claus (Forrest's faith in him is as great as ever). The make up was splendid. A sailor had made a fine large Tam, with a long new manila rope wig and beard which was combed out. We were afraid Forrest would recognize Ron by his eyes, but we kept the light turned down on account of it hurting them. He changed his voice and acted it out splendidly. It was really fun for us all. We had ginger and sandwiches for him and again Santa was delighted with the tree we had ready for him to trim later. We had already put on the popcorn, tinsel, and bags of nuts. Forrest awaked early this morning and was not disappointed in any of his wishes. Everybody was remembered. We invited all the sailors in to see the tree and gave them a cigar. The steward gave who wanted it a strong drink and for the others ginger beer. They had a good dinner. They were supposed to have a holiday instead of which have been hauling yards since 7 AM. Ron had dinner with us which, we all decided, could not have been better had we been in Port. A beef steak pie took the place of turkey, but we had squash, mashed potatoes, boiled ham, jelly, etc. Forrest is just going to bed, tired out, wishing next Christmas was not so far off—Good-night.

30th Dec. ~ We ought to get in soon, now are only 30 miles from Buenos Ayres, but have been stuck 4 times already in the mud. We are drawing more water than there is in the River. We came to an anchor last evening at 6 in Montevideo roads—could see the City very plainly and all the Ships at anchor. In a short time a pilot came off in a tow boat. Since then we have been trying to get up here. It is a beastly place to get to. The poor sailors are completely tired out. Ron knows what real hard work is, but he has done well and our letters will make us forget every thing to-morrow. I have written to Arth and Flo. I know they are so anxious to hear of Ron and it would be so much longer to have to wait to hear from you. Fred and Forrest and Ron join in love to all.

Yours affectionately

Grace F. Ladd

P.S. Forrest has not managed to answer his letters. Has made several attempts but would get tired. He still thinks he will write.

G.F.L.

The Belmont *anchored at Montevideo the next day, but was held up by protocol concerning the death of Charlie Ritchie. Losing a crew member this way was a lamentable and yet all too common occurrence. It weighed heavy on the captain, in this case even more so since Charlie Ritchie was a Yarmouth boy. The news reached Yarmouth by telegraph as soon as the* Belmont *arrived at port. Charles E. Brown wrote about the incident in his journal on December 31, 1897:*

> Mr. Ladd called up to tell us of the arrival yesterday at Buenos Ayres of the *Belmont* but with the sad accompaniment "Charles Ritchie drowned." Poor boy! He was about Ron's age, & like Ron, on his first voyage & they were roommates. We should be thankful that it is not we that are called to mourn & can feel for the mourning mother & friends. It will be a month before we shall know the particulars.

In fact, it was to be more than a month. Grace's letter (above) finally arrived in Yarmouth on February 14. In his journal entry for that day, Charles E. Brown responds to the news of Charlie Ritchie as delivered to him by Grace:

> A long letter from Grace by the evg mail written at different dates during the voyage, concluding with the date of their arrival at B. A. Dec 30. As we had supposed, Charlie Ritchie

fell off the main yard into the sea in heavy weather near Cape Horn. The Capt. threw him a life buoy which he caught & [———] & the mate with 4 men in a light boat risked their own lives to find him, but in vain. And it was with great difficulty they regained the ship, at one time having been given up. Ron wrote that he should never forget when Fred went forward & said, "Boys! We've lost the boat too."

The "Account of Wages and Effects of a deceased Seaman" lists Charlie Ritchie's possessions, which would have been sent to his next of kin (in this case, probably his mother) as the following: "1 Bag, 1 Quilt, 1 Pillow, 1 Pannikin, 1 cup, 3 shirts, 3 prs. socks, 4 prs. Dungarees, 2 pr. trousers, 1 coat, 1 pr. shoes, 1 suit oilclothes, 1 cap." In addition to personal belongings, Charlie was owed $56.47 in wages.

The Ladds' unsettling passage around the Horn ended with a long South American stay, some of which is described in Grace's next two letters from Colonia, Uruguay.

Bark *Belmont*
Colonia Uruguay
9th March 1898

My dear Papa

This is such a funny little place with about 2000 inhabitants. Our vessel is moored half a mile from the town. We came over here on the 25th Feb. and for a week was the only ship, when the *Stalwart* came along, and now the *Anglo American* is outside waiting for a fair wind to come in over the shoals. Then there is a Uruguayan "Man of War" anchored close by. We get very little news here. There are no English people living in the town. Fred met a young Englishman. The other day he came along to help F—with his Spanish, saw I suppose he needed assistance, introduced himself,

Charlie Ritchie of Yarmouth was 19 years old when he fell from the mast of the Belmont *near Cape Horn and drowned. The Ladds were deeply affected by his loss.*

said his name was Nino. He lived out in the Country ("Camp" they call it), would bring his sisters in to see me, and would like for us to come and see them. We have a sail in our boat. There is nearly always a breeze so we enjoy the boating. Forrest does the steering. He has not yet learned to swim well, can go about two strokes alone over the side. While we were in Buenos Ayres Fred used to take him to a swimming bath nearly every day. Half a mile below the town there is a nice farm. We land on the beach with our boat and get such nice vegetables. One day we bought a turkey alive, the only one they had. We get milk every day and fresh eggs. It was a great change to come here after B.A. We met so many Yarmouth people there it seems I must have been at home a few months ago instead of over a year. I was never in a port before where so many Captains had their wives. It was pleasant. Every evening we met on some of the ship[s] to play cards or, if there was a piano, music. Ron was always called on to sing when they met here and was invited out with us several times. I do not know why I had formed such a poor opinion of Buenos Ayres. It is a very fine City. The suburbs are beautiful. The climate is much better than out East, nights always cool. We are all well, will be loaded in about two weeks, go to Queenstown for orders. I shall write lots of letters on my way to make up for lost time here. All join in love,

Yours affectionately

Grace F. Ladd

Bark *Belmont*
Colonia Uruguay 29th March 1898

Dear Papa

I was very glad to receive two letters from you last Sunday dated 10th & 16th Feb. It is a comfort to know Fletch is so much better before starting off on our homeward passage. Ale is probably just what she needs.[111] The *Hillside*, after all, loaded at Rosario.[112] Diamante is a small place, three hundred miles up river from Rosario in the Argentine Republic. It is astonishing how little the people living here even, know about the places round about; for instance, before coming here we could not find out anything about the place—were told we could not buy vegetables or fruit—whereas we get fine vegetable[s] fresh from a farm, also certain kinds of fruit—melons, figs, apples (very poor), potatoes are very dear, $1.55 a bushel. A bushel is nothing with our old cook. Fred says all he does is peel potatoes. We have a number of extra men, the Stevedore's men. What a mixture about our going to Ensenada. We have never seen the place. Ensenada is the shipping part of La Plata. We did intend going to La Plata to see the Museum, but gave it up. It rained or something the day we were going. You write "Freight insured from Ensenada." Fred cannot understand that as we go direct from Colonia to Europe, not via Ensenada, and if it was the lumber freight, why insured for there, when we were bound to Buenos Ayres? We did see green grass waving on a small uninhabited island of the Falkland group. We were not sure but said perhaps it is tassel. There are no vessels trading between River Plata and the Falklands. The only communication between there and here is a man-of-war, perhaps once in three months. There is a man-of-war here now, or Gun boat, the *Beagle*. The officers have been on board. Fred, Forrest, and Captain Lovitt returned their call two evenings ago. They sent us fourteen partridge. They were a great treat. The American Consul has invited Fred and I out to breakfast with some of the officers Wednesday morning. We will not be able to go as we tow several miles out into deeper water to finish taking our cargo and can only come onshore when our men are not working as it is not safe to come so far in a small boat—these pamperos* blow up so quickly. We were pleased to hear of the arrival in the Armstrong family. I suppose Malcome is delighted. May took so much care of him, she will have her hand in. Poor Mr. Hickey. I am so sorry he is dead, always expected to come across him again sometime. Shall keep that slip and put it with the other papers which are at home.[113] Forrest has quite a collection of birds eggs, some very pretty ones. We do not know the names of the birds. We have met several very nice English families: the "Eastons," Mother and two daughter[s], keep a boarding school. They have a very nice place and the children belong to ranchmen who live many miles inland. We think it would be a good place to leave Forrest for a few years. These children all have their own ponies and learn to ride with a sheep skin, not a saddle. Several boys have gone straight from this school into business houses in Monte Video and got good positions. I feel curious about all of these people and wonder what brought them out here. This seems such an out of the way place and the country is not beautiful. The oldest, Miss Easton, came out first as Governess and saw an opening here for a school, so sent for her Mother and sister. They came off one afternoon and a pampero came up so they had to stay all night. There were six of them, three of them were seasick, and a boat from the *Anglo America[n]* with five men could not reach their ship, just managed to get to us. It was very amusing. The Eastons were in great distress about their school. The children had a holiday of course. Captain Lovitt is well but he looks on the dark side of life, is worried about his boys. Thinks May did well to get Henry K—. I do not believe he ever heard about that money scrape of Henry's.[114] The *Stalwart* won't get away for a fortnight yet. We expect to get away this week if the weather keeps fine. I will write again and send back by Pilot. With love to all from all,

Yours affectionately

Grace F. Ladd

It took a month to load the Belmont *with 31,797 bags of wheat. Loading was completed on March 31 and the Ladds departed for Queenstown the next day. It was a slow start—the vessel repeatedly got stuck in the mud as they began to make their way out through the Rio de la Plata. To make it worse, Fred was plagued with a toothache that drove him finally to try—unsuccessfully—to pull out his own tooth.*

As they neared the end of the century, Grace and Fred were sailing through an unsettled world. Fred noted in his logs on June 9: "We get Accts that War has been declared between America & Spain & that Mr. Gladstone is dead." The former British prime minister William Ewart Gladstone died in May 1898, and the Spanish-American war— fought between Spain and the United States over control of Cuba and the Philippines—broke out the same year. The battle of Manila Bay, which was won by the Americans, was fought on May 1, 1898, just over a month before Fred mentioned the war in his logbook.

On June 10, Grace and Fred arrived at Queenstown, where Fred received orders to proceed to Bordeaux, France. Instead of going with him, Grace and Forrest travelled to Ainsdale, and they appear to have met up with Fred later. Fred loaded ballast, after which he set out again for New York, unhappy with his pilot who was apparently incompetent— "an old woman frightened out of his life." On their way to New York, as they were passing to the south of Newfoundland, the Belmont *sailed past a number of fishing vessels and Fred's logs record another incident of trading at sea:*

Set sail in the Midst of fishing fleet of Barks & Bktines & Brigs. Could see 30 at one time. Up to noon had passed altogether, including last night, 55 Sails. One came onboard from Bkentine *La Liberté* of Fécamp, brought 3 letters for us to Mail & he brought us 3 cod fish, one for each letter. We gave him two buckets potatoes & ½ bucket onions. Grace waved her hat to Another who came over bringing us 8 More Cod. We gave him Some potatoes & onions, a piece of Beef & Pork & 10 Cigars & a French newspaper.

Grace and Fred arrived in New York on August 31st, went home for a short time, and then left again at the end of September for Shanghai with a cargo of oil, this time without Forrest. Grace's younger brother, Ronald Brown, signed on once again as "bosun" (wages, £3.50). Before the end of this voyage, he was promoted to second mate (mentioned in Grace's letter of September 12, 1899) with a raise in wages to £4.10. Grace and Fred arrived at Shanghai in mid-February, and sailed next to Newcastle, Australia.

One more letter from Charles E. Brown to Grace that was written around this time managed to end up in the Brown family file in the Yarmouth County Museum Archives. The letter is dated April 2, 1899, written just after Charles E. Brown learned of the Belmont's *arrival in Shanghai and its subsequent chartering to Newcastle. In it, Grace's father elaborates on life back in Yarmouth, including details of various family members that Grace herself frequently mentions. Among them are Grace's sister Georgie and her husband John Allan (living in New York at this time), her aunt Elizabeth and Uncle George, and her other sister, Flo (who became a nurse) along with details of her courtship with the man she was eventually to marry, Hamilton Byers. The letter also alludes to the war and the consequent demand for coal in Manila, which is what sent the* Belmont *to Newcastle in the first place (something Grace does not appear to be happy about in her next letter). Finally, Charles E. Brown tells us much about Forrest at home, what his interests are, his character and his activities—and behind the stories he tells, Grace's father inadvertently reveals some enticing facets of his own personality. The following is Charles E. Brown's letter to Grace:*

2nd April 1899
Yarmouth, Nova Scotia

Dear Grace,

We were agreeably surprised to hear of your arrival at Shanghai in 142 days, 164 being the average of your three previous arrivals there. Your letter of 19th reached us on the 23 Mar = 32 days; by last mail your letters to Forrest & to Eth & Ron's and Fred's to me, came duly forward. I wrote last to you and to Ron on the 17th Feby, sending to Each under separate cover, a Photo of the Milton Whist Club of this season of which Flo & Stayley were Members. We hear lately of the ship's being chartered to load at Newcastle for Manila, at 187 per ton for coal, which is thought to be a very good freight. We at home, however, would much rather the freight to N.Y. loading at Shanghai & at Hong Kong had been accepted—since there's no knowing when this coal business may come to an end. Just now it looks as if the War might be prolonged indefinitely, and Coal will be in lively demand for years to come.

It was a great comfort to know you were all well. Fred says you promise to overtake in [——], even Aunt Eth, but she is going steadily along, and fairly shines with fat, 207, I think, was the last I recorded for her. You are doing well at 153, but you do not need to go beyond that. Breathing gets wheezy & you can't run up stairs or up a long hill. Aunt Elizabeth for instance, is a warning. She is scarcely able to walk about alone now. Georgie with John called to see Aunt Eliz. & Uncle George after their return and Uncle George saw them off for Washington, where they made a delightful visit of about 10 days, were introduced to Prest. McKinley,[115] visited Mt. Vernon. I don't suppose they saw the cherry tree, but may have seen the hatchet. Called on Mrs. Garrison and saw all the notable institutions of the City. Georgie wrote that she was glad to get back to New York, unpack her cases and get settled down. Their friends were very generous to them. John's business connections made them a lot of presents. I will [——] over Georgie's letters & as you intimate to Eth, you would like to see a list of her presents. I will perhaps send you one in some future letter as it will take some time to go through the letters. Georgie writes very often to some of us, so that hearing from her so regularly we do not miss her so much.

We are all quite well now. We have had two or three cases of Grippe. I attended meetings at Wolfville & at Annapolis in Feb., staying at Mrs Owen's and having a very delightful visit in distinguished company for two days. Mrs. Daniel (Alice Baker), the Hon. Minister of Agriculture & Prof Shutt from Ottawa & the *Hon Mr Longley, Attorney General of N.S.* were among the guests. The house was full all the time, but Mr. Longley had to *sleep* on a sofa, & Mrs. Daniel at a neighbour's, while I had a most luxurious bed & the best room in the house. The two boys, Dan & Farish sat at the table, and you could not imagine their conduct. Once at dinner, Dan called out to the Hon. Mr. Longley "'Long*legs*,' do you know who you look like"? No! "Well! You look like old Jim Richardson," a disreputable old darkey of the neighborhood. On another occasion, the two boys were having a fight at a lunch and one giving the other a hearty punch in the wind, extorted the bran[d] new oath, "Holy Communion"! At Breakfast, each plate was supplied with three knives, one small, plated, for fruit, oranges being the first course, one shaped like a fish knife, for fish cakes, and the ordinary bread knife. One morning one of the boys called out loudly and reprovingly "Mrs. Daniel! Mrs. Daniel! You're cutting your orange with a fish knife!" Mr. Longley told me that these cases were nothing to what he has witnessed on former visits, that one on each side of him would yell "Longlegs" at him for five minutes together. But it's too bad to fill my paper with these instances of lack of training.

Forrest is a model in comparison—I caught the Grippe in the Cars coming home and kept house for a week or two but was not seriously ill. Forrest probably & Fletcher caught it from me but cases were all light—Forrest has in a week lost 3 lbs but has gained 4 lbs, now 72, the heaviest yet.

(With my love this 3 day of April 1899
Forrest Arthur Ladd)[116]

Feb 9th & 10th were two of the worst storms of the winter. On the 9th, Thursday, Henry drove me to the Bank in the sleigh, no cars running & the right side of my face got frozen. The storm was so bad there was no school but Forrest with other boys were out coasting down the first [——] field for hours & enjoying it. The *Prince George*[117] was due here at *8 AM on the 9th* but she did not arrive until *3.30 P M on the 10th*—The next day, Saturday, 11th Feb, the therm. stood at 2° at 8 A M. 14° at 12 N., 10° at 6. Forrest was away nearly all day helping Malcolm Davis deliver parcels from the Paper store.

Thursday 16 March, there was a carnival at the Rink, & Forrest was very anxious to go. Flo readily agreed to go with him while rigged up in that fancy suit of his and they had a grand time.

On Saturday, 18th I record[ed] this in my journal: "Forrest at the Rink in the afternoon, and although I gave him 40¢ to cover any possible expenses, (and he was free to call about 20 of this his own) he brought back 38 and had lent a boy one cent (which he collected later) out of this two cent expenditure. The money was partly his own too, and Hubert Cann had tried to persuade him to spend it, so there's lots of virtue in Forrest Arthur Ladd.

Walked down & up too instead of taking the cars." He is quite contented, and likes books & school, rec'd honorable mention for regular attendance. Last evg. he read to me all the verses in the first Reading Book—I have offered him a dollar to learn to recite Drummond's "Habitant," a most humorous descriptive French dialect poem, which I have lately learned myself & which was one of the recitations at the recent festivities at Annapolis.[118] Forrest recites "Jes fore Christmas" with good taste & appreciation of the points.[119] I wish you could see him today [———] from Easter service, white vest, pretty neck tie, new coat & pants and as rosy & hearty looking as any boy between us of his years.

He was much pleased with your letter and with the dollar for a Birthday present, which he handed to me to take care of for him. He does not like to keep money about his own person, the temptation to spend is too strong & then there are always gluttonous boys or girls who want to be forever eating or drinking…who would encourage him to spend any money they might see in his possession—the shops are full of these temperance drinks, to incite people to waste money, & to me it seems little worse to spend money for liquor than it is to spend it on ginger ale, or any other of these fancy soft drinks—We have a neighbor, Dan, the Blacksmith, on the Loch, who must spend about half his Earnings at McMullens on this stuff. There is nothing so wholesome as good pure water and the Doctors say every adult should drink from one to two quarts per day, to cleanse the system, drive out rheumatism & flush all the outlets—Do you know John F. McLauren of Lower Argyle? One of John's friends, keeps a stock of goods & does a large business—He suffered so much from rheumatism a year or two ago that he was obliged to give up business. To the surprise of every one he recovered entirely, resumed business & looks as well as ever in his life. T. A. Crowell asked him what had cured him. He said it was simply taking a *swallow* of a solution of Epsom salts, every night before going to bed. Crowell began at once; that was nearly three months ago, and he says there's no trace now of rheumatism left in him.—There is no more prevalent or troublesome disease in our Province. Every one nearly has it in some form & the hospitals say it's incurable & will not receive patients.

Mrs. Byers has been ill for some time with some obscure trouble, possibly cancer. The Doctors performed an operation which was temporarily successful & prolonged her life, but the tumor remains.—Flo yielded to a request from the Doctors that she should act as nurse at the time of the operation, & she was there for a day or two at the house, until another nurse relieved her. Ham. Jr. came home to see his Mother, the last of February, called here several times & seemed taken with Flo but did not venture to propose to her. After his departure he sent Flo from Boston a box of the finest roses, Carnations & Violets that were ever seen in Yarmouth. I was fairly astounded. It looked like a confession, but Flo says they have only agreed to correspond. Ham is carrying on a Hardware & Miner's supply business in three places in British Columbia, and is said to be doing a very large business, making $10,000 a year. He is quite fine looking, & healthy-appearing and is generally liked. He is said to have told some of his friends here that he would have proposed to Flo but that he dreaded a refusal as Flo is credited with having declared that she would not marry any man. Arthur had heard of the matter and asked me if there was any thing in it to which I replied something as above & told him that if he knew of any objection to the match that now was the time. The same applies to all Flo's friends.—Stayley is still at home, but will likely ship in the S. A. Trade, when the winter is fairly over. He has been quite well, has been regular & steady & always at home in good season at night.

Fletcher is only middling, but has kept up and about fairly well. Forrest has his crib in her room and she is his chief care taker. Flo & he have frequent quarrels, but of course nothing serious, & Flo takes him to Church & to any places she visits herself.—Maria has had her turn with Grippe, but is well now. The winter has been dreadful, cold & stormy & no let up at all—Wrecks Willow's End. A large Steamer on Sable Island and a fine new 8000 ton Allen liner at Gannet Rock [——]—Cargo mostly saved and sold here, cattle, horses, sheep, cheese, Bacon, Apples, etc. I notice there has been a terrible drought in N. S. Wales, Millions of sheep &

Grace's sister, Florence Isabel Brown. She married Hamilton Byers and moved with him to Nelson, British Columbia, where he owned a hardware business.

Cattle perished—the Whole country dried up & no water.—I shall try to write to both Fred & Ron by this Mail & you will see one another's letters.

Yours affectionately

Charles E. Brown

Grace began her next letter home as they approached Newcastle, about one week before their arrival.

Bark *Belmont*
South Pacific Ocean
12th May 1899

Dear Papa

We are now beating down the Australian coast. For ten days, we have had this South East wind. After making a good passage this far, it seems too bad to have it spoiled now, but some way it is our luck. After leaving Shanghai we sailed due East through the Liu Chotins [?] to 158 E., then passed West Marshall Group, and East of Caroline Islands crossed the Equator 165 E 23 days, then between the Solomon Island and Santa Cruz, and West of New Caledonia. We must have passed over the place the *Ancona* put in such a miserable time but we had no calms.[120] Light winds brought us quickly through those belts. We have not sighted a single island out of all the number we have passed and only one sail in 2' N. too far away to signalize, bound North. Yesterday we killed one of our pigs. It seemed almost impossible to give them enough to eat. One is all right. Today I have been busy making sausage meat and head cheese. The weather is warm, so we shall not be able to keep it for any length of time. Our Langshans are fine for the table but we do not average more than 1 dozen eggs a week.[121] I do not see why they do not lay better as they are in a fine place down in the ballast. In a few days now I suppose the fruit trees will be in bloom and everything looking lovely. Down here it is the Fall but the climate will be fine. I expect it is very nice here. Every day we say this must be a beautiful day on the shore, but we don't enjoy them at sea. We are too disgusted with getting sent here. I wonder how Hermann will stand the hot weather. It is very trying at first until one learns how to dress for it. I am glad Arth is in better spirits. I felt quite miserable about him when I was home. The only way to do is to take things as they come in this world, good or bad ————— [?] (never mind) as the Chinese say.

New Castle, N.S.W. C.E.B.[122]

20th May. ∽ We arrived here last evening. Had to beat every mile of the way. We were under every Lighthouse on the coast, down 52 days passage. The *Andromeda*, which left some time before us, was 49. Fred bet with a man in Shanghai that both vessels would be under 60 days. He is very glad to have won. The place is full of Shipping. The *Jane Burrill* arrived yesterday morning; the *Celeste B*—is also here. The old *Haddon Hall* is right along side of us but Capt. Dixon is not in her now.[123] The *Oweenee*, Capt Burchell, is in Sydney—also the *William Law*. It is very cool mornings, or it is this morning. The Board of Health require every vessel to pump all the water out, such a farce. Here we have been drinking this water all the passage; and all of our ballast has to be sent to sea. Dot (a small dog) has to go ashore in quarantine and we have got to kill our little pig. We can keep the hens. The doctor is now on board. Fred will not be able to go on shore until the water is out. I believe that will...

[hand-writing change to Fred Ladd]

Grace put this by for me to do some writing & went on deck. In Coming down Stairs, she moved towards the Fore Cabin* in which there is a trap door leading to Lazaretto. It was open and she did not see it, & so fell into it or across [———], her right arm striking the edge & broke the bone between the elbow & Shoulder. It is a straight break and I'll close this & write again tomorrow.

Yours Affectionately

Grace F. Ladd
per F.A.L.

Capt. Fred A. Ladd. The photo was taken in Newcastle, New South Wales, perhaps when the Ladds were last there in 1899.

Evidently, Grace did not start out her stay in Australia in a positive way. Her frustration about being sent there is obvious in the previous letter, and breaking her arm was not likely to have cheered her. The Belmont remained in Newcastle until the end of June and then departed for Manila with its cargo of coal. The Philippines was still a region of political instability as the Americans struggled to maintain control. As they approached the area through the Basilan Straits, Fred noted in his logs that they sighted a number of canoes and that "Grace says they are getting ready for war."

Grace still sounds discouraged and tired at the beginning of her next letter, but seems relieved when they reach Manila on September 18.

Bark *Belmont*
Mindoro Straits 12th Sept. 1899

Dear Papa

74 days out and still 80 miles from Manila. At the rate we are going we shall be many days yet. We are all dreadfully tired of this tedious passage. Two weeks ago yesterday we came through Basilan Straits, thought our troubles were over as we fully expected to get the South West monsoon, but not a sign of it have we had. Nothing but light airs and calms. Feel happy if we make 15 miles a day. We used to growl at 30 coming along the Equator. We had a good run from New Castle up to New Ireland, sighted Solomon Islands afar off, came along the equator for 1,500 miles about, kept on the look out for the high mountain as we passed New Guinea. Saw nothing of it, did not see a sign of life on any of the Islands we passed. It was lively enough coming through Basilan Straits. I never saw as many native canoes. They seemed to be crossing the Straits in all directions but did not come near us. In places we passed near the shore, could see villages etc., even men walking along the shore—and on the Island of Tobago, an old derelict. We have another one in sight now on Apo reef, a good place for all sailing vessels high and dry.[124]

18th Sept. ∞ 80 days out. In sight of the light, but winds and tides are against us. However, we feel better. Last Thursday an American Bark, the *St. James*, passed close by. We put our boat out and Mr Ellis[125] went on board to get some news. You can imagine we were surprised to know that "old derelict" was the *Jane Burrill*. We were not nearer than seven miles as we kept close under the south shore. All vessels are making long passages so we are not alone. If we could only have come Torres Straits, we would have been in Manila long ago. Fred wrote both "Hall" and "John Black" from Shanghai to arrange for this, but they did not and he did not feel like taking the whole responsibility as the Charter Party "prohibited" Torres Straits.[126] I do hope you went to Boston. You would enjoy the change. Notwithstanding my broken arm I enjoyed my self in Australia. We had a delightful trip to Sydney. Capt. Burchell is a fine man and it was a treat to see Clara. She has changed very much. I should not have known her. Her Father's second wife is dead. She was a pretty hard case I think. She did not have any money and got the little bit of land Mr Blethen had in her own name and made it over to her own daughter. Charlie's wife is left with nothing and two children. She kept house for Mr. Blethen. George married a [——] girl and lives out West. Nettie's boy Lou is with Capt. B. He does not like going to sea. They are going to send him home from London. We have a splendid crew and a healthy one although our second Mate was laid up for two week[s]. Ron took his watch and did well. The second Mate is a Scotchman. We shipped him in New Castle. He is not a bit of good.

20th Sept. I went on deck to watch a nice little breeze coming on the water and did not come below again until we were at anchor. Yesterday we got our letters, three for me from you, June 23rd, 30th, July 21st. It was too bad you should worry about Ron when there was not the least cause. On the contrary, Fred put more confidence in him than he does in Mr Ellis. You cannot imagine a more useless man. As soon as Mr Fields (2nd) leaves, probably to-morrow, Ron moves aft. I shall be glad. He will also get more wages, £ 4.10. I do not imagine he will save any more; for instance, he will go on shore with Mr Ellis and perhaps pay all the expenses. He does not value money at all. In New Castle he met lots of nice people, always went in good company etc. Stayley is far better off in the Cotton Mill than at sea. I am glad Flo interfered. I have not had a line from the latter since I left home. I am so afraid Lem will change his mind. He is so changeable. If this vessel goes across to the Sound,[127] you can look for me home. I almost hope she will. I had letters from Fletch, Arth, Maria & Charlie. Shall have lots of time for writing letters here. With much love to all,

Yours affectionately

Grace F. Ladd

Grace wrote the next two letters while they were in Manila discharging and then loading sand ballast, waiting to receive orders to their next port and the next load of cargo. The American presence was evidently strong (as Grace describes it below) and the fighting ongoing. The unrest made it difficult to obtain a cargo, as Grace mentions, but it also must have been an uncomfortable place to be.

Bark *Belmont* Manila
9th Oct. 1899

Dear Papa

During last week I received your two letters dated 20th & 27th Aug., also one from Fletch. The mails are very irregular, nearly all coming by transports which are arriving every day. They anchor near us. The men are sent on shore in lighters* towed in. Sometimes they are kept on board two or three days. They have no places for them on shore, poor fellows. They are sick of the American Army long before they get to Manila. Imagine—the Americans have had Manila for over a year. The bay is only twenty miles in [———], yet they are fighting on all three sides of it. We hear the bombarding daily. At night we can see the burning villages and see them signalizing from different stations by throwing lights in the sky. It looks as if this fighting may go on for years. It does not interfere with us at all except prevents our getting a cargo. We are not able to get vegetable[s] of any kind and the beef is very poor. Fortunately an English steamer is here with a load of ice and frozen mutton consigned to Luneth [?] Bell & Co. We are able to get through and both of these. We share the sheep with Captain Abbott. We get potatoes and onions from a Government store house. Both are very dear. Oh well, we are working two gangs now. If the weather keeps fine, shall be discharged in about ten days. Fred is going to put a full set of sand ballast in. We can not form the least idea where we will go to load. You will probably know before we do. If the Pacific Coast, Fred has made up his mind to go home with me for a year, so I hope it will be there; but it will be better for the ship if it is Singapore or Hong-Kong.[128] Fred is much flattered that you should send to New Castle for some more of those photos. I thought them good too. It was too bad Ron did not have some taken there, but I discourage him in all of his vanities. Just now we all feel pretty dusty with coal. It is dreadful. We are obliged to shut everything up, and it is so hot. There is one consolation.

Quite A Curiosity

There is not a happy looking Captain here. They console each other going and coming in the Launch. Some Ships have been here 100 days. Captain Trefry in the *Celeste Burrill* has had an awful siege.[129] Flo's conscience must have troubled her when she received Grandma's handsome present. I wonder what has struck her, Grandma I mean.[130] I should like to have been home this Summer, am so glad we left Forrest. He would feel the heat very much here. He must be having a very happy time. I expect we shall have about three or four weeks more here. On shore every spare lot of land is taken up with soldier's tents. "Otis" is not very popular with the men. They say he is making money.[131] I believe Mr and Mrs L Johnson are expected here in about ten days from Iloilo. Fred saw his partner the other day. The weather has been so rough there has been very little visiting among the shipping. Now the N.E. monsoon seems to be setting in and the day[s] are finer. Fred has given me a Post Office order to enclose made payable to you. It is for Forrest, $5.00 for Christmas money and $5.00 for anything else he may want. He asked for a cart but he probably wanted that for garden work. Fred joins in love to all.

Yours affectionately

Grace F. Ladd

Bark *Belmont*
Manila 28th Oct. 1899

Dear Papa

We are not sorry, I can assure you, to be sailing tomorrow for Astoria. Fred does not like the idea of going for orders, is afraid the brokers will wait until freight begins to fall before chartering. Give us plenty of time as we expect to have a hard beat from here up as far as Japan. Ships coming in report strong N.E. winds. I have sold my piano here, had to let it go for very little but did not see the use of leaving it in the Ship. We also are sending a box and barrel of things by Captain McKenzie of the Osberga. He is going to New York.[132] Fred still says he is going home with me. He may change his mind but I shall not. I should like to see Flo. Perhaps we shall be able to arrange it.[133] Last evening I wrote to her. We have all kept well. No sickness at all, and only one new sailor. We have a fine crew. I think Ron is writing. We have a new steward. He is willing, that is all I can say. He speaks very little English. The cook is the same, and good. We shall kill our pig going across so that we shall all be enjoying fresh pork at the same time. This evening several of the Captains have been on board to say Goodbye. We sail as soon as possible in the morning. I must write Forrest a few lines. Any letters that come for us will be forwarded. With love to all in which Fred joins,

Yours affectionately

Grace F. Ladd

Grace and Fred set off from Manila to sail north, then east toward Astoria, Oregon. However, as Grace tells us in her next letter, the northeast monsoon kept them from making progress until finally they gave up and sailed into Hong Kong instead. There, they put the Belmont in dry dock* and had the vessel cleaned and painted while awaiting more favourable conditions. The last letter from Grace was written in Hong Kong, an unexpected stop on their voyage back to North America.

Bark *Belmont*
Hong Kong 10th Nov./99

Dear Papa

We imagine how surprised you will be when you hear we are in Hong Kong. It is a surprise to ourselves. After leaving Manila, worked up close under the land to the North end of Luzon. As we opened up the Bashi Channel, got the full force of the North East monsoon. The vessel would not work at all, neither tack nor wear. She drifted to leeward like a crab, would not sail at all. We felt pretty blue I can tell you. The only other way was around Australia, 15,000. Measured the distance to H.K. Found it 290 miles. Concluded the only thing to do was to come here and Dock. From the time we squared our yards* until we had arranged for the Dry Dock was just 48 hours. We got in Dock this morning, will get out Monday afternoon, sail Wednesday or Thursday, are going down Mindoro Straits through Basilan Straits and up to the Eastward of the Pelew Islands, then across. It will be a tedious passage but with a clean Ship, ought [to] save time. Last Sunday, quite an interesting incident happened to us. In the afternoon, about four o'clock, we were in a calm just off the coast of Luzon when a U.S. Transport *City of Rio de Janeiro* passed close by us. We hoisted our ensign when he was within about 200 ft. Their band played "God save the Queen" and as we dipped our flag, the hundreds of soldiers on board cheered. They then played their Anthem. We again dipped our flag and our men cheered them. They also dipped their flag. At dark we could just see a little smoke in the direction of Manila. Hong Kong is delightful now. I did not know it was ever so cool here, a pleasant change from what we have been having. We were all beginning to feel the effects of so much hot weather, lazy, etc. I wish we were going to load here. As it is, I shall be home sooner, of course—some time in February.

14th Nov. As a mail leaves today for America, will finish this and write Forrest again before we leave. Got out of Dock last night. Today it is raining but I am going on shore as it is my only chance. A Typhoon is now passing North of Luzon. I am thankful we are not over there. On the 5th of Nov. one passed to the Southward. We were North. It is strange how we seem to escape them coming to Manila from New Castle. Captain Abbott got two and we had nothing but calms. I prefer the calms. We are all well. With much love from all to all,

Yours affectionately

Grace F. Ladd

P.S. Ron has written Fletch.

Grace experienced some calms and some rough seas on their passage back to the west coast, and a hurricane on January 10 that left the Belmont short of sails. In his logs, Fred comments, "I never saw it worse. The Wind & Sea are something fearful." Nevertheless, they arrived safely at Astoria.

The above is the last of Grace's letters to her father and the last in the collection. One letter written by Fred to his brother-in-law in mid-February 1900 also survives. From this, we know that the Ladds were still on the west coast at this time. The letter was written from Portland, Oregon, and in it Fred describes some of the ordeal they went through in Manila as well as their passage over. There is an unmistakable touch of weariness to his tone:

> Since I last saw you, have sailed about enough to sicken most anyone. Finally got to your American Colonies. Witnessed the taking of Subic Bay, then drank Sherry

cobblers at the club with the officers & knew all about fighting Philippinos. Was in hopes of getting a cargo for New York when General Otis closed the Hemp Ports. This meant a trip over here. We sailed to Hong Kong, Docked & painted the *Belmont* then sailed around the Philippine Islands. Here, we arrived after 70 days....We didn't have any picnic but got here in time to save our Charter & some time I'll give you an idea of the whole affair.

Fred's letter was written on February 15. Two days later, Grace's father, Charles E. Brown, died suddenly in Yarmouth of heart failure. Grace was once again absent for the death of a parent. Charles E. Brown had kept his journal unfailingly each day up until the day before his death. Beneath his last entry is a black horizontal line drawn across the page and then the journal resumes in a different handwriting. One of his children (perhaps Charles F. Brown) took up a pen and finished the story of his father's life, movingly describing his last moments and paying tribute to a life well-lived:

Saturday February 17th 1900 18° - 28° - 24° Wind West. It becomes my duty to chronicle the doings of my Father today, it, being his last day on Earth, and the hand that has written these pages for fifty years or more is now still in death.

He arose at the usual time in the morning apparently as well as ever, after breakfast went to town for the mail, as was his custom on boat days. I met him in town about ten o'clock and talked with him for a few minutes and he seemed in excellent spirits. This was the last time I saw him alive.

He enjoyed a hearty dinner after which he went to the shop to write some letters. Wrote to A. V. Metcalf, Brunswick, [———], Dr. Fletcher, Ottawa, Hermann and had partly finished one to Georgie. It was then about 2.30. He then left for the house to make arrangements with Fletcher about attending Mrs. Metzke's funeral. He then returned to the shop to finish his letters. Mr. Ladd came in and after a few minutes, he went to the house again on some errand leaving Mr. Ladd reading a paper. He went to the kitchen, and finding Sadie, the girl, who was the only person in the house besides himself, gave her a brush and comb, remarking that he had always intended to give her some little remembrance, and on turning to go, fell dead. This was in the sink room. He never spoke afterwards. Sadie at once ran out to the road and called in Mr. Doty of [——] who was passing in a tram. He saw that it was something serious and went at once for Dr. Williamson who came immediately, but life had gone.

Thus ends a life of integrity, honor and uprightness, which virtues he tried to instill into the lives of his children, the life of one whose word was never questioned.

We mourn the loss of an affectionate and indulgent Father, his friends, at home and abroad will long remember him for his many acts of kindness, the children going to and from school will never forget the shop on the corner, where he always had an apple or some little treat for them, and the poor were always kindly received and never turned away without an encouraging word and assistance of some kind.

As a consequence of the sudden death of Charles E. Brown, Grace's evident expectations to see her father when they returned "some time in February" went unfulfilled. The death of her father is also the reason there are no more letters from Grace available to us even though she sailed with Fred on and off for another fifteen years. Charles Brown took a keen interest in the voyaging life of his daughter. As evident from Grace's letters, he painstakingly kept in touch with her whereabouts, keeping records and saving the letters themselves, including the one Grace wrote to her mother that sadly never reached her.

It is because of Mr. Brown's meticulous gathering of documents and recording of events that we know as much as we do about Grace's life at sea. The letters carefully kept and passed on give us just a glimpse of a spirited woman and of a spirited time in Nova Scotia's past.

The Ladds at Sea
1900 to 1915

After returning to Yarmouth in early 1900, Fred kept his promise to Grace and stayed home for over a year. The Belmont *was sailed by others during this time. Captain P. R. Hilton (of Yarmouth) sailed from Portland to Queenstown, then to Cardiff and finally to Rio de Janeiro, arriving at the latter port in November 1900. From Rio, Captain J. Durkee (also of Yarmouth) took the* Belmont *to Taltal up to Pisagua and then back to New York by July 1901. In August, the* Belmont *arrived at Boston where Fred Ladd once more took over as captain and sailed out for Buenos Aires on September 19.*

This must have been a difficult departure for Fred. Grace gave birth to their daughter, Kathryn Ladd, on September 22, just three days after Fred sailed away from any means of receiving the news. Shortly after his departure, Fred recorded some of his anxiety and sadness in his log records. He wrote on September 27, "this is my first real homesick day. I feel as if I had a big lump in the Pitt of my stomach. Terribly lonesome." The fear and worry that came from not knowing the outcome of Grace's pregnancy must have been tormenting, especially when the Ladds had experienced the loss of a child at birth many years previously. The evidence that such memories remained to haunt Fred reveals itself in his log entry of October 5, 1901: "Dreamed I was home. Saw Grace. She was sick and cried. Said the baby was dead."

Fred presumably learned of the baby's birth and good health after he arrived at Buenos Aires on November 25, but even so he clearly was not enjoying this voyage and struggled throughout with feelings of homesickness and isolation. From Buenos Aires, he sailed to Cape Town, where he remained for just over two months. His logs while in port frequently speak about boredom and, above all, a hatred for holidays, at which times he was forced to confront many hours of time alone with only the occasional letter from home to bring him into contact with the family he left behind:

> March 23rd. Sunday. Baro. 30.35 falling. S. Easter all day long. Clear Sky. Find Sunday lonesome enough....

Forrest Ladd with his younger sister, Kathryn. The photo was taken in the studio of Enos Rogers Parker, one of Yarmouth's best known photographers.

March 26th. Mail a day late. Got one letter from Grace....

March 31st. Easter Monday. Another holiday. The devil take the holidays...

April 1st. Went onshore with [———]. Loafed Around & did nothing. Mailed Photos of Cape to Forrest....

April 21st. Onshore loafing around. Nothing doing.

At the end of May, Fred left Cape Town for Singapore and then finally turned back towards home, departing Singapore for Boston on September 19, 1902, exactly one year from the day he left. On the way back he stopped at St. Helena to pick up the welcome mail that was waiting for him there: "got a whole armful papers from Grace and seven letters, six from Grace & one from Forrest. Grace sent me five snap shots of the Baby. They are fine" (Nov. 15, 1902). *This may have been his first glimpse of his daughter, and he did not see her for real until Christmas when he finally arrived home and Kathryn was already 15 months old.*

The next time Fred set out, he took his family with him—all but Forrest who was now getting older and attending school at home—so the young Kathryn began her childhood days at sea. Fred's first reference to her was made a few days after they started out when Kathryn was evidently having some trouble adjusting to her new environment:

...heavy gale and heavy sea. The seas going over deck load. Kathryn very sick ever since leaving. Grace has been in bed with her for three days. She won't let her leave her for a moment" (Feb. 17, 1903).

Within a few days though, Kathryn's condition began to improve and soon afterward, Fred noted that she was spending time with them on the Belmont's *deck, enjoying the fine weather they experienced that was much* "like summer."

The Ladds at Sea

Grace with Kathryn on the poop deck of the Belmont. *Kathryn was a year and a half old when she went to sea for the first time.*

The voyage this time was to Buenos Aires where they loaded wool and goat skins to take back to Boston. The Boston/Buenos Aires circuit became the basis of the Ladd routine for the next twelve years. Usually they transported lumber down to Buenos Aires; in later years, they loaded quebracho (the name given to a number of hardwood trees grown in South America) to take back to Stamford. No longer did they go across the Atlantic to the Pacific as they did in former days. Times were changing for sailing vessels with the steady increase in reliance on steam and, as Kathryn recalls in later years, steamers were used more frequently for long ocean voyages, leaving the sailing ships "just going up and down the coast." Consequently, Kathryn did not get the same exposure to the world as did her older brother, Forrest. Instead, her experiences at sea were essentially divided between North and South America.

Kathryn and Grace joined Fred on most of the earlier voyages throughout this period, and Forrest was with them for one voyage in 1907 during which he helped with various maintenance tasks aboard the vessel. Grace and Kathryn stayed home more and more frequently after 1909 so Kathryn could attend school. Not surprisingly, Fred was evidently more content to have them nearby. Whenever they were absent in the earlier years, his logs reflect a languor, perhaps more

The crib Kathryn slept in as a child aboard the Belmont. *The suspended crib would have swayed with the motion of the vessel.*

139

pronounced at this time than it was in his younger days. A tired voice emerges, for instance, in Fred's log entry for Christmas, 1905, spent at sea with his family at home: "Xmas day a lonely one at sea thinking of home & those there. Jim celebrated the day. Turkey, Boiled Ham, Tomato soup, Green Peas, Cranberry Sauce, Xmas pudding, German Sauce.... Nothing in sight (Lonely lonesome)."

At other times, when the family was together, Fred's logs reflect the same enjoyment of a domestic environment that was there when Forrest was young. The *Belmont* became a home with Grace and Kathryn onboard and Fred took pleasure in recording Kathryn's antics in the same way he used to delight in writing about his son. And Kathryn, on occasion, seemed to get herself into much worse trouble than Forrest did:

Forrest holding his catch. He is standing on a deckload of lumber. Behind him is a temporary rail which had to be constructed when the deckload was as high as the regular rail. The photo would have been taken in 1907, the one voyage Forrest went on after Kathryn's birth.

April 3rd [1904]. ... Kathy cut her curls off with the scissors. Got into the white zinc paint with a pair tongs. Then got at the black paint. She was a sight.

August 14th [1904]....Again [Kathryn] went into the Store room after sugar. Crawling over the flour Bbl, the head slipped & she fell in the flour. Imagine the sight. She must have gone right under.

Kathryn watching over her cat and dog. A sailor is at the helm in the background and Grace is standing just behind the after cabin skylight.

Releasing a tired yawn, Kathryn is leaning against the Belmont *chart house. She is wearing a sou'wester and sea boots. The photo is looking toward the bow of the vessel.*

For Kathryn, the combination of home and workplace made the Belmont *a world full of intriguing possibilities which she evidently did not hesitate to explore.*

Fred's final fifteen years at sea appear to have been successful and prosperous with very little major trouble. Overall he spent a remarkably long time sailing just one vessel without many mishaps, or without much loss of life. There were difficult passages of course, times when the Belmont *was in danger due to weather conditions or potential accidents, and Fred comments more than once that a particular day was the worst he'd ever seen. One such trip occurred from January to March 1905 when the* Belmont *suffered an exceptionally trying passage back to Boston from Buenos Aires. An account of the ordeal appears as follows in the* Saint John Globe:

> The barque *Belmont* arrived at Boston on Tuesday, after a passage of seventy days from Rio Janeiro. Her commander, Capt. Ladd, stated that the voyage was one of the most trying in his many years experience, northeasterly winds being encountered from the very outset. Capt. Ladd expressed his heartfelt thanks to Capt. Wier of the British steamship *Clara McIntyre*, which arrived at Philadelphia from Cheribon, Java, recently for his kindness in steaming off his course and running down close to the *Belmont*, while in the latitude of Delaware, and taking the trouble to display signals notifying him of a submerged wreck which was directly in his track and a very dangerous menace to navigation. (March 4, 1905)

Just over a year later, the Globe *again cites the* Belmont*'s difficulties while returning from Buenos Aires. This time, the culprit was the northeast winds that plagued the vessel's progress from Cape Hatteras* onward. Several times the gales impeded the Belmont's attempts to head toward the lightship on the Nantucket shoals. After succeeding finally, they were met by a "furious northeaster...accompanied by thick snow and intense cold," and, despite the Belmont's best efforts, they found themselves the next morning, "sixty miles southeast of her position on the preceding day" (Saint John Globe, November 3, 1906).

But such incidents were typical for any sailing vessel and they were among the trials that Captain Ladd probably expected to face on any given voyage. A much more serious incident occurred in 1908, one that could have destroyed the vessel completely. Surprisingly, the incident occurred not at sea but at dock. On July 8 at about 4:15 PM, a fire thought to have been caused by spontaneous combustion or a locomotive spark broke out in one of the warehouses at the East Boston harbour. The fire spread quickly, destroying four piers, three warehouses, several freight cars, and a grain elevator loaded with 30,000 bushels of grain.

A number of vessels moored nearby were not able to be pulled out in time, and the Belmont was one of the most unfortunate. The cabins were seriously damaged, the lifeboats ruined, the spars and rigging badly burned, and the paint scorched off the steal hull. In a sad state indeed, the ship was towed to a dry dock and was assessed for $23,000 to $27,000 damage. Valued at $40,000 before the fire, the Belmont was insured for that much. When temporary repairs were completed in Boston, the ship was towed to New York for permanent repairs. After being off duty for many months, in mid-November the Belmont left New York for Boston; in January 1909, after being loaded once more, it left Boston for Buenos Aires.[134]

About three years later, one other mishap put the Belmont in significant danger. On November 29, 1911, they left Buenos Aires for Barbados. At about midnight on December 14 when the Belmont had reached latitude 29S, longitude 44W, it collided with a vessel whose

After the fire of 1908, the Belmont *needed extensive repairs. Here the hull plates, which were damaged in the fire, are being replaced.*

identity could not, at the time, be determined. That vessel was en route to Buenos Aires, and because it was running before the wind, Captain Ladd was not at fault. In his logs for December 15, Fred wrote, "...at 12.15 had a collision. We were on Starboard tack steering by the wind. Sighted red & green light right ahead. Our hulls did not strike but our yards hooked." In the end, the other vessel disappeared into the darkness and Fred was forced to take the damaged *Belmont* back to Montevideo to have the spars and rigging repaired.

Grace and Kathryn were not with Fred on this voyage, but they received news of the accident soon after the Belmont *reached Montevideo. Later, in her notebook of recollections, Kathryn remembers her father's version of the incident and she also recalls what it was like for her and Grace at home:*

> I remember my father saying he was below (in his cabin) when the Mate called. He rushed up. There were no other lights showing on the vessel. They shouted "Ship Ahoy," etc. but received no answer.
>
> The only thing to do was "about ship" and sail back to Montevideo which was the nearest port equipped to handle the situation. Lloyd's Insurance immediately took over and searched everywhere for the unknown vessel which was definitely at fault. No blame was attached to my father or the *Belmont*. Nothing was ever heard of the other vessel. There was no serious damage done to the *Belmont*. She was, if I remember correctly, put in dry dock. But it was thought the other vessel could have been more seriously damaged. On Feb 1st, set sail from Montevideo to Barbados.
>
> At the time, Mother and I were at home so I could attend school. I remember being in the kitchen when mother received a telegram from John G. Hall & Co. She kept rushing around telling me not to worry, that every thing was all right—that my father was all right. Of course no one had heard about it until the Belmont sailed into Montevideo—when Hall's were notified by cable.

One of the greatest fears of those at home was to receive news like this, but for the Ladds, it could have been much worse. In this case, the fact that the news reached them after the vessel arrived back at port was clearly a good thing because, as Kathryn implies, they knew then that Fred was safe. The repaired Belmont *was ready to leave Montevideo on February 14 (and not February 1 as Kathryn reports). The guilty vessel (which was later identified as the* Brynhilda, *Captain Schmeisser) continued on to Buenos Aires, arriving on December 22. The ship set sail for Boston at the beginning of March, presumably after undergoing repairs.*[135]

In the last five years of Fred's career at sea, the collision was just one incident that perhaps contributed to his evident lack of patience on a number of occasions. Perhaps Fred was growing tired as he entered his fifties. Perhaps the *Belmont*, aging along with him, no longer sailed as efficiently. Fred may also have grown bored with the coastal route, especially as he sailed more frequently without the company of Grace and Kathryn. Whatever the reason, his later logs return to a chiefly technical record without the detail and elaboration present in logs from the earlier days when he and Grace were younger and when they sailed around the world. Mixed in with the technical data are more and more frequent expressions of frustration, mostly with weather conditions, but occasionally with the crews and, on one voyage in particular, with a lingering illness that caused Fred much digestive suffering, diarrhea, and weakness: "It is a mean place to be sick onboard ship. The Steward is very kind & does everything. Gives me a sponge bath every day. I must have been sick when I left the river," (Oct. 25, 1913). No doubt Fred missed Grace on this passage.

A particularly rough time was had by Fred in 1912/13 both on the passage down to Buenos Aires and on the passage back. On the way down, the vessel met with days of calms and slow progress followed by gales from the southwest and then from the southeast that impeded the *Belmont's* journey down the coast of South America. On the way back, northwesterly winds slowed them down, ending in days of blinding fog and finally snow. The log records tell the story of the climatological difficulties, but they also tell a more compelling story about Fred and his increasing unwillingness to patiently put up with such challenges:

> 2 knot current to SW. No chance to get out of this hell hole. (June 25, 1912)...If this keeps on will make a devil of a passage (July 4)...Could imagine I was at home if could only see familiar faces (July 5)...wonder if we are ever going to get a breeze (July 12)...don't understand this damn weather...A gale would be a welcome change (July 16) ... we are simply having a hell of a time (July 31)...hard old chance to get southward...looks like more bad weather (Sept. 1)...can't do anything (Sept. 9)... This is the last day of the old year 1912....Hope the New Brings better luck. (Dec. 31)...The year begins with a strong Breeze from the North...No luck to start the new year (Jan. 1)...If we ever get a breeze to keep sails full, a damn poor chance since the

new year started (Jan. 4)...We are having a poor chance to get north, the same as we had to get south (Feb. 10)...A hard gale from NW and a heavy sea and making ice on deck...a hell of a chance (Feb. 24)

After a longer than usual passage down (86 days) and then a long passage back up (79 days), Fred ends his logs for this voyage with a tired sigh of relief: "if ever any one was glad to get to port it was your Honorable servant" (March 5).

Despite these mishaps, Fred persevered as master of the Belmont *up until the start of World War One. In an unexpected turn of events, the war brought a prosperity to sailing vessels that hadn't been seen since the booming days of sail in the mid-1800s. Because so many vessels (especially steamers) were taken up by the war effort, sailing vessels were left to carry the weight of the mercantile traffic. Moreover, the involvement of Europe in war meant a reduction in trade between European countries and South America. Vessels sailing out of North American ports benefitted from this and the* Belmont *was no exception. Kathryn recollects in later years that, by sticking with the vessel and buying up shares, her father was able to do quite well: "Then, of course, when the war came, ships were as scarce as hen's teeth," Kathryn recalls, "and they needed the sailing ships for carrying cargo, so the vessel began to make money hand over fist."*

On his second to last voyage in 1913, Fred notes in his logs that he is painting Kathryn's cabin. This may have been in hopeful preparation for his last time out when, as though to celebrate the end of a long career, Grace and Kathryn joined him once again. They departed in June 1914, arriving at Buenos Aires in mid-August. While there, Fred, who was granted power of attorney, visited both the British and American consuls to see to the sale of the Belmont *for $24,000 U.S. from the Belmont Shipping Company based in Yarmouth (Irving G. Hall, manager) to the Hall Shipping Company (Irving G. Hall, president), the latter located in Searsport, Maine. This transfer, which may have been primarily one of name and location, meant that the* Belmont *was now officially owned by an American company. American ownership enabled a further change to take place in early 1915. On his way back from Buenos Aires, Fred stopped at Barbados (leaving Grace and Kathryn there for a holiday) and picked up a provisional American register. Presumably, the change in registry from British to American was a way of protecting the vessel from attack now that the war had broken out, allowing it to carry the flag of a country that was, at least at this time, neutral. After Barbados, Fred arrived at Cove Harbour*

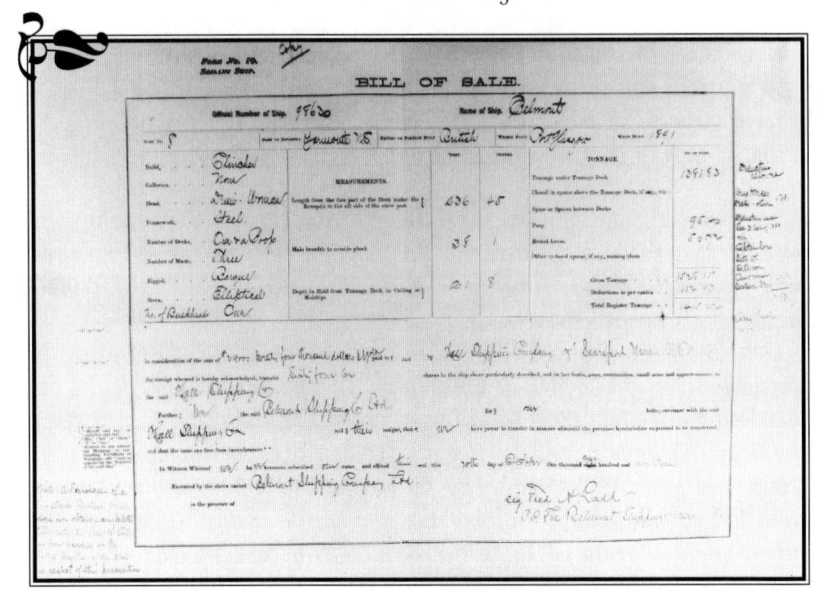

The "Bill of Sale" detailing the transaction that changed the ownership of the Belmont *from the "Belmont Shipping Co." to the "Hall Shipping Co.," the latter based in Searsport, Maine. Fred Ladd was given power of attorney to sell the vessel and it is his signature on the document. The* Belmont *was sold for $24,000 U.S. gold.*

(Stamford), where he participated in a ceremony marking the Belmont's American conversion. A local newspaper reports:

> The bark Belmont, a vessel of 1415 tons, had the Stars and Stripes hoisted to her peak at the wharves of the Stamford Manufacturing Company, this afternoon, and the vessel was changed from the British to the United States registry. The affair was marked by a celebration. The owners of the vessel were aboard, as well as a number of friends of the owners from Boston and other points in New England....A dinner was held aboard the vessel, beginning about 1 PM, then there were speeches.

    The article fittingly pays tribute to both Captain Ladd's long relationship with the Belmont *and the vessel itself, noting the comfort of the captain's quarters and the crew's quarters which, it says, are "something above the ordinary." The article also takes note of the* Belmont's *resilience: "She was built for heavy work and she looks the part. The great steel ribs and strong curves of the bow and the steel masts that taper high above the cross bars of steel, all have the appearance of great strength and endurance."*[136]

The "Certificate of Registry" indicating the transfer of the Belmont *from a British to an American vessel in 1915. American registry protected the vessel from attack now that Britain was involved in the war.*

And so the Belmont *began a new career just at the time Captain Ladd left the ship. From Stamford, he sailed to New York where he met with Grace and Kathryn, who had steamed up the coast from Barbados. Before the vessel left New York in March to head back to Buenos Aires, Captain Ladd had handed over command to Captain H. W. Fancy, from Queens County, Nova Scotia, who sailed the* Belmont *throughout the war. In 1921, the ship was sold and converted to a coal barge. It eventually sank somewhere near the coast of Florida in 1933.*

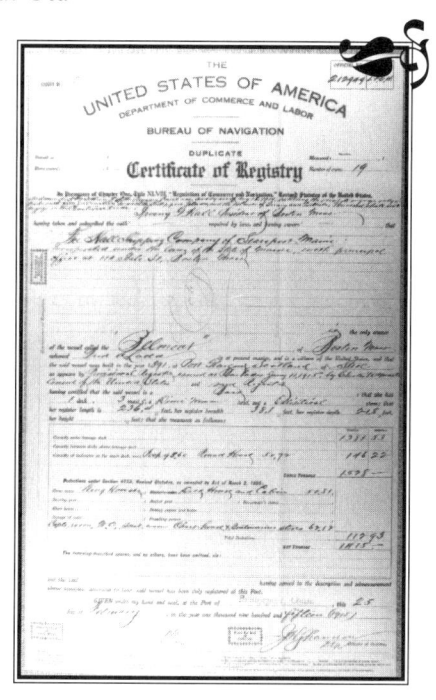

Despite the Stamford article's cheerful assertion that the Belmont's *last passage from South America as a British vessel "was a particularly delightful one," Fred's logs once again tell another story. As he sailed from Barbados for Stamford, he seemed to be worn down. One last time he was forced to confront some nasty weather when he was anchored at New London waiting for a tow to Stamford and his logs do not indicate that he was feeling a great deal of nostalgia over his last days aboard the* Belmont:

> 1st Feb. Monday. Still at Anchor 60 fths. Wind went right around N.E., East, S.E., S.W., N.W. & N.W.E. Thick all Night. First snow, then rain & sleet.
>
> 2nd Feb. Blowing Strong All Night N.E. 75 fths. Strong spring tides. Raining, sleet & hail & snow, everything frozen. At 10 AM Shoveling snow overboard. Cloudy & thick all the time. Again I was up All night. Getting tired of this.

This was Fred's last log entry. After over twenty years in the same vessel, his expression of fatigue reads as a bit of an understatement. Added to Fred's apparent weariness, the Ladds no doubt had other matters on their minds. By the time Fred retired, the war had broken out and Forrest had enlisted. Not long after they returned to Yarmouth, a short report in the Yarmouth paper reveals that the Ladds had just received some relieving news about Forrest:

> "Capt. Fred Ladd has received a cable that his son Forrest had survived the recent great battle in Flanders, in which so many Canadians were killed and wounded. Forrest is in the 2nd Brigade, 1st British Columbia Regiment, 7th Battalion. For 72 hours he was in the trenches during that action," (*Yarmouth Light*, May 6, 1915).

It had been awhile since Grace, Fred, and Kathryn had seen Forrest. They were soon to meet him again.

Kathryn Ladd's Travel Journal
1915

Before he enlisted in 1914, Forrest had been in British Columbia, possibly working as a clerk in his uncle's hardware store in Nelson. At the start of the war, he joined the B.C. 7th battalion out of Vancouver as a private with two close friends. They were sent to Valcartier camp and on to Salisbury Plains, England, becoming part of the Canadian 1st Contingent. Forrest was eventually promoted to captain and was wounded several times. The first was a slight head wound in January 1916, followed shortly by a bullet wound in his left hand that took him out of service for a month. In August, 1917, Forrest suffered a fairly serious shrapnel wound that left him considerably lame in the left leg. This was enough to have him sent home with a recommendation for light duty in Canada. He was fortunate to have made it back. The two friends who enlisted with him were both killed, one of whom, Kathryn later reports, "died in my brother's arms."[137]

In 1915, the Ladds learned that Forrest would have a five-day leave which he would spend in London, England. When reminiscing about this time, Kathryn describes the bustle and excitement that took place at home as her father "pulled every wire he could to get us over to England." She kept a travel journal throughout the trip, and it offers glimpses of the family holiday, a different sort of account from Grace's letters which described the sometimes challenging conditions aboard

Another E. R. Parker photograph. This is Kathryn with her dog, Pilot. As Kathryn explains in her recollections, the dog was named after the Argentinian pilot at Montevideo who gave her the dog.

a sailing vessel at sea. What is especially telling in Kathryn's journal, however, is the vivid picture of Grace that still emerges. Kathryn recollects later in her life that, while in England, "Mother felt that she had to take me to museums and art galleries, Windsor Castle, Eaton, I don't know where I wasn't taken. Mother was untiring, but she was interested in these things herself." And so Kathryn's journal confirms the many tourist attractions they visited—Westminster Abbey, the Tower of London, Madame Tussaud's wax museum, the British Museum, Hampton Court, the homes of Charles Dickens and Samuel Johnson, etc. etc.—and one can almost picture the forever energetic Grace, still with the curiosity that motivated her to travel around the world, leading her 14-year-old daughter from place to place, and standing over her shoulder to make sure she kept a record of her experiences in her journal.

Below is a short excerpt from Kathryn's journal that covers the days the Ladds spent with Forrest. It begins with Kathryn's description of their passage across the Atlantic in September 1915 while the world was at war.

1915 K. Ladd

[Thursday, September 23] ∽ We left New York on the 11th September on the S. S. *New York* of the American Line. We had a very nice trip as to weather, but the food was very bad. We entered the war zone two days before we arrived and some of the passengers were nervous and they said they would stay up all night & they did too. It was very funny to see them with life belts in their hands sitting or lying on chairs or sofas. Father, Mother, and I did not sit up. We went to bed and to sleep as did lots of others.

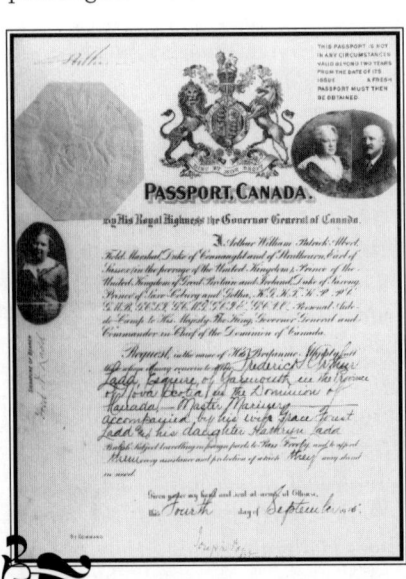

On each side of the boat in white letters against the black about 4 ft. high was printed "American Line" with an American flag at each end of the words. At night after we had entered the war zone,

The Ladd's passport, issued just before their trip to England in 1915.

lights were played on the words so that everybody could see we were an American boat. We also had a flag at the stern. One night a British battleship pointed his guns at us and asked if any Germans were onboard. The Capt. said no and the battleship went away.

I made friends with two English girls on the voyage. I liked them very much. Their names were Flora de Breton & Tara Fischer.

When we landed at Liverpool we immediately got on the Train and left for London. I think the English scenery is very beautiful. There are no wooden houses in England and the Red brick houses are so pretty in a green field or close to some large green trees. The English trains are very funny and they have only a very few street cars. The gray stone churches are mostly covered with ivy and they look so quaint and pretty.

We got in London about half past six Sunday night [Sept. 19] and we had a great time getting our luggage. Everybody made a grab for their own luggage and we got our shawl strap and 2 valises alright but we could not find our trunk so we left our name in the lost luggage office and went to the Grosvenor Hotel and had supper and then we went to our room to have some sleep. We asked a porter to wake us at one o'clock (we had had a letter from Black Moore & Co. saying Forrest would arrive in London in the Victoria Station at two o'clock Monday morning) and we went to the station to meet Forrest (the station was nearby). They said that there were 1800 soldiers coming in on three different trains so we went to the platform where the first train was coming in and Mother stationed herself at one part of the platform and Father and I at another part. When the train stopped and the soldiers started coming they looked very much alike. But Forrest saw Father, so we did not miss him. We stayed up till four o'clock talking and then we went to bed. The next day [Monday Sept. 20] we came here to this private hotel, 51 Torrington Square.

In the morning we went to St. Paul's Cathedral. It is so

Fred, Kathryn, and Grace.

large and high. I do not see how people could have built it. We went down into the crypt. It is vast, dark and gloomy and the things I remember best are Nelson's and the Duke of Wellington's tombs and the Duke of Wellington's burial carriage which was made out of the guns he had captured. It is huge.

We then started up to the "Whispering Gallery." It seemed as if there were a million stairs. On the way we stopped at the library and looked in. Along the walls are shelves and along the shelves are pieces of granite and plaster and the things churches are made out of all carved. They were pieces of the old St. Paul's and of the churches that were there before even that. This present church was built after the fire of 1666 by Sir Christopher Wren. In one room in the library (there are three rooms) the guide showed us a lot of curios and a book of writing with Sir Christopher Wren's signature, also a painting two hundred years old and a lot of old jubilee coins of the different reigns. And some idols and carvings the Danish kings had in about 1,000 A.D. The guide was very funny. I could hardly keep from laughing. He talked very fast, never changing the tone of his voice, once hardly stopping to take a breath just like a machine wound up. He most likely had memorized all he said. It was hard to understand him. Then we went on up to the "Whispering Gallery." Along the sides of the walls in the room the curios were in, were old books which were used for references. From the Gallery you can look right down into the church. It looks and is a great distance. After lunch we did some errands. And in the evening, Mother and Forrest & I went to the theater to see a play called *The Man Who Stayed at Home*. It was a comedy and a very good one too. Father did not go because he had a headache.

Tuesday [Sept.21] we did errands in the morning. We went around London with

A portrait of Forrest in military uniform and Kathryn, taken while the Ladds visited Forrest in London.

Forrest. In the evening we all went to see a play called *Peg o' my Heart*. Peg was a dear and the rest were all good.

Wednesday [Sept. 22] ⁓ Yesterday was my birthday and I got some very nice presents: a snakeskin wristlet to put my watch in and it is a great deal prettier than my other one, 1 box of writing paper with my initials on it and a pretty grey hand bag. Father gave me £1 to buy anything I wanted with. We had been all this time trying to locate our trunk and we got it in the morning. About 11 o'clock we left Charing Cross station on the train for Shorncliff. It is over two hours ride. Then we had lunch at a crazy little shop. They said it was the first in town and if it was I would not brag of it.

We went to a garage and got an auto to take us to Otto Pool camp where Ralph Harding was. It is 14 miles to the camp. The Roads are lovely, so smooth and the country is very beautiful. After a mile or so we came to the beginning of the camps. It was very interesting. When we at last got to the camp, Forrest went in search of Ralph. Father & I got out of the auto and walked around a bit. We saw the inside of a tent with its cot and oil stove and things and as for the horses!— There were hundreds of them. This was at an artillery camp. There were two long ropes to which they tied the horses like this (see diagram 1) facing each other. Those little marks along the line are horses. I also saw the men on horseback drilling. There were over a hundred of them. It

Diagram 1

was a great sight to see them trotting or galloping along and when the horses were walking along, two and two, sometimes they kept such perfect step you would think there was only one horse. When we met Ralph he said that Wilfred Doan & Eric Burrill were at another camp not so far away, so we got in the Auto and Ralph came with us. We met his Colonel and his Captain. We also saw Mr. Durland. We went to the camp and saw Wilfred Doan and Eric Burrill. Wilfred is all well again & Eric is well enough to be on duty. They said Arthur Rogers was at a hospital near so we said good-bye and started off to find him. When we got to the hospital they said he had been removed that very morning and after a great deal of hunting we found he had gone to a place about 20 miles away so we had to give it up. While we were waiting at the hospital a byplane was flying over our heads. It made a great noise and is rather pretty in the air. Driving about the hospitals you have a beautiful view of the English Channel. We were on a high hill and you could look right down into the

Channel and across. We could see the mist over France though we could not see the land itself. We went back to Folkestone and had a very stylish dinner. Ralph was with us. We saw lots of men marching on the road. We came home in the evening and got here about half past 11. Ralph went back to camp. There were all Canadian soldiers at Shorncliff. We saw some of the soldiers with all their equipment starting for the front and others starting for a march and others on the march and others drilling and others washing their clothes and others coming back from the front and others wounded. I forgot to say anything about Lord Roberts' tomb. It is in the crypt of St. Paul's Cathedral. I was very much disappointed about it. There is only a rail around a part of the floor with Roberts engraved on one of the slabs.

24 Sept. [Friday] ∽ We met Mr. Elliot yesterday and he had lunch with us. We went shopping in the afternoon and had dinner with Mr. Elliot and his friends and went to the theater with them to see *The Scarlet Pimpernel*. It was very good. I liked Sir Percy Blakeney best.[138]

The other day I saw the Bank of England. It is very strong looking. I saw no windows on the outside. We came through under the arch of the war office and past 3 of the life Guards guarding the gate, one on foot and the other two on horseback. The horses were beauties, coal black, and the guards had bright red coats and silver helmets on. Forrest gave me two lovely little gold spoons for my birthday present. One with a picture of Westminster Abbey on [it] and the other with a picture of the Houses of Parliament on it.

25 Sept. [Saturday] ∽ We met Mr. McLennan and his mother Mrs. McLennan yesterday. They had lunch with us. Mr. McLennan and Forrest left on the 5.40 train for France. It seems lonely without Forrest.

Retirement Years

Cynthia Roberts, a long-time friend of Kathryn Ladd, remembers when, as a child, she once met Grace Ladd, probably in the late 1930s or early 40s. She was sitting at a table in the Ladd home when Grace and Kathryn walked into the room. Cynthia was told to get up and offer her seat to Mrs. Ladd. When she hesitated because she hadn't yet finished drinking her milk, Grace responded tersely: "It'll go down much easier when you stand up," a retort that left Cynthia without much of an argument and also without a chair.

Like Grace's letters, such anecdotes convey the sense of an intensely animated character. But these stories are the products of memory, and memory is not always reliable. Trying to piece together some sort of profile of Grace and her family in the years after she went to sea is an exercise in sorting through a few available facts and a few remembered moments. If there is a commonality to the few stories I heard about Grace, it's that many of them alluded to Grace's sense of humour and mischievous nature. Cynthia Roberts remembers a story that illustrates both Grace's humour and her talent with needlepoint. At some period during her days at sea with Fred, Grace embroidered a tulip and a rose on the buttocks of Fred's pants. Despite the obvious invitation for mockery in this extremely masculine environment, the sailors apparently had so much respect for their captain that "no one said a thing." Another memory comes from Mary Clulee, a cousin of the Ladds, who recalls a naked statue—one of Grace's "curiosities"— in the Ladd home.

Grace on a hammock under the apple tree on Elm Street in Yarmouth, circa 1918.

Young's Mary's fascination with the statue's nakedness prompted Grace to tease her relentlessly for many years afterward.

Mary Clulee recalls Grace's sense of humour and her quick wit, qualities that were perfectly matched to Fred's occasional sharpness, as he was a man, she says, who "did not have the patience of Job." Grace's wit was perhaps a strong ally in her many years at sea with Fred, probably contributing to her ability to adjust to constant change. It may also have helped her reintegrate to Yarmouth when she began to stay home more frequently and, finally, when she took up permanent residence there after Fred retired from the sea in 1915. To find themselves so settled in one place after so many years of travel that, in the early days, took them around the world must have been an adjustment for both Grace and Fred. Yet if we can reach some conclusions from the evidence left, it appears that both of them were strong participants in the community, volunteering in several societies and contributing in whatever way they could to the Yarmouth region.

Grace, who spent so many years without the regular company of women, took part in a couple of clubs reserved for ladies only. One was the Milton Improvement Society, begun in 1913 by a group of local women, including Grace. This group initiated various horticultural projects to beautify the town of Milton, including the development of Milton park and the planting of a row of trees on Brunswick Street in memory of those who lost their lives in World War One. The other organization Grace joined was a unique literary society called the Kritosophian Club (Kritosophian means "council of the wise"). This club was started by four women (Grace's sister, Florence Brown, was one of them) in 1888 with the original goal of studying the works of Dickens. Eventually the group's repertoire expanded to include a wide variety of literary classics and touched upon non-literary subjects (scientific, social, and other artistic fields) as well. Grace was once asked to give a talk on the Alfred Noyes poem "A Salute from the Fleet"[139] and to provide with it some information on "saluting at sea." Both the Milton Improvement Society and the Kritosophian Club are thriv-

The Ladd home on Elm Street in Yarmouth.

ing in Yarmouth still, with daughters and granddaughters taking over when their elders become too frail to continue.

With their volunteer work, Grace and Fred perhaps found a way to continue the partnership they developed through so many years together on a vessel at sea. They each contributed in their own way to the Yarmouth Hospital, an effort that may have been precipitated by the needs of the hospital after World War One. Grace belonged to a group called the "League of Mercy," founded just after the war in an effort to help fulfill hospital needs by making sheets and pillow cases and by holding an annual bazaar to raise funds. For his part, Fred put his management skills to use on a committee that worked to build a new hospital wing in 1925. He was rewarded with a gift and a letter lauding his efforts as particularly valuable:

> The hospital society is under deep obligation to all who assisted in thus enlarging the hospital equipment to meet increasing demands, but the Directors feel that the society is especially indebted to your own good self in their regard. Your never-flagging interest in the work and your willingness to devote so much of your time to it have been, and are, deeply appreciated by every member of the society. The marked executive ability displayed by you in meeting conditions as they arose merits our sincere admiration, and will, we hope, be again exercised in our behalf when occasion arises.

Fred Ladd died on May 5, 1937. Grace followed five years later on March 8, 1942. While it is easy to find documentation of rewards and praise given to Fred, it is much more of a challenge to find acknowledgment of Grace's accomplishments. While Fred's obituary honours him for his many years as a successful sea captain as well as his follow-up years serving the Yarmouth community (his work for the hospital is specifically mentioned), Grace's obituary makes no mention of the 30 odd years she travelled with Fred at sea.

Kathryn Ladd won the Nova Scotia provincial golf tournament in 1934.

Considering how major this sea travel was to Grace's life overall, the omission is odd. It suggests that, for a wife, going to sea was not an active contribution or a notable accomplishment—just as a wife's domestic role at home was largely taken for granted. And so the tribute paid to Grace after her death focuses on what she did for the community through the societies she belonged to rather than on her earlier years as a partner to Fred on his many voyages.

Grace and Fred did not leave any grandchildren behind, another block to establishing a clear picture of their later years. Forrest married Mary Elizabeth Holden of Shelburne in 1920, but they had no children, and Kathryn remained single all her life. Forrest worked for the Nova Scotia Provincial Police, and joined the local RCMP in 1932 as a special constable, becoming a regular constable two years later. He retired in 1946 and moved to Wellington, where he is remembered as having done some work for the SPCA. (Mary Clulee recalls getting his advice once when her dog was injured and that he was "helpful and sympathetic.") Forrest died in Wellington on April 28, 1963, at 73 years old. He is said to have been much more quiet than his sister and is remembered as being somewhat frail (his war wounds may have played a part in such frailty). However quiet he may have been in life, he is noticeably the one unheard voice in this book. While Grace speaks through her letters, Fred through his log records, and Kathryn through her journal and reminiscences, Forrest left behind neither a journal, nor a single letter or note that I have been able to find. Other than the childhood remarks on board the Belmont *that were recounted by Grace and Fred, Forrest's thoughts, words and perceptions are somewhat of a mystery. But he too lived a varied and challenging life, spending his childhood years at sea visiting many distant ports, as well as surviving a number of years at war. While combing through his military records I came across the usual medical report that recorded Forrest's height as 5 feet, 10 inches and his weight as 158 pounds. My mind flashed back to Grace's letters from the* Belmont *where she too would often provide a record of Forrest's*

The Ladd tombstone in Yarmouth's Mountain Cemetery. Fred, Grace, Forrest, Mary Elizabeth (Forrest's wife) and Kathryn are all buried here.

height and weight, proudly taking note of how much her young son had grown, and I wondered what she would have thought if she could have seen what dark days awaited him in the early part of the twentieth century.

Kathryn Ladd died on July 17, 1989, at the age of 88, and is therefore the one most easily remembered. Although she never married, she may have had a romance in her young life with the son of a school principal, but Grace apparently disapproved and Kathryn was sent off to Boston to study piano at LaSalle Junior College. When she returned to Yarmouth, she taught piano for many years, organizing a concert by her students each year for which she spent days baking and preparing. She was also an avid golfer who attained a level of fame when she won the Nova Scotia provincial tournament in 1934. Like her mother, then, she had some athletic ability, and also like her mother, she participated in various community organizations, the Kritosophian Club and the Milton Improvement Society among them.

Unlike Forrest, Kathryn did leave behind her memories and perceptions of a childhood aboard a sailing vessel, and much of what she recollected both orally and in writing appears in the pages ahead. The impact such a childhood had on her is obvious, but whether the impact was positive or negative is not easily ascertainable. Her experiences at sea did, however, shape her character in various ways. Several people I talked to told me that they were initially afraid of Kathryn because she had a particularly brash and blunt manner. She did not seem to be one to concern herself too much with social niceties, and was probably even more outspoken than her parents. One story describes how Kathryn used to sit with her legs spread slightly too wide and her skirt hiked a few inches too high, something that always annoyed her father, who would go over to her and grab at her skirt to try to get her to sit properly. Perhaps her early days at sea exposed her to a rougher comportment that left her less attentive to some of society's restrictive codes of behaviour for women. Whereas Forrest would have at least had masculine role models aboard the Belmont (the most important being his father, who, as captain, was respected and powerful), Kathryn would have lacked such

Forrest Ladd in uniform for the RCMP. The photo was taken in 1936 when he was 46 years old.

models, outside of Grace. In her recollections she recalls the loneliness of life at sea, acknowledging that she had no friends except for those she made in port at Buenos Aires. For a female child, especially, life at sea away from the stability of home, society and friends must have brought with it its own challenges.

    Cynthia Roberts remembers one or two comments Kathryn made that show her in a struggle with her past. Once, as she was looking at an exhibit of ship paintings, she was pulled back in time, obviously transfixed by her memories; she quietly said, "I'd forgotten how awful it was." Other times she was able to distance herself more completely and take a more philosophical stance. She was heard to sum up her early days with the comment, "If I had gone to school and stayed at home, I'd have been a more stable but much less interesting person." In the end then, she seemed to accept the bad with the good, appreciating the value of her early experiences. With her later involvement in the Yarmouth Historical Society and her attempts to save and record her history, she at least ensured that the interesting stories she had to tell would not be lost over time. Such stories, memories and remnants are what Kathryn preserved and left for the enlightenment of others. The last pages of this book feature her words.

Kathryn's Recollections

As she grew older, Kathryn Ladd nurtured a strong interest in her connection with the sea and in her parents' lives, which were so typically a part of Nova Scotian history. She became a member of the Yarmouth County Historical Society and an active participant in the affairs of the Yarmouth County Museum. Eric Ruff, the curator of the museum, tells stories of Kathryn sitting and working at a desk with her Little River Duck Dog (a Yarmouth County breed) by her side. The dog was named "Charlie Brown," no doubt in honour of the grandfather she never met, or perhaps in memory of her uncle[140] (rather than in reference to the popular Charles Schultz character).

Both Eric Ruff and Cynthia Roberts recall how she used to beautify the museum with fresh flowers cut from her garden, another connection perhaps to Charles E. Brown via his interest in horticulture. Kathryn also spent much time polishing museum exhibits, which was one of her favorite things to do as it reminded her of her days aboard the Belmont *when she would help polish the brass instruments. She contributed greatly, not only with her presence, but with her experiences. And her wish to share such experiences encouraged her to leave behind many fragments of her family's history, which remain in the museum and archival collections, including her memories told in her own words. One such collection of memories is a transcript of Kathryn's stories (originally told orally and recorded) of her own childhood and of the*

The sailor sitting beside Kathryn in this photo is polishing the binnacle cover. Kathryn is polishing one of the lights that goes in the binnacle to enable the compass to be seen at night.

Kathryn and Forrest with Kathryn's dog, "Pilot," in 1907.

Grace and Kathryn on washday. The laundry is hanging on a line just behind Grace.

lives of her parents while they were at sea.[141] I have already drawn from this transcript at other places in the book. Below are more extensive selections from it.

My mother went to sea for twenty-five years out of father's forty. He had gone ten years before he married her. My father was twenty-seven and my mother was twenty-one when they married. On their first trip they went to Shanghai. The trip lasted six months and they ran out of [———]. He wasn't used to having food for a lady. The rough soldiers had hardtack and salt beef, salt cod, but so did we. That's what we lived on—salt cod, salt pork, herring, salt mackerel, and a few cases of bully beef, which I suppose was considered fresh meat. Once a week we had fresh meat. I liked the salt fish better than I liked the fresh meat, ... but this first time, my mother was a bride, they ran out of everything, except for a little bully beef and hard tack and they ran out of water. The trip was very long, so they caught rain water. You put something into the rain water. First of all it goes bad and then it cleans itself and becomes purified, but mother said to the first mate "this water tastes awfully funny. I don't believe it is good," and he said, "Oh no, it is perfectly alright," but of course it was bad. ...

My parents had three children. Their first baby died and is buried on the Island of St. Helena.[142] My brother, twelve years older than I, was born in England. Father's ship was being built in Scotland and my father was there overseeing the process. My mother was in England. An aunt lived there. Her husband was a sea captain too.[143] Mother took a house near her, just outside Liverpool, while she was expecting my brother, and he was born there. I was born right here in this house.

Yes, when my parents were first married they went all around the world, but then the steamers came, and they could go around the Cape so much more quickly. They also went through the Panama Canal, so that left the sailing ships just going up and down the coast to places like Buenos Aires and Capetown. My brother had gone around Cape Horn when he was young. He went with them when he was small for several years, but when I came along we went only to Buenos Aires.

My childhood was different. I didn't lead the kind of life that most children lead. I had bronchitis, which was caused by an allergy, but then they didn't know about allergies. But they found that on board ship I didn't get ill, so when I was eighteen months old my mother took me to sea and I didn't get home until I was about five or six. Even then I had such awful croup that they took me back to sea. There was plenty of fresh air and no dust. I am allergic to feathers.

On board there was not a great deal to do. In the mornings I would have my lessons, as soon as I was old enough to remember. I don't remember what I did as a very small child. But around six or seven I had spelling, and reading, writing, history and

Kathryn and "Pilot" standing beside the skylight to the forward cabin. The photo is looking forward.

Both the pig and Kathryn are unhappy in this photo. Forrest is above. The ship's cook is holding the pig. Fred Ladd took the picture instead of rescuing his screaming daughter.

geography. Mother taught me those every morning. At eleven o'clock I would go up to father and he would give me arithmetic. As I got a little older, I remember I was twelve, and was supposed to be doing decimals, my father looked at the book and after two days he called it perfect foolishness and proceeded to teach me navigation instead. I had my own charts. He gave them to me and I charted my own course. I had to draw in the course wherever we went, down South America; we went way out down to the Canary Islands in order to catch the fair winds and then we came back. We made a sort of triangle and then went to Buenos Aires. On the way back we came straight along the coast of South America. I had my charts—unfortunately when I got home, I gave them to my schoolteacher whom I was very fond of. Of course, she wasn't particularly interested in having these charts, but she accepted them very graciously. I should never have been allowed to give them away. They would have been very interesting today.

I remember one trip took about seven months. We had a lot of bad winds. It was nearly 91 days going down, but we came back in 56 days. It was much shorter.

These are some pictures. The sitting room was very comfortable. It had a fireplace, beautiful paneling, it even had a piano. I took a few lessons when we were home, and was supposed to practice but the piano got out of tune. This is the hen coupe. We kept chickens on board. And here I am cleaning brass with one of the sailors. My father didn't really want me to help, but he allowed me to do it. I was very much the spoiled darling. This picture is of my mother hanging up the family wash. The cabin boy brought up tubs of water. Mother washed just the sheets and our personal clothes—used to hang it up on deck on a fine day. On a day after the rain we washed, when there was lots of water.

Here is my brother with my dog. He came on one trip with me.[144] He used to go when he was smaller, but my father wanted him to go to school so he could go to college and wouldn't have to go to sea. My brother was bored on that trip, and here he is. He put the pig into the barrel with me while I was taking a sea bath. I was supposed to be delicate and they used to put salt water in a big pork barrel and I used to take a bath every day in warm salt water. So my brother got the cook to put the pig in and there is the picture of the pig and I both in the salt barrel together. The pig didn't like it any more than I did. I called my father. I remember that very well because I knew he would rescue me. But when he came out he disappeared again quickly. He came back with the camera and took this picture.

Kathryn's Recollections

And here is a picture of myself with the dog. The dog came from Argentina. When I was a baby, we went up by Montevideo, and the pilot came aboard. It takes two or three days to sail up to Buenos Aires and the pilot guides the boat through the huge river with flats and sandbars. The pilot was Argentinian and they loved children. He said the bambino should have a dog and he had a lovely puppy, just the thing for the baby. So they sent the cook with a big basket. He didn't come back for a long time. Hours later he appeared dragging this tall six-months-old dog on a string, flea bitten, dirty, never been washed in its life. We called it Pilot. He became a good pet. He was also a good watch dog. The vessel was never robbed, as so many other vessels were.

Here I am with the chickens, and here I am scrubbing the deck with the sailors. I was only allowed to work with two of the older sailors. I could never understand why, but I suppose the others were sort of rough.

I remember we had a funny watchman. His name was McGill. He was squat and bowlegged, cross-eyed and bald, with a salt and pepper beard. One night the family had gone out and they heard me screaming when they returned. McGill was shouting down through the skylight of the cabin, but he couldn't get to me and I couldn't get to him. My brother was in the other stateroom sound asleep. He was supposed to watch me. So when mother and father returned they saw McGill and he said "Capitain, Capitain, the bambino she cry, she want McGill." But mother and father thought it the funniest thing that I wanted this awful old bum to come to me, but I was not scared of McGill. I thought McGill was lovely. I wanted him to come and rescue me.

Shipboard life was very lonely, extremely lonely. I had no friends. However, Buenos Aires was beautiful. I used to enjoy going there. I had friends there. But on board, on stormy days, we just stayed in bed. My mother stayed in her bed and I in mine. My bed was

Kathryn among the chickens. The skylight to the forward cabin is at the left of the photo. Behind it is the chart house, the after cabin skylight, and a sailor at the helm.

Kathryn at work scrubbing the deck.

a stateroom bed, up high with dresser drawers underneath. I used to climb up on the settee and there was a big high board so I wouldn't fall out, and sometimes it would be three days that you'd be in bed. When one of these storms would come up, the only thing I would be able to do was to look out of the port hole, and my mother never felt well when these big storms came up. She wasn't scared, but didn't feel well because the boat pitched. I was a good sailor. It didn't bother me at all, but I had no one to talk to. I don't remember how we got our meals, but the cabin boy must have come in with food on trays for us. Aside from that nothing happened. My father would come down every so often to look at me to cheer me up and then he'd go to mother and talk and then go back up on deck. During these stormy times he never slept at all. He just stayed on deck and never left, even when the first mate or the second mate were in charge on the watches. It was very scary, I mean, the vessel would roll a lot. You'd be up, you'd roll way over to starboard and then you'd look up and you'd see the sky and then slowly she'd roll back again and you'd be looking down and see her racing through the foam and terrific waves. The waves would be so high you could barely see out of the window. That might go on for three days. The weather always kept one in suspense. Other than that, it was monotonous and very lonely.

Christmas was quite different on board ship. We took days to get ready for it. Of course, life had to go on with the kitchen and so forth, so we had to make the cake one day and something else another in getting ready and I would help with the citron, mostly eating it, but I was supposed to cut it up for the cake. I have never been able to eat citron since. I ate so much at that time. We also made a lot of molasses candy. My father would come down. He'd pull it. He was a great puller of candy, so that it became white and hard as could be. Then you'd have long twisted pieces. Then you'd cut it up and do it up in wax paper. They had a slop chest, which was really kind of a half-a-store. It was a room and when the sailors came on at port, they'd perhaps come on with just their shirts and trousers which they had on. These sailors were kind of shiftless, most of them, scum of the earth. Some of them were alright, but most of them were just the dregs of humanity. They would come on board like that. They wouldn't have anything for cold weather, not have the right clothes, so father always had this; they could buy it from their wages—warm trousers, warm shoes and socks. They'd buy this from the slop chest. So he also had lots of dark briar pipes. I would do up a pipe and a plug of tobacco. They always chewed tobacco, most of them did, and the candy and what all. [We'd] put it in the basket and on Christmas Day I'd go around and take it to them as a present. If we had a turkey, we would have it then; if not, they might have a goose or we might just have chickens for Christmas dinner instead. The turkey would be just for the family and the officers. One time, they gave the sailors chicken for Christmas dinner because they had lots of chickens, and a delegation of sailors arrived up to my father and they said that the "Articles" said that they were allowed so much salt beef and they did not have to eat chicken. They didn't want chicken. They wanted their salt beef. Father was perplexed because he had thought they would like chicken. But apparently chicken did not stick to a man's ribs. So they would be given whatever was their favorite meal. Of course, if they had a pig, they'd all have fresh pork with the rest of them. We only took one pig each trip, and as soon as it got fat enough, they'd kill it. The sailors didn't mind having fresh pork once....

Mother was sort of Victorian and very strict with me, but my father spoiled the life out of me, and I could have anything. He would do anything I wanted. We were great pals. I used to go with him in Buenos Aires when I was a small child (when I got older he wouldn't take me) to the billiard parlor where all the Captains went and I would just sit there and watch them play cards. But the last time we went to Buenos Aires he wouldn't take me. I was too old. It wasn't really a girl's place. Mother tried to interest me in going with her to look at the shops, but I didn't want to look at shops. I wanted to go with father.

When I was small my mother dressed me beautifully. She bought all my clothes from a child's shop in New York called Beth's. I had a black silk coat with an Irish lace collar and once while going for a walk with my parents in Buenos Aires I wanted to walk in back of them. I was walking along with my coat out, like children do, when my mother suddenly looked around and said "Kay, where is your coat?" I answered, "a shadow took it."

Some Argentine had come up and quietly smiled at me and had taken my coat. I wasn't old enough to be scared. I hadn't said a word. He literally stole the coat off my back. Needless to say, I walked in front of my parents after that, which I didn't like at all.

Life on board ship never seemed to me the least remarkable. As far as I am concerned, it was the most natural way of living. My mother was not afraid of anything, for instance, storms at sea. ... I wasn't scared because mother would say, "don't be silly, Kay." I was brought up with the idea of being fearless. My father was so wonderful that I didn't feel I had to worry about the storm. He would take care of it. My only phobia is feathers. ...

On my last trip when we came up north my father dumped my mother and me off in Barbados and we stayed there two weeks. He went on up the coast. It was January weather, and after two weeks my mother and I took a steamer up the coast to New York. We went to the hotel as soon as we got in and mother contacted the shipping agent to see what they were expecting and they said father's ship had been sighted off Nantucket Point and she would be in that evening, and sure enough father arrived upon the scene and there was great excitement. We had hoped but didn't think we would be so lucky to arrive on the same day. We had expected one of us to be first, probably mother and I. So he had another captain take over.[145] My father had been to sea for forty years. We then came back to Nova Scotia and there we heard that my brother was posted and was going to be in England. He had gone to officer's training school. We had not seen my brother since I was seven years old. My parents decided to go and see him in England....

When I got back to town I didn't have any trouble catching up with my studies. I had a tutor who would come in and teach me after school. Mother had taught me many things, but to this day I can't spell properly. On board ship we didn't have a blackboard, so she wrote with soap on the large mirror in the livingroom of the ship. I could never see the words very well, so I never learned to spell. A friend of mine, who has been teaching me to spell all her life, once said, "Kay, if you don't know what to do, you just double a letter."

After I finished school I taught piano. It didn't make much money, but it kept me busy. My father never worked after he retired, but he did a lot of volunteer work and kept occupied. This house is getting too big for me. We have lived here in this house all our lives. I am going to be very busy getting ready to move. I have to get rid of all the stuff that I have here. It takes so much time.

Kathryn's Notebook

The elderly Kathryn recounted part of the story of her childhood at sea and the sea-going life of her parents in a small green notebook. Included in the notebook are random excerpts from Grace's letters, and Fred's log accounts copied in Kathryn's hand (with the addition of the odd comment or explanation), interspersed with the occasional anecdote written out by Kathryn from her memory. The anecdotes recall her own life as a child aboard the Belmont *as well as events she was likely told of by her parents about their life before she was born. Below are a few of the stories Kathryn recorded:*

In times of storm the Captain never left the deck unless to go into the chart house to check the charts. He would be sailing by "dead reckoning*" then and when the better weather came and the sun would appear even for a few minutes, the captain would take the sight (of the sun) and check his navigation. Great relief when it was found that they were only a few miles off course. If the storm happened when they were near land, the vessel was immediately turned around and headed out to sea and safety. My father once said the longest he ever had to stay on deck without any sleep during a storm was seventy-six hours. Of course the crew and two mates would get their hours off to sleep except when they heard the shout—and my father had a pair of lungs, that his voice could be heard all over the vessel—"All men on deck!"

In my little bunk, it seemed only a minute later I would hear the sailors running over my head. Sometimes the piercing scream of a sail as the wind whipped it in two, and the sound of the mate and father shouting orders, and all sorts of mixed-up sounds—ropes running through their blocks, more sails being lowered, orders to the man at the wheel who always repeated the given order. In big storms there would be two men at the wheel as one man could not hold the vessel against the storm.

* * *

On the *Belmont* there were two brass clocks kept in a large teak [———] case. They were fastened by brass so when the vessel rolled they would swing and keep upright. Next to water they were the most precious thing on the vessel. They kept the mean time of Greenwich, England. And even a minute out could mean grave error in navigating. I was never, never allowed to touch these precious clocks which were in Mother and Father's stateroom. Mother wound them and when my father would "take the sun," would call up to him the exact time. Usually 12 noon, if I remember correctly.

* * *

I remember when I was younger hanging my Xmas stocking by the grate. Also Mother, making Molasses Candy—Father would be called downstairs to pull the candy which he did beautifully until it was a lovely creamy color—Cut it in pieces and my job was to wrap it in (Brown? wax?) paper. Then that was dealt out to the sailors as the Christmas Candy. I remember one year we had to wait for a day or so for a smooth enough day to celebrate.

* * *

So much of the story told in this book centres on the bond between Grace and Fred Ladd. What brought them through so many years of a tough and unsettled life was their obvious commitment to each other, a commitment that brought them together to face the often dangerous sea, the unpredictable profitability of cargoes, and the great distances between them and their families that could only be bridged through letters. As I spoke to Mary Clulee, someone who had the good fortune of knowing both Grace and Fred, she took a gold wedding band off her finger and dropped it in my hand. It was Fred's wedding ring, with his and Grace's initials engraved on the inside. To have in hand something so personal to them, such a powerful symbol of their years together, was a moment of great impact.

The short anecdote below is another that Kathryn included in her notebook. It looks back on the Ladd's honeymoon voyage to Shanghai in 1886, and clearly reveals the mischievous side of Grace that Mary Clulee described. And so we end in Shanghai where Grace's marriage to Fred began, her first voyage at sea on which she started the letters collected in this book:

Kathryn's Notebook

In Shanghai they did a lot of sightseeing. One day my mother coaxed my father to hire two bicycles. Father had never ridden on one. But mother told him it was easy. You just had to steer by turning the handle bars. So off she started and father started after her, downhill, calling for her to wait for him. Up the hill toiled a coolie with a cart full of vegetables and oranges, etc. Father yelled for him, in English, to get out of the way. Too late. The terrified coolie saw the red-haired white devil flying at him. Father, the coolie, and the loaded cart landed in a heap with the coolie screeching at my father, while mother gaily disowned him and went on her way.

The Swallow's Progress

[written for Grace Ladd by the Baron Harden-Hickey when he spent time with the Ladds in Calcutta (December 1888–January 1889) on the occasion of her birthday.]

I come a feathered visitor
from climes far, far away
where now reigneth cold,
   bleak winter,
night long & shortest day;

where the water fresh & shal-
   low
is shackled by the ice,
Hence cometh the wandering
   swallow
To the saving lands of spice.

By the stormy breezes wafted
O'er the angry main of salt
By no beings animated
Oh! how I yearned to halt,

And upon my weary feather
As I was want to do,
on a tree or 'midst the
   heather.....
at last I descried you.

My fogged wing just brought
   me
On to the *Morning Light*
Your gentle hand, it sought
   me
And quieted my fright

But life too fast is flowing
from the little swallow's
   breast
So fare-thee-well, he is going
To sleep in his last rest

May she who gave it shelter
Be blessed for the same,
May God from heaven protect
   her
Who loveth in his name!

Grace F. Ladd (1864–1942)

Endnotes

Introduction

1. Directed by Kent Martin; produced by Barry Cowling and Rex Tasker, 1979.
2. For a useful description of a captain's responsibilities, see Sager, *Seafaring Labour*, pp. 78–88.
3. This question is discussed in Bonham, "Feminist and Victorian," pp.203-18.

The Letters Of Grace Ladd

4. The captains were comparing their chronometers, verifying their accuracy. An accurate chronometer was of utmost importance since captains depended on accurate time to calculate their longitudinal position.
5. "Mollyhawk" or sometimes "Mollymock" or "Mollymoke" was a sailor's term derived from the Dutch mollemuck, meaning "foolish gull." It was usually applied to a smaller species of albatross, or sometimes to jaegers or to immature gulls. "Cape pigeons" were one of the most common petrels and were known for following ships.
6. The log entry for October 30 records these incidents as follows: "Two canoes came off with 10 men in each, they had only a few lines & Shells to trade. I boght a boy for four lbs Tobacco. He is about 12 years age. The Natives were Naked & Tatooed very fine. At 3 AM Same date Sighted the Island of Sonsoral & at daylight saw twenty canoes coming off with ten men in each. I hauled Ship to the West, thought we would get Skinned out by these natives. At 7 AM they were close alongside hollering like Mad. I would not let them come onboard. We traded some tobacco for Turtles, Cocoanuts, Shells & Sponges. These natives were Also Naked & Tatooed."
7. The *City of Florence* did survive the ordeal as it shows up later in both *Lloyd's Register* and the *New York Maritime Register*, but I was not able to find reference to the date of its arrival at Shanghai.
8. Rev. Y.K. Yen was an episcopal missionary who had studied in America and returned to his native Shanghai. He was head of St. John's College, a Christian college, in Shanghai (Grace mentions the college later in her letter). Grace had been given a letter of introduction to him and he and his wife acted as guides while the Ladds were visiting Shanghai.
9. What is now part of central Shanghai used to be surrounded by a three-mile wall. The wall was removed in the early twentieth century.
10. Mr. Hall was from John G. Hall & Co. of Boston, Ship Brokers and

Commission Merchants. The Ladds had close business connections with the Halls.

11 Since the first letter in this collection was written on Grace's passage out to Shanghai, perhaps her letter did get through to her father after all.

12 The narrow strait between Denmark and Sweden called Øresund.

13 Robert and Sophia Caie of Yarmouth. Sophia was a daughter of Samuel Killam. Her sister, Annie, married J. O. Biederman. Clara may be Clara Killam or Clara Caie. The "contemptible thing" that Mr. Biederman did is, unfortunately, lost to history.

14 Grace's sister, Charlotte Ethel, married Thomas W. Stoneman in 1884. Their daughter, Grace Muriel Stoneman, was born in 1887.

15 Grace is referring to the book *Yarmouth, Nova Scotia: A Sequel to Campbell's History*, which was written by her uncle, George Stayley Brown, in an effort to improve upon a previous history of Yarmouth written by J. R. Campbell and published in 1876. Brown's book was published in 1888 in Boston by Rand Avery Co.

16 The castle must be Kärnan, the surviving centre tower of the medieval fortifications of Helsingborg. The word *Kärnan* means "the keep."

17 Grandma Brown was Ellen Grantham (Farish) Brown, the second wife of the Honourable Stayley Brown. His first wife (and the mother of Charles E.) was Charlotte (Fletcher) Brown; she died in 1847.

18 "The electric street lights were installed [in Yarmouth] in November 1887, five in number, on poles 40 feet high, located at the junction of Main and Albert, Cliff, Alma and Parade streets, and opposite the Seminary. The full complement of lights was put in circuit on the 2nd of April, 1888" (Lawson, p. 635). Charles E. Brown's journal confirms that the lights were also lit in Milton at the same time and that the "light at the Devil's Half Acre [was] apparently the best in the whole place diffusing a strong light over a larger area."

19 Many versions of this song exist. The one most likely referred to in Grace's letter had the alternative title of "Goodbye, Fare-ye-well" and was popular aboard French and Norwegian ships.

20 The health spa Grace mentions, located in Helsingborg, became well-known in the early eighteenth century as a place of healing. Today, the mineral water from this area is sold under the name Ramlösa.

21 The Nordic Industrial, Agricultural and Art Exhibition opened in 1888 and attracted over a million visitors to Copenhagen. It featured products and artistic displays from various European countries.

22 Christian IX, king of Denmark, came to the throne in 1863.

23 "The French home" is a reference to the large Acadian population of Yarmouth and Digby counties.

24 The Canns were a major seafaring family from Yarmouth.

25 The church is Vor Frelsers Kirke, or Church of our Saviour. It is 292 feet tall (not 280 ft. as Grace records) and was built from 1682 to 1696. It was designed by the Dutch architect Lampert van Haven. He did not, however, throw himself off the top as legend would have it.

26 The bracketed passage was crossed out in the original letter.

Endnotes

27 Leeches were used medicinally for centuries to draw blood off an infected area. It was a popular form of treatment in Europe in the nineteenth century.

28 Coolies were unskilled East Asian labourers contracted by Western merchants to work in European colonies for low wages. The coolie trade developed to fill labour shortages after the abolishment of slavery. Conditions aboard "coolie ships" were often crowded, as Grace notes, and the cause of much sickness and death.

29 The battle that Grace refers to is the long conflict that began in the eighteenth century and carried through most of the nineteenth between the Kafirs (or Xhosa), a South African tribe, and the European colonists. Eventually the Xhosa were defeated and their territories were annexed by the European settlers. The term *Kaffir*, when used to refer to a black African, is now considered offensive.

30 The garden is that of Grace's childhood home on Vancouver Street in Milton. The house was situated close to where the river entered the harbour and it was once a popular Mi'kmaq fishing site. Residents at the house were still finding arrowheads in the backyard as late as the 1950's.

31 Grace's eye problems were probably a combination of astigmatism and far-sightedness. It is difficult to ascertain what she means when she says the condition was often treated incorrectly, unless only one of these conditions was commonly treated rather than both together.

32 Belle Farish (daughter of James and Mary Farish) married Jacob M. Owen on October 24, 1888.

33 Kalighat (the origin of the city's name, Calcutta) is the temple of the goddess Kali, whom Grace describes in her letter. Kali is the black wife of the Hindu god, Shiva, and she represents the dark side of divine energy, or Sakti. She does indeed frequently have a long tongue as well as a necklace of human skulls; she is often depicted holding a dagger and sword in two of her four hands and severed heads in the other two. Up until earlier in the nineteenth century, worshipers of Kali, known as thugs, would kill human beings and bring the corpses to her temple as sacrifices. By the time Grace visits Kalighat in the late part of the century, the thugs had been suppressed and worshipers sacrificed goats to the goddess instead.

34 Grace has counted the days incorrectly. From January 27 to May 15 is 109 days. In the end, Mr. Brown's prediction was impressively accurate as the *Morning Light* did indeed come to anchor at Boston on May 15.

35 Minnie Ladd (Fred's sister) married Charles Pratt on September 5, 1888, in Milton.

36 Captain Lemuel Robbins and his wife (Grace's aunt) Margaret (or Maggie).

37 Grace was fortunate to have a cabin fire, which the "poor sailors" likely did not. Fire was a hazard aboard a vessel (especially a wooden vessel) and was used with caution. With Grace aboard, a fire in the cabin was less dangerous because she would have been available to tend it.

38 These French islands are rugged with steep cliffs and were the site of many shipwrecks. They are now a designated national conservation area.

39 "Old friends"—a constellation of stars Grace was familiar with. As she travelled through new regions, even the night sky was often strange.

40 New Zealand was ceded to Great Britain by the Treaty of Waitangi in 1840.

41 Stayley Brown's first wife, Charlotte, was the daughter of Dr. Richard Fletcher and Mary McKinnon, so "Grandfather McKinnon" would have been Grace's great-great grandfather. The "photo" is a bit of a mystery since photography wouldn't have appeared in his lifetime, but perhaps Grace had a photograph of a portrait.

42 Edward Payson Roe (1838–1888) was an American writer whose books were published throughout the 1870's and 80's, the last one, *Miss Low*, completed from his diary after his death.

43 Kaurie gum from the Kauri pine was dug out in a semi-fossil state from the sites of previous forests. It can be used for making varnishes, lacquers and linoleum. A specimen of Kaurie gum collected by Grace is on display at the Yarmouth County Museum along with the stone and axes she mentions earlier in this letter. Also on display is a pair of tusks from a wild boar shot at Wairua Falls by friends of the Ladds.

44 The scarcity may be due to the extinction of the moa, an ostrichlike flightless bird, native to New Zealand, a couple of centuries earlier! However, a few of the smaller species may have survived into the nineteenth century.

45 See the *Yarmouth Herald*, 25 March, 1891, p. 3, for the "Public Notice" announcing the formation of The Belmont Shipping Co., under The Companies Act.

46 Unlike the *Morning Light*, the *Belmont* was made of steel. Consequently, fire was not as much of a hazard and stoves in the sailors' quarters were less of a danger.

47 Walter Nesbitt Davis, the second mate, was a first cousin of Fred. He later became a captain.

48 Fred echoes Grace's complaints in the log book entry for December 11: "Ship dirty. The Mate and Steward a useless pair."

49 J.J. Teasdale and W.H. Langille were both Methodist clergymen in Yarmouth.

50 Ralph, whom Grace mentions frequently in her letters, was Ralph Robbins, son of Captain Lemuel and Margaret Robbins (aunt Maggie), and Grace's first cousin. He boarded the Belmont in Wales as a cabin boy for his first voyage. He was 16 years old. He later became a captain like his father and his grandfather before him. Ralph's roommate, Tom, was Tom Moore, another 16-year-old first-time sailor who boarded with Ralph and who also worked on this voyage as cabin boy. See crew lists for the *Belmont*, 22 Sept. 1892 to 1 Aug. 1893, Maritime History Archive, Memorial University of Newfoundland. Later, it appears that Tom and Forrest became friends.

51 The Neptune ritual was an initiation rite that was practiced when vessels crossed the equator. In this special ceremony, a more experienced member of the crew (one who had crossed the line before) would dress as Neptune (the Roman god of the sea) and shave and "baptize" the young sailors to bring them into experience and manhood. There are many accounts of this frequently practiced ritual and it was not unusual for the initiation to be rough.

52 A disorder believed to be caused by excessive excretion of bile from the liver. The symptoms, according to Dr. Ira Warren, whose book Grace mentions in the next letter below, are fever, chills, lack of appetite, a tongue

Endnotes

"generally covered with a yellowish, or a dirty-white fur" and "frequent evacuations of dark, offensive matter" from the bowels (pp. 411-12).

53 M.F.G.L. were the signal letters of the *Belmont*.

54 The Oxford English Dictionary defines the verb *mash* as follows: "To fascinate or excite sentimental admiration in (one of the opposite sex)." It was also used as a noun in the expression "to have a mash on (someone)," which is similar in meaning to the more familiar expression used today: "to have a crush on (someone)."

55 Most probably a goat and a sheep-Billy goat and bellwether (the leading sheep of a flock).

56 This is probably Forrest's cousin, Grace Muriel Stoneman (b. 1887), the daughter of Grace's sister, Charlotte Ethel, and Thomas W. Stoneman.

57 Warren, Ira. *The household physician: for the use of families, planters, seamen, and travellers*. (Boston: Bradley, Dayton, 1862). The book was revised and reprinted in 1871, 1884, 1885 and 1898.

58 Forrest probably "picked it up" from the crew, since sailmakers and carpenters were commonly called "Sails" and "Chips."

59 "Little drops of water/Little grains of sand,/Make the mighty ocean/And the pleasant land," Julia Fletcher Carney, *Little Things* (1845).

60 In his log entry for April 16, Fred records that since April 6, they "have only made an average of 50 miles per day."

61 Mr. G. K. Vickery as first mate and Mr. F. J. Sullivan as second would each take charge of one watch.

62 This ship, built by Sewall's of Bath, Maine, was a four-masted barque 3154 tons, 300 feet in length, and able to hold 5300 tons of cargo. The ship was "famous," as Grace says, because it appeared on many American shipping documents (see Carr. *The Medley of Mast and Sail*, p. 106.) The signal letters for the *Shenandoah*, however, were KHST and not KHCT as Grace records.

63 Probably the same weapons that are on display in the Ladd collection at the Yarmouth County Museum.

64 i.e. Rio de la Plata

65 In his log, Fred notes on July 7 that Grace and Captain Dixon of the Haddon Hall "bet pr. of gloves who would arrive first."

66 Billy (a horse) would have worn blinders at the side of each eye to prevent him from taking fright at the sight of other vehicles around him.

67 At the back of Fred's log book, there is a collection of recipes Grace must have used aboard the vessel. One of these is the recipe for ginger beer: "12 qts water; 3 ozs ginger, bruised; 3 lbs white sugar. Let this boil 1 hour, then add 1 oz cream of tarter and two sliced lemons. When cool add 1 cup yeast. Leave 24 hours and bottle."

68 The names were all signed by each individual in the original letter.

69 Grace's brother Arthur W. Brown attended Springfield Training School in Massachusetts, which opened in 1885 and provided physical education and training for YMCA executives. Arthur graduated in 1894 and accepted a position as physical director of the YMCA in Meriden, Connecticut. In 1898, he moved to Grand Rapids, Michigan, to work in a similar position.

70   John Boyd (1826–1893) was appointed lieutenant-governor on September 21, 1893, a position he held until his death on December 4 of the same year.

71   The common name for this plant is bird-of-paradise. It is an exotic plant, native to South Africa. Perhaps C. E. Brown got the seeds from Grace.

72   In his logs, Fred estimates that one of the icebergs was "1/3 of a mile long & 80 to 100 feet above the water."

73   "Findlay" was Alexander George Findlay (1812–1875), an English geographer who published numerous atlases and nautical directories and charts. What Grace is probably looking at is his directory for the Indian Ocean, which is where the island of St. Paul is located. This work is entitled "A directory for the navigation of the Indian Ocean with descriptions of its coasts, islands, etc. from the Cape of Good Hope to the Strait of Sunda and western Australia," and it was published in 1866. The Island of Bourbon, which Grace mentions in her next sentence, is now Réunion, part of the Mascarene Island group located to the east of Madagascar. The sketch enclosed by Grace in her letter must have been lost.

74   Scott, Rairden & Co. operated out of Anjer, servicing incoming vessels by forwarding letters and orders on board to them, as well as providing them with papers, water and other supplies. See Crowell, *The Noviascotiaman*, pp. 218–20; 246. This is probably who Grace means when she refers several times to "Scott's boat."

75   "Troop" may refer to the well-known Troop fleet of ships built in Saint John, New Brunswick. J.W. Parker & Co. were Ship Brokers and Commission Merchants located in New York.

76   Probably the nursery rhyme, "Sailing, Sailing," the chorus of which runs "Sailing, sailing over the bounding main./For many a stormy wind shall blow/E'er Jack comes home again."

77   The visit to the plantation was also part of their stay at Semarang.

78   The Yarmouth County Museum displays a model of this well-known vessel in the front entrance. The *Lancing* began as an iron steamer, built in 1866 and called *Pereire*. In 1888, it was converted to a four-masted sailing vessel by Captain George Hatfield (of Yarmouth) and renamed. The *Lancing* was known for its strength and speed, once beating a Danish mail steamer by a day on a passage from New York to Denmark. See also Morris, *Atlantic Sail*, p. 174. Batavia is now Djakarta or Jakarta.

79   Captain Trefrey's ship, the *Celeste Burrill*, encountered a boat containing sixty pirates while sailing through the Malay Archipelago on route to the Sunda Straits. The pirates tried to board the ship, but did not succeed: "The savages all wore long garments, shaped like women's wrappers, and it's supposed that they formed part of the wreckage from some vessel that had been engaged in carrying female passengers from China to Japan. Before the coast of Java was lost sight of Captain Trefry saw his unwelcome visitors land on an unnamed island, where they seemed to live in a floating bamboo village. Many vessels have been wrecked in the vicinity of where the Burrill encountered the savages, and the islands are known to swarm with pirates, who so frequently attack vessels that a Dutch warship is kept mov-

ing in and about the archipelago for the protection of shipping" (*Yarmouth Light*, Feb. 22, 1894). In her letter, Grace refers also to the "wrappers" worn by the pirates, clarifying that they would have been "sarongs," a garment worn by both sexes. She must have read the same account of the incident.

80 In his logs, Fred notes "I haven't had 12 hours sleep in the last 14 days & am near crazy. The fever has taken all the life out of me."

81 "Jonah," from the Biblical story of Jonah and the whale, was a term commonly applied to someone who brought bad luck to a vessel.

82 The "brownie," a mischievous fairy found in English and Scottish folklore, was popularized in the late nineteenth century by a Canadian writer, Palmer Cox, who published an illustrated book, *The Brownies, Their Book*, in 1887. By the 1890's, the brownie figure appeared on all sorts of toys and games and was even used by Kodak to advertise their "Brownie" camera.

83 Sidney Jones was a first cousin of Fred. According to the Oxford English Dictionary, the expression "to pay for one's footing" referred to "a fee demanded of a person on doing something for the first time or on being admitted to any trade, society, etc." It was common practice at the Neptune ceremony to demand a fee from the uninitiated; a refusal to pay would result in shaving and "baptism." See also Beck, *Folklore and the Sea*, p. 117.

84 There were a number of superstitions connected with pigs aboard a vessel. Many considered it unlucky to say the word "pig," and it was considered necessary to call a pig "Mr. Dennis," as the Ladds do here. See Creighton, *Bluenose Magic*, pp. 117–18. However, the naming of their next pig after Lord Howe Island shows that the Ladds did not always follow the "Mr. Dennis" superstition.

85 To "try out the fat" was to render oil from blubber in a large pot. (See also Glossary, "try out the oil.") Fred provides the following description of this particular attempt in his log for March 7th: "Saved his Pelt & got 1½ Gals good oil. Only we tried it out wrong & lost a lot. Should have put water in with the fat as the oil burnt up on the Side of the Kettle without water."

86 "Snug Harbour"—a sailor's expression for a nice place in which to settle down.

87 The Chinese/Japanese war begun in July 1894 in which the Chinese were defeated. A peace treaty was signed on May 8, 1895.

88 The *Celeste Burrill*, captained by Clarence Trefry, left New York on December 6, the same day as the *Belmont*. It did not arrive at Shanghai until July 6, over six weeks after the *Belmont*.

89 Hattie Hibbert was the daughter of Captain William Hibbert, of Yarmouth. She married Captain Fred A. Brown in Hong Kong in December 1891.

90 Captain Clarence Hemeon was lost at sea along with his ship, the *George W. Homer*, in 1897 en route to Shanghai with a load of oil. See Lawson, *Yarmouth Past and Present*, p. 189.

91 i.e. rickshaws

92 The willow pattern was a landscape design (blue on white) developed in England in imitation of the Chinese. It includes a weeping willow, pagodas, three figures on a bridge, and two swallows. An English legend developed around the pattern, which told the story of two lovers whose love

was forbidden by the girl's father. They escaped over the bridge helped by a servant in one version, chased by the father in another; the swallows represent the lovers transformed after their deaths.

93 Henry Carter Harrison (1825–1893) was elected mayor of Chicago in the years 1879, 1881, 1883, 1885, and 1893. He completed a voyage around the world in 1887–88 which was the basis of his book, *A Race with the Sun*, published in 1889, in which his visit to Canton is described. He was assassinated in his home in 1893 by an angry man whom Harrison had turned down for employment. H. J. Stockard (1858–1914) was an American poet, born in North Carolina. His poems were widely published in various periodicals in the 1890's and early 1900's.

94 A pomelo is a fruit, also called shaddock, that resembles a grapefruit and is native to Malaysia and Polynesia. It is yellow in colour with a pallid or red pulp, and has a tart flavour.

95 The logs inform us that Captain Scott died in February.

96 George Clunies-Ross of the Keeling Islands established the first settlement on Christmas Island, which was annexed by Great Britain in 1888. He and John Murray were granted a 99-year lease to mine phosphate and cut timber. Later, Ross became part owner of the Christmas Island Phosphate Company Ltd.

97 The muskcat, also called musk-deer, is the animal from which the perfume musk is obtained. It is small (about 2 feet high at the shoulders) and hornless with a short tail, large ears, and long canine teeth. The "musk pod" on its abdomen produces the musk.

98 This is probably Mrs. Hattie Anderson, wife of Captain J. W. Anderson and daughter of Mr. Zebina Goudey, a Yarmouth ship owner. She died on February 23, 1897. Despite Grace's unflattering comment, Mrs. Anderson's obituary states, "She was of a sunny temperament and her society was much prized by those who had the good fortune to enjoy her acquaintance" (*Yarmouth Light*, Feb. 25, 1897).

99 The reef was named after Captain Cann's vessel, the *Ismir*, a 1259-ton Yarmouth ship built in 1878.

100 i.e. the west side of the South China Sea. This would be the most advantageous position because of the expected southwest winds.

101 On May 24, 1896, Grace and Forrest were not at sea. It is possible that the good time they had was connected with celebrations of Queen Victoria's birthday at home. The *Yarmouth Light* reports "carriages, coaches and bicycles conveyed hundreds to the country to engage in picnicking, fishing, etc....In the evening the Yarmouth Band played a fine program on Main Street" (May 28, 1896).

102 The *Ancona* (Captain L.E. Robbins) left New York for Shanghai on August 19, 1896, and did not arrive until April 19, 1897.

103 Linseed meal is from flaxseed and was used medicinally in poultices. Ira Warren instructs, "Put boiling water in a basin, and stir in flaxseed meal to make a thick paste. Spread on linen and apply" (p. 680).

104 Diego Ramirez Islands—a small island group to the southwest of Cape Horn.

105 Charles Ritchie was a native of Yarmouth, which made his death a personal loss to the Ladds. He was 19 years old. As indicated on the "Account of Wages and Effects of a deceased Seaman" (Maritime History Archive, Memorial University of Newfoundland), his death was the completion of a bizarre circle—not only did he die at sea, but he was also born at sea.

106 This seems to be a lesson that Fred remembered. Many years later, in January 1909, the *Belmont* lost another sailor after he fell from the rigging into the sea. Fred wrote in his logs: "We could do nothing. No boat could live in a sea like that even if we could have got a boat out & if the Boat once got away from the ship you would never get the boat again. I couldn't send a boat and crew to certain death."

107 Because the *Belmont* was stopping at Buenes Aires, the Ladds would be able to send the letters via steamer. The *Corinnea* was probably on a longer passage to North America or Europe.

108 Also known as Isla de los Estados.

109 The bottom of the *Belmont* was covered with seaweed and marine life that would have slowed it down.

110 i.e. the ship was going too slowly.

111 "Fletch," Grace's older sister, seemed to have various health problems. In his journal for January 11, 1898, C. E. Brown records this problem as "an hysteric attack," and notes, "she had seemed so much better lately that I hoped she had become permanently stronger." A few days later, he did indeed send to Halifax for some ale.

112 The *Hillside*, Captain R. W. Morrell, and the *Stalwart* (mentioned in previous letter), Captain G. B. Cann, were both Yarmouth vessels. The *Hillside* left Yarmouth on November 1 and arrived at Rosario on February 10.

113 Various newspaper clippings of unknown origin saved among the Ladd papers reveal that Baron Harden-Hickey, a French citizen of Irish descent, was undoubtedly an eccentric character. While on a voyage aboard the vessel *Astoria* in 1888, he discovered the existence of a small island, "Trinidad," about 700 miles off the coast of Brazil (not to be confused with the larger Trinidad and Tobago situated off the coast of Venezuela). He took possession of the island in 1893 proclaiming himself King James I of Trinidad. However, his kingdom didn't last. The British eventually claimed the island in the name of Queen Victoria in 1895. In February 1898, Baron Hickey killed himself while staying at a hotel in El Paso, Texas. He died from an overdose of morphine; found with him was a suicide note to his wife (who never recovered from the shock and was eventually committed to a sanitarium) and a copy of his own book, *Euthania, or the Ethics of Suicide*. The Ladds had some contact with Hickey when they stopped in Calcutta in December 1888/January 1889. There are a couple of letters that survive written by the Baron Hickey to Fred Ladd at this time, as well as a poem he wrote called "The Swallow's Progress," which he dedicated to Grace. The poem is reprinted on page 172.

114 Annie May Lovitt, daughter of Captain Edward H. Lovitt, married Henry Austin Killam on June 2, 1894.

115 William McKinley, president of the United States from 1897 to 1901.

116 Written in Forrest's hand.

117 A steamer (built in Hull, England; 2041 tons) that ferried passengers from Boston to Yarmouth, beginning in 1898.

118 William Henry Drummond (1854–1907) was born in Ireland and moved to Montreal in 1864, where he eventually practiced medicine. His poems imitated the broken English dialect of the habitant farmers. His book, *The Habitant*, was published in 1897. The first stanza of the poem Forrest is asked to learn reads as follows: "De place I get born, me, is up on de reever/Near foot of de rapide dat's call Cheval Blanc/Beeg mountain behin' it, so high you can't climb it/An' whole place she's mebbe two honder arpent."

119 "Jest Fore Christmas" is a children's poem written by Eugene Field (1850–1895). The first stanza is as follows: "Father calls me William, sister calls me Will,/Mother calls me Willie, but the fellers call me Bill!/Mighty glad I ain't a girl-ruther be a boy,/Without them sashes, curls, an' things that's worn by Fauntleroy!/Love to chawnk green apples an' go swimmin' in the lake -/Hate to take the castor-ile they give for bellyache!/Most all the time, the whole year round, there ain't no flies on me,/But jest 'fore Christmas I'm as good as I kin be!"

120 The *Ancona* was an English iron ship. At the time Grace refers to it, its captain was Jim Ellis, of Maitland, Nova Scotia. The "miserable time" had by the *Ancona* became quite a famous story. Sailing through the Solomon Islands in 1892, the ship was boarded by armed natives who held the captain and crew under siege. The story, as it was told many years later, was that the native chief, who initially showed potential for violence, calmed down completely when he found a Bible onboard the vessel (having learned about Christianity from missionaries). He then offered Captain Ellis a shell as a gift, which turned out to be the rare conus gloria maris, or glory of the sea. The story appears in MacMechan, *There Go the Ships*, pp. 211–24, and in Barrett, *Tales Told*, pp. 173–80.

121 Langshan is a breed of domestic fowl originally from China.

122 The heading indicating place was inserted later by Charles E. Brown. Arth's problems seemed largely due to stress over finances. C. E. Brown's journal tells part of the story that unfolded when Grace was home: "Grace called me aside for a confidential talk. She said Arthur had told Fred that he was much broken down & needed to rest, also that he was much worried over his financial position & was anxious to sell out his shares in the *Belmont* to reduce his liabilities" (Sept 10, 1898). A few days after this, both Arthur and Hermann Brown left Yarmouth to start a new life in Grand Rapids, Michigan.

123 The captain of the *Haddon Hall* at this time was O. Pritchard. The *Jane Burrill*, Captain W. D. Robertson, the *Celeste B*[urrill], Captain C. A. Trefry and the *William Law*, Captain B. A. Abbott, were all Yarmouth ships.

124 As it turned out, both derelicts were familiar vessels. Fred records in his logs that they were surprised to find that the ship on Apo reef was the *Selkirk*, built in South Maitland, Nova Scotia in 1886. The *Selkirk* was totally wrecked, but the captain (James Crowe) and his crew survived. See also Crowe, *In the Days of the Windjammers*, p. 41. The other derelict was, as

Grace notes later, the *Jane Burrill*, built in Little Brook, Nova Scotia, and wrecked while transporting coal to Manila. Once again the captain (D. Robertson) and the crew survived. See also Lawson, *Yarmouth Past and Present,* p. 190.

125 Mr. J. W. Ellis—the first mate.

126 Torres Strait, the passage between Queensland, Australia, and New Guinea, would have been a more direct route to the Philippines, but it must have posed some danger to the vessel due to navigational hazards or perhaps even piracy, and so the shippers did not want to risk losing their cargo. Fred was evidently trying to gain support for the Torres Strait route from others who had an interest in the vessel, but was not able to do so.

127 i.e. Puget Sound

128 Eventually, the Ladds do go to the Pacific coast and Fred takes time off from the sea beginning the following February (1900) until he returns to the *Belmont* again in September, 1901.

129 The *Celeste Burrill* arrived at Manila on July 18, eighty-three days ahead of the *Belmont*. Wallace mentions that several ships were forced to give over their cargo of coal to the American army at Manila, and that a Burrill ship from Yarmouth was one of them (p. 164). So perhaps the loss of coal to the war effort was part of the *Celeste Burrill's* "awful siege."

130 The present was probably a wedding gift. Grace's sister, Florence Isabel Brown, married Hamilton Byers on August 23, 1899.

131 Elwell Stephen Otis (1838–1909) was an American general in command of troops in the Philippines from May 1898 until May 1900.

132 The *Osberga* arrived in New York on March 7, 1900. Grace must have sold her piano and sent back some of their possessions in anticipation of their time away from the *Belmont*.

133 Florence Isabel Brown and Hamilton Byers moved to Nelson, British Columbia, where Mr. Byers had his hardware business, after their wedding. Grace must have been planning to take advantage of their stay on the west coast by arranging to see her sister.

Ladds At Sea

134 See the *New York Maritime Register*, July 15, 22, August 12, 19, and October 7, 21 1908; *Yarmouth Light*, July 9, 1908; *New York Times*, July 9, 1908.

135 See the *New York Maritime Register*, December 27, 1911.

136 From a clipping found among the Ladd papers. The name of the newspaper was not identified.

Kathryn Ladd's Travel Journal—1915

137 Kathryn met both these friends, Norman McLennan and Fletcher Elliot, on her trip to England and both are mentioned in her journal.

138 The Ladds saw a number of theatrical productions while in London. *The Man who Stayed at Home* was written by Lechmere Worrall and J. E. Harold Terry and was playing at the Royalty Theatre at the time of Kathryn's visit.

Peg o' my Heart, a play by J. Hartley Manner that was playing at the Globe Theatre in Shaftesbury Avenue, ran for 709 performances in all. *The Scarlet Pimpernel* was written by Baroness Orczy. The character Sir Percy Blakeney was routinely played by actor Fred Terry who became quite well-known for the role. The Ladds would have seen the play at the Strand theatre (see *The London Stage, 1910-1919: a Calender of Plays and Players*. Metuchen, N.J.: Scarecrow Press, 1982).

Retirement Years

139 Published in *A Salute from the Fleet and other poems* (Toronto: Copp, Clark, 1915).

Kathryn's Recollections

140 Grace's brother, Charles F. Brown, who worked for the Maritime Telegraph and Telephone Co., died in 1965 at the age of 97.

141 The interview was conducted by Ingrid Prosser as part of a social studies project. Three other women were interviewed along with Kathryn Ladd, all of whom were in their eighties at the time.

142 This child is a bit of a mystery. No one else I spoke to seems to remember such a child. However, Grace and Fred stopped at Lord Howe Island (not St. Helena) on April 1st, 1895, and several months later (June 7, 1895) the following notice appeared in *Lloyd's Shipping Gazette Weekly Summary*: "Sydney, April 29—the steamer Bishsgate [?] reports that the Nova Scotian barque *Belmont*, from New York for Shanghai, called at Lord Howe Island on April 1 and reported the death of the captain's child and one case of scurvy and one of consumption on board." (emphasis mine). Grace's letter (begun on December 31, 1894) covers this passage, including the visit at Lord Howe, extensively and so does Fred's log record. Neither give any indication that Grace was pregnant or that she gave birth to a child that died. Perhaps the *Shipping Gazette* report was in error, but the fact that Kathryn also has a vague memory of a child buried on an island suggests something may have happened at some point.

143 Aunt Maggie and Captain Lemuel Robbins. When Forrest was born, Fred was at sea, still sailing the *Morning Light*.

144 This would have been the first six months of 1907.

145 Captain H. W. Fancy.

Glossary

Aback ～ to position a sail so that the wind is on the forward side, pushing back against the sail. This is done to stop a vessel's progress through the water.

After ～ toward the stern of a vessel. Also "aft."

After Cabin ～ the cabin nearest the stern.

Athwarts (n) ～ as used here, Fred means to refer to the "thwarts" or the rowers' seats in an open boat. The seats are positioned across (athwartships) the boat.

(to) Back the main yards ～ to bring the yards around so that the wind is on the fore side of the sail in order to stop or slow the vessel. See also aback.

Beam ～ timber that runs from one side of a vessel to the other, supporting the deck.

(to) Beat ～ to sail into the wind in a zig zag pattern. See also tack.

Bells ～ the ship's bell was rung each half hour to mark the passage of time in a four-hour (or two-hour) watch. Time was then told by reference to bells. When Grace refers to seven bells, she means the beginning of the last 30 minutes of a four-hour watch.

(to) Bend a sail ～ to join a sail to the yard or gaff. The verb "to bend" was generally used to describe the act of attaching one thing to another by rope (or the act of attaching one rope to another).

Binnacle ～ a stand of wood or metal in which the ship's compass and a lamp were housed.

Boat skid ～ one of a pair of beams supporting the ship's boats.

Boom ～ a spar to which the bottom of a fore-and-aft sail is attached.

Braces ～ ropes attached to the yard arms that are pulled from the deck to change the yard's position or to trim sails.

Bridge ∾ a partial deck extending from one side of the vessel to the other.

(to) Break off ∾ i.e. the wind had broken them away from their course. The wind direction was not helping them progress on their desired course, so Fred decided to use the wind to go to Lord Howe Island instead.

Bulwarks ∾ planking or steel plating around the sides of a ship to prevent water from rushing on board and to keep people from being washed overboard.

Bumboat ∾ a boat that carried provisions and sold them to vessels in port or offshore.

(to) Carry sail ∾ to spread enough sail to get out of the path of the cyclone as quickly as possible.

Case oil ∾ Oil was shipped in small drums that were packed two to a wooden crate or case. Hence, cargoes of oil were often referred to as "case oil."

Chalks ∾ blocks of wood used to prevent objects from shifting on a moving vessel. They were also used as connecting, reinforcing or filling pieces. The correct term is "chocks."

Chart house ∾ See chartroom.

Chart room ∾ A room either on or near the bridge that contained a chart table and charts, and in which the captain would do his navigational work.

Clew ∾ one of the two lower corners of a square sail.

(to) Clew up (sail) ∾ to haul the clews up to the yard by the clew lines when furling a sail.

Coaster ∾ a vessel sailing along a coastline, and/or conducting business in ports of the same country.

(to) Copper the ship ∾ to apply sheets of copper to the bottom of the hull of a wooden ship to protect it from ship worm and from damage due to weeds and barnacles.

Cross trees ∾ timbers laid across the upper ends of a mast to spread and support the shrouds to the next higher mast(s).

Dead reckoning ∾ a rough estimation of a ship's position from records of courses sailed when cloud cover makes it impossible to obtain accurate observations with the sextant.

Deck load ∾ goods (often timber) that were carried on the open deck either because they could not be stowed anywhere else (due to size or inflammable nature) or because the holds below were full.

Dry dock ∾ a dock with water-tight gates. Vessels were floated in, the gates locked and the basin emptied, so that work could be done on the ship's hull.

Glossary

Foot rope ~ a rope suspended below the yard, and attached to it by smaller ropes (or stirrups), on which a crew member could stand while working on a sail.

Fore cabin ~ in a larger vessel, the captain's quarters were often divided into two, the fore cabin being the one closer to the bow of the vessel. Compare after cabin.

Forecastle ~ the crew's quarters, located in the bow of the ship in front of the foremast. Pronounced "foc'sle." In her letter of December 25, 1891, Grace refers to "a stove in each forecastle." By the 1880s, the seamen lived in a house on deck which would have been divided into several rooms. The port and starboard watch each would have had their own forecastle.

Fore top ~ a "top" is a working platform for the crew located at the lower masthead. "Fore" refers to the foremast, the mast nearest the bow of the vessel.

Forward house ~ See forecastle.

Forward ~ toward the bow of a vessel.

(to) Furl (a sail) ~ to gather up a sail and secure it to the yard arm.

Gaff ~ a spar to which the upper portion of a fore-and-aft sail is attached.

Galley ~ the ship's kitchen.

Gasket ~ a line attached to a yard, boom or gaff and wrapped around a furled sail to secure it.

Gig ~ a light ship's boat designed for speed and adapted for either rowing or sailing.

Glass ~ a barometer.

Good sails ~ these are the best sails that would be used in harsher climates. Older and worn sails would be used in regions where the climate was gentler. On a long voyage, the sailors would have to change the sails several times.

Goose-winged sail ~ a square sail is goose-winged when the middle part is hauled up to the yard and the clews hauled down, so that the two sides of the sail are spread and resemble wings.

Gripes ~ ropes and other gear used to secure the ship's boats.

Halliards (or halyards) ~ the ropes with which the sails or yards are hoisted up or down.

(to) Haul yards ~ to pull on ropes in order to move the yards after the course of the vessel is changed. The sails/yards would have to be adjusted to accommodate the wind from a different direction.

(to) Heave to ∽ to prevent the vessel from continuing on its forward course by directing the wind onto the forward side of the sail or by causing the sails to counteract each other. At this point the vessel is said to be "hove to" or "lying to."

Helmsman ∽ the crew member steering the vessel.

Holystoning ∽ the cleaning of the ship's deck with soft, white sandstone. This would whiten the wood and give it a smooth surface.

House ∽ a cabin on the after part of the deck, often called a "roundhouse," not because it was round in shape, but because it was possible to walk around it.

Junk ∽ a Chinese or Japanese sailing vessel with a flat bottom, a high stern and up to five masts with square sails made of cotton or matting.

(to) Keep off ∽ Used twice in two different senses in Grace's letter of Oct. 24, 1889. Fred "kept off to speak to him," meaning that Fred "kept off the wind" or sailed at a disadvantage to himself in order to get close to the other vessel. The vessel, however, "kept off," in the opposite sense. It increased its distance or kept away from the *Morning Light*.

(to) Keep the ship off before the sea ∽ Fred altered the ship's course away from the head sea so that it was moving with the wind rather than against it. This would have kept it from "tossing about" quite so much, thereby allowing all aboard to enjoy a Christmas dinner.

(to) Lay to ∽ see heave to.

Lazaretto (or Lazarette) ∽ a compartment, frequently in the stern, for the stowage of provisions and, in this case, of sails.

Lee side ∽ the side away from the wind.

Leeward ∽ on the lee side.

Light ship ∽ a stationary vessel exhibiting a bright warning light which marks a dangerous area.

Lighter ∽ a barge used to transport goods to shore from a vessel, or to a vessel from shore.

Log ∽ an instrument used to measure the speed of the vessel. In this case, the log (a "taffrail log") was attached to the rail on the stern (or "taffrail") and towed behind the vessel. The log would revolve with a speed proportionate to the vessel's speed and readings on a dial could be taken at any time.

Pampero ∽ a violent storm which forms in the pampas of Argentina and frequently comes off the land to the sea.

(to) Pay off ∽ to provide a crew member with the balance of

Glossary

pay owing to him when he was discharged from duty at the end of a voyage.

Pilot ∽ a navigator specializing in a specific coast taken aboard a vessel in order to guide it, for a fee, either into or out of a port through rivers or channels. Pilots would wait near a port onboard cruising vessels to be picked up by incoming ships and dropped off by outgoing ships.

Pilot chart ∽ a track chart issued monthly which gave detailed information relating to meteorology, hydrography and navigation. Average conditions for wind and weather for the month following its issue are marked on the chart, as well as information relating to the previous month, including the position of derelicts.

Poop (deck) ∽ a raised deck at the stern of the vessel.

Port ∽ the left side of a vessel, as viewed from aft.

Port trim ∽ trimmed and painted for port. It was customary to want a vessel to look its best when it reached port.

(to) Put the wheel hard down ∽ push the helm as far down to the lee side as possible to put the vessel into the wind.

Rail ∽ the upper edge of the bulwarks.

Reefed sails ∽ sails that have been reduced and secured by means of reef points.

Reef points ∽ short pieces of rope attached at intervals to a sail so that only a portion of the sail could be furled and secured to the yard.

(to) Report a vessel ∽ to give notice when having reached a port that one has seen or communicated with another vessel at sea, giving that vessel's position (latitude and longitude) and condition.

Rig ∽ the way in which the sails and masts of a sailing vessel are arranged. A rig can be either "fore-and-aft," where the sails are hung parallel to the ship's length; or "square-rigged," where the sails are hung across the vessel. There are a number of different combinations of these rigs. Some of the more common are the following:

Brig ∽ two masts, both of them square-rigged.

Brigantine ∽ two masts, the foremast square-rigged, the main mast fore-and-aft rigged.

Barque (or Bark) ∽ three (or more) masts, all square-rigged except the aftermast which is fore-and-aft rigged.

Barquentine (or Barkentine) ∽ three (or more) masts, the foremast square-rigged, the others fore-and-aft rigged.

Ship ⌘ three (or more) masts, all square-rigged.

Schooner ⌘ two (or more) masts, all fore-and-aft rigged.

Rigging ⌘ a term that applies to all ropes, chains and wires used aboard a vessel. Those used to support the masts and yards are the standing rigging. Those used by the crew to work the sails are the running rigging.

(to) Run off ⌘ to sail with the wind aft.

(to) Run across ⌘ See run (our) eastern down. The run from Tristan da Cunha to Tasmania would have taken the Ladds into the "roaring forties." The beneficial westerly winds were the reason for the distance they made in such a short period of time.

(to) Run (our) eastern down ⌘ The usual expression is "to run our easting down." This was something that happened in the area that stretches from Cape of Good Hope to Australia, between 40° and 50° south latitude (commonly called the "roaring forties") where prevailing western winds would help the progress of eastbound vessels. They were able to sail before the wind, hence "run."

Saloon ⌘ a large cabin on a vessel for the use of first class passengers

Sampan ⌘ a small Chinese utility boat used for passengers or the transportation of goods.

Short sail ⌘ reduced sail.

Shrouds ⌘ supporting ropes that extended from the top of the mast to the sides of the vessel.

(to) Signalize ⌘ See Speak a vessel.

Sky light ⌘ a window, normally glazed, built into the deck to allow air and light to reach the lower decks.

Slatting ⌘ the shaking of sails due to the wind when the sail isn't properly set. In this case, Fred had no time to set the sail properly, and consequently, it was damaged in the wind.

Slop chest ⌘ a place where clothing and other provisions were kept for sale to the crew. The slop chest and its profits belonged to the captain.

(to) Speak a vessel ⌘ to use one of a number of ways to communicate with a passing vessel at sea. This communication might be accomplished directly (using the ship's boat to visit another vessel), or by megaphone or signal flags. By the late 19th century an International Code of Signals was established to replace earlier and less effective codes. It consisted of a series of flags and pendants, one flag for each letter of the alphabet and one pendant for each number between zero and nine. These flags were hoisted in various combinations to convey messages to passing vessels. Note that one would "speak" a vessel rather than "speak to" a vessel.

Speaking tube ~ a tube used to carry a voice from one part of the vessel to another, in this case from the captain's cabin or bedroom to the quarterdeck.

Square run before the sea ~ bringing the boat perpendicular to the direction of the waves, making it less likely that it would be swamped.

(to) Square the yards ~ to place the yards at right angles to the ship's fore-and-aft line.

Stanchions ~ upright posts that supported rails, bulwarks and other structures.

(to) Stand in ~ to sail towards land.

Starboard ~ the right-hand side of a vessel, as viewed from aft.

(to) Tack ~ to move the vessel into the wind in a zig zag fashion so that the wind blows alternately on the starboard and then the port side of the vessel.

Tanks ~ for the storage of fresh water. These tanks were located near the deckhouse and would hold up to two thousand gallons each.

Ton/Tonnage ~ The tonnage of a vessel (both gross and registered) does not, as many erroneously believe, refer to the weight of the vessel, but instead to its capacity. The word "ton" comes from the French word for barrel. Ships were once measured according to how many barrels they could carry, hence in tons. When the Ladds sailed, a ton was equal to 100 cubic feet of space.

(to) Try out the oil ~ to render oil from blubber in a large pot.

Tug ~ a small vessel used to tow ships at sea or to help them navigate through confined areas.

Under the tip ~ about to load coal. The "tip" was a mechanism that tilted a railway truck so that the coal inside would spill out into the ship's hold.

Watch ~ The twenty-four-hour day was divided into work periods called watches. There were four 4-hour watches in addition to the evening watch (from 4 to 8 pm) which was divided into two 2-hour watches (commonly called the dog watches), making a total of seven watches in a twenty-four-hour period and ensuring that no crew members worked the same watch two days in succession. The term "watch" also referred to the group of crew members who worked together. The crew was divided into two groups--the "starboard watch" (these were the sailors housed on the right side of the vessel) and the "port watch" (those housed on the left side). Traditionally, the mate was in charge of the port watch and the second mate was in charge of the starboard watch.

Watch below ∞ time off between watches.

(to) Wear ship ∞ to change to the opposite tack by turning the stern (instead of the bow) into the wind.

Weather ∞ an adjective that applies to anything that is on the side of the wind. Opposite of lee.

(to) Work ship ∞ to do whatever was necessary to keep the vessel sailing.

Yard ∞ a large wooden spar mounted across the mast from which the sails are carried.

Yawl ∞ fore-and-aft rigged with two masts. The mizzenmast is located far aft and is much smaller than the mainmast.

Bibliography

Alexander, David & Gerry Panting. "The Mercantile Fleet and its Owners: Yarmouth, Nova Scotia, 1840-1889. *Acadiensis* VII (Spring 1978): 3-28.

Alexander, W. B. *Birds of the Ocean*. New York: G.P. Putnam's Sons, 1963.

Allan, Wilfred H. *Index of People, Places & Vessels to Yarmouth, Nova Scotia: a Sequel to Campbell's History* by George S. Brown. Tusket, N.S.: The Society, 1995.

Armour, Charles. *Sailing Ships of the Maritimes: An Illustrated History of Shipping and Shipbuilding in the Maritime Provinces of Canada, 1750-1925*. Toronto: McGraw Hill Ryerson, 1975.

Austin, B. F., ed. *Woman: Maiden, Wife and Mother: A Study of Woman's Worth and Work in all Departments of her Manifold Life, Education, Business, Society, Housekeeping, Health, Physical Culture, Marriage and kindred Matters*. Toronto: John C. Winston & Co., 1898.

Babcock, F. Lawrence. *Spanning the Atlantic*. New York: Alfred A. Knopf, 1931.

Balano, James W., ed. *The Log of the Skipper's Wife*. Camden: Downeast Books, 1979.

Barrett, William C. *Tales Told Under the Old Town Clock*. Halifax: Imperial, 1944.

Bathe, Basil W., ed. *The Visual Encyclopedia of Nautical Terms Under Sail*. New York: Crown Publishers, 1978.

Beck, Horace. *Folklore and the Sea*. Middletown, Conn: Wesleyan University Press, 1973.

Bonham, Julia. "Feminist and Victorian: The Paradox of the American Seafaring Woman of the Nineteenth Century." *American Neptune*. 37 (1977): 203-18.

Bowen, Frank C. *A Century of Atlantic Travel: 1830 - 1930*. London: Sampson Low, Marston & Co., n.d.

Brown, George Stayley. *Yarmouth, Nova Scotia: A Sequel to Campbell's History*. Boston: Rand Avery, 1888.

Carr, Frank G. G. *The Medley of Mast and Sail: A Camera Record*. Sussex: Teredo Books Ltd., 1976.

Cordingly, David. *Women Sailors & Sailors' Women: An Untold Maritime History*. New York: Random House, 2001.

Creighton, Helen. *Bluenose Magic: Popular Beliefs and Superstitions in Nova Scotia*. Toronto: McGraw-Hill Ryerson, 1968.

Creighton, Margaret S. "'Women' and Men in American Whaling, 1830-1870." *The International Journal of Maritime History IV* (June 1992): 195-218.

Creighton, Margaret S. & Lisa Norling. *Iron Men, Wooden Women: Gender and Seafaring in the Atlantic World, 1700 - 1920*. Baltimore: Johns Hopkins University Press, 1996.

Crighton, Whitcomb. *The Struan: From Saint John to Sandlake*. Halifax: Nimbus, 1999.

Crowe, John Congdon. *In the Days of the Windjammers*. Toronto: Ryerson, 1959.

Crowell, Clement W. *The Novascotiaman*. Halifax: Nova Scotia Museum, 1979.

De Pauw, Linda Grant. *Seafaring Women*. Boston: Houghton Mifflin Co., 1982.

Dictionary of American Biography. New York: Scribner's, 1927-1964.

Dictionary of National Biography. London: Smith, Elder, 1885-1900.

Doane, Benjamin. *Following the Sea*. Ed. Heather M. Doane Atkinson. Halifax: Nimbus Publishing and Nova Scotia Museum, 1987.

Druett, Joan. *Hen Frigates: Passion and Peril, Nineteenth-Century Women at Sea*. New York: Simon & Shuster, 1998.

Fingard, Judith. *Jack in Port*. Toronto: University of Toronto Press, 1982.

FreeHand, Julia. *A Seafaring Legacy. The Photographs, Diaries, Letters and Memorabilia of a Maine Sea Captain and His Wife, 1859-1908*. New York: Random House, 1981.

Gardiner, Robert, ed. *The Golden Age of Shipping: The Classic Merchant Ship, 1900 - 1960*. London: Conway Maritime Press, 1994.

Greenhill, Basil & Ann Giffard. *Victorian & Edwardian Merchant Steamships from Old Photographs*. London: B. T. Batsford, 1979.

Greenhill, Basil & Ann Giffard. *Women Under Sail: Letters and Journals Concerning Eight Women Travelling or Working in Sail Vessels Between 1829 and 1949*. New York: Great Albion Books, 1971.

Grosvenor, Melville Bell, ed. *National Geographic Atlas of the World*. Washington: National Geographic Society, 1963.

Home Knowledge Atlas: Geographical, Astronomical, Historical. Toronto: Home Knowledge Association, 1888.

Howell, Colin & Richard Twomey, eds. *Jack Tar in History: Essays in the History of Maritime Life and Labour*. Fredericton: Acadiensis Press, 1991.

Hugill, Stan. *Shanties and Sailors' Songs*. London: Jenkins, 1969.

Hugill, Stan. *Shanties from the Seven Seas*. London: Routledge & Kegan Paul, 1961.

Kemp, Peter. *The Oxford Companion to Ships & the Sea*. London: Oxford University Press, 1976.

Kerchove, René de. *International Maritime Dictionary, 2nd. ed*. New York: Van Nostrand Reinhold, 1961.

Lawson, J. Murray. *Yarmouth Past and Present: A Book of Reminiscences*. Yarmouth: Yarmouth Herald, 1902.

The London Stage, 1910-1919: a Calender of Plays and Players. Metuchen, N.J.: Scarecrow Press, 1982.

MacGregor, David R. *Merchant Sailing Ships, 1850-1875*. London: Conway Maritime Press, 1984.

MacMechan, Archibald. *Tales of the Sea*. Toronto: McClelland & Stewart, 1947.

MacMechan, Archibald. *There Go the Ships*. Toronto: McClelland and Stewart, 1928.

Maginnis, Arthur J. *The Atlantic Ferry: Its Ships, Men and Working*. London, 1892.

Montgomery, Martin, ed. *The Illustrated Atlas of the Nineteenth Century World*. London: Bracken Books, 1989.

Morris, Roger. *Atlantic Sail: Ten Centuries of Ships in the North Atlantic*. London: Aurum Press, 1992.

Bibliography

National Cyclopedia of American Biography. Clifton, N.J.: J.T. White, 1926-1978.
New York Times, "Children on Blue Water." December 22, 1889
Perkin, Joan. *Victorian Women*. New York: New York University Press, 1995.
Piers, Harry, ed. *Biographical Review: Province of Nova Scotia*. Boston: Biographical Review Publishing Co., 1900.
Robertson, P. W. "Coolies in the Ship *Rhine*." *American Neptune* 19 (1959): 227-31.
Sager, Eric W. *Seafaring Labour: The Merchant Marine of Atlantic Canada: 1820-1914*. Montreal & Kingston: McGill-Queen's University Press, 1989.
Spicer, Stanley T. *Masters of Sail: The Era of Square-rigged Vessels in the Maritime Provinces*. Halifax: Petheric Press, 1968.
Simpson, Raymond A., ed. *If We are Spared to Each Other: Love and Faith Against the Sea*. Hantsport: Lancelot Press, 1995.
Times Atlas of the World, The. 2nd ed. Boston: Houghton Mifflin Co., 1971.
Villiers, Alan. *The Way of a Ship: The Story of the Square-Rigged Cape-Horner*. London & New York: White Lion, 1974.
Walker, Benjamin. *The Hindu World*. New York: Frederick A. Praeger, 1968.
Wallace, Frederick William. *In the Wake of the Windships*. Toronto: Musson, 1927.
Warren, Ira. *A New, Enlarged and Revised Edition of Warren's Household Physician*. Boston: Bradley, Dayton, 1862.

Newspapers and Shipping Registers

Lloyd's Register of British and Foreign Shipping. Register Books, 1880-1900. London: various publishers.
New York Maritime Register. 1886-1915. New York: Maritime News, Co.
New York Times. New York, New York.
Saint John Globe. Saint John, New Brunswick.
Yarmouth Herald. Yarmouth, Nova Scotia
Yarmouth Light. Yarmouth, Nova Scotia.
Yarmouth Registry of Shipping, Yarmouth, N.S.

Original documents

Account of Wages and Effects of a deceased Seaman, the *Belmont*, 16 July 1898. Maritime History Archive, Memorial University of Newfoundland, St. John's, Newfoundland.
Brown, Charles E. Personal Journals. Various excerpts from the years 1887, 1892, 1894, 1895, 1897, 1898, 1899, 1900. Yarmouth County Museum Archives, Yarmouth, Nova Scotia.
Brown, Charles E. Letters written to Grace Ladd while she travelled aboard the *Belmont*, 25 December 1893 and 2 April 1899. Yarmouth County Museum Archives, Yarmouth, Nova Scotia.
Crew Lists for the *Belmont*, 22 September 1892 to1 August 1893 and 30 September 1898 to 30 July 1900. Maritime History Archive, Memorial University of Newfoundland, St. John's, Newfoundland.

Hickey, Harden, Baron. Letters to Fred Ladd and poem written for Grace while they were in Calcutta, 16 January 1889 and 19 January 1889. Yarmouth County Museum Archives, Yarmouth, Nova Scotia.

Ladd, Fred. Letters to Charles Pratt, 6 January 1897, 29 January 1897, 21 September 1897 and 15 February 1900. Yarmouth County Museum Archives, Yarmouth, Nova Scotia.

Ladd, Fred. Ship logs for the *Morning Light* and *Belmont*, 1886-1915. Yarmouth County Museum Archives, Yarmouth, Nova Scotia.

Ladd, Grace. Letters written to her father from the ship *Morning Light* and the barque *Belmont*, 1886-1899. Yarmouth County Museum Archives, Yarmouth, Nova Scotia.

Ladd, Kathryn. Personal Journal, September/October 1915 and Notebook containing transcriptions of passages from Grace Ladd's letters and Fred Ladd's logbooks along with commentary. Yarmouth County Museum Archives, Yarmouth, Nova Scotia.

Ladd, Kathryn. "A Social History of 'K' as told to Ingrid Prosser." Typed Transcript. Yarmouth County Museum Archives, Yarmouth, Nova Scotia.

Military Records for Forrest A. Ladd. The National Archives of Canada, Ottawa, Ontario.

Yarmouth Hospital Society. Letter to Fred Ladd, 1925. Yarmouth County Museum Archives, Yarmouth, Nova Scotia.

Image Sources

All images appear courtesy of the Yarmouth County Museum Archives, Yarmouth, Nova Scotia except the following:

Mariners' Museum, Newport News, VA: page 48.

Nichols, Louise: page 158.

Photographs on pages 8, 9, and 139 were taken by Nathan Bain and photographs on pages 11, 22, 31, 45, 63, and 65 were taken by Louise Nichols, with permission of the Yarmouth County Museum.